THE CAMPUS CURE

THE CAMPUS CURE

A Parent's Guide to Mental Health and Wellness for College Students

Marcia Morris, MD

ROWMAN & LITTLEFIELD
Lanham • Boulder • New York • London

Published by Rowman & Littlefield
A wholly owned subsidiary of The Rowman & Littlefield Publishing Group, Inc.
4501 Forbes Boulevard, Suite 200, Lanham, Maryland 20706
www.rowman.com

Unit A, Whitacre Mews, 26-34 Stannary Street, London SE11 4AB

British Library Cataloguing in Publication Information Available

Library of Congress Cataloging-in-Publication Data Available

Names: Morris, Marcia, author.
Title: The campus cure : a parent's guide to mental health and wellness for college students / Marcia Morris MD.
Description: Lanham : Rowman & Littlefield, 2018. | Includes bibliographical references and index.
Identifiers: LCCN 2017019028 (print) | LCCN 2017027762 (ebook) | ISBN 9781538104538 (Electronic) | ISBN 9781538104521 (cloth : alk. paper) | ISBN 9781538104538 (electronic : alk. paper)
Subjects: LCSH: College students—Mental health. | College students—Mental health services.
Classification: LCC RC451.4.S7 (ebook) | LCC RC451.4.S7 M68 2018 (print) | DDC 362.1968900835/2—dc23 LC record available at https://lccn.loc.gov/2017019028

♾ ™ The paper used in this publication meets the minimum requirements of American National Standard for Information Sciences Permanence of Paper for Printed Library Materials, ANSI/NISO Z39.48-1992.

Printed in the United States of America

CONTENTS

Acknowledgments   vii

Author's Note   ix

Introduction   xi

PART I: PROBLEMS   1

1 Anxiety: The College Years Are Now the Age of Anxiety   3

2 Depression: When College Is Not the Happiest Time in Life   21

3 Substance Use Disorders: Should You Just Say No When It Comes to Drugs and Alcohol?   39

4 Academic Failure to Thrive: Attention Deficit Disorder and Other Ailments   53

PART II: PRESSURES   73

5 Loneliness: The Importance of Social Belonging in College Success   75

6 Perfectionism: The Dangers of Duck Syndrome   93

7 Culture, Sexuality, and Gender Challenges: A Time to Heal   103

8 Financial Stress: Debt Bubbles, Depression, and Health Care Blues   115

PART III: CRISES   133

9 Suicidal Behaviors: A Parent's Worst Fear   135

10 Sexual Assault and Intimate Partner Violence: Being There
   in Their Darkest Hour   153

11 Eating Disorders: Drunkorexia and Other Dangerous Trends   163

12 Psychosis: Heartbreak and Hope   177

Epilogue   195
Notes   199
Bibliography   219
Index   229
About the Author   235

ACKNOWLEDGMENTS

The theme of this book is how collaboration among parents, patients, and health care providers promotes wellness and mental health in college students, and in writing this book I have learned about the power of collaboration to bring these ideas to print.

I thank my husband, Michael, and my children, Andrew and Alyssa, for their love, encouragement, and patience during the writing process. I also thank my parents, Bernerd and Arline Delman, who have provided a lifetime of cheerleading and unconditional love.

I am grateful to all the people—students, parents, friends, family, and colleagues—who have offered feedback and ideas about this book, including Beth-Anne Blue, Ludmila De Faria, Richard Hahn, Deborah Kalb, Susan Cohen, Haleigh Klem, Jeannie Latimer, Joan Listernick, Barbara Lewis, Linda Lewis, Charlotte Martin, Gabrielle Marton, Amy Poon, Linda Siemens, and Lauren Taub. Buddy Martin, a mentor and friend, was instrumental in getting me to turn my passion for writing and college mental health into action. I appreciate the encouragement of the faculty and students at the Harvard Writing, Publishing, and Social Media for Healthcare Professionals Conference, who told me, "You are going to write this book!" To my patients and their parents, you have shown me the power of resiliency and hope. Finally, I want to thank my wonderful agent, Diane Nine, and my thoughtful editors, Suzanne Staszak-Silva, Will True, and Kimberly Giambattisto, for their expert guidance during the writing and editorial process.

AUTHOR'S NOTE

The stories in this book reflect the common problems, pressures, and crises I and my colleagues see in the college mental health setting. The characters in these stories do not represent any single patient; the names are fictitious and any identifying information has been removed.

The medications mentioned in this book are recommended according to practices described in medical literature and the medical community. Most but not all have U.S. Food and Drug Administration approval for the specific disorders that are mentioned. If the medications are not approved for the specific disorder, they are mentioned based on medical literature showing a benefit. Readers should consult with their medical provider and the medical literature before making any decisions regarding medication or any other medical treatment.

INTRODUCTION

I remember leaving my son for the first time in his freshman dorm room, with half unpacked containers and a sense of unease in the air. My womb ached! He called me two nights later. He had lost his room key and was ready to come home; college was not for him. My womb ached even more, but I told him to give college a chance, that everything would work out, and it did, with some bumps along the way.

Sending your child to college may be one of the most momentous times of your life and also one of the most frightening. For eighteen years you have provided your child food, shelter, and, most importantly, rules to keep him or her safe. You have felt his or her failures and shared his or her successes. But now he or she is entering a wilderness where danger could lurk in every corner—drugs, alcohol, and unprotected sex. He or she could face all kinds of obstacles—his or her first F, unrequited love, roommate conflict. And you are not there to help him or her. Will he or she survive and thrive in his or her new environment?

Every child will run into small bumps, large bumps, and major roadblocks in the college years, something I have witnessed firsthand as a college mental health psychiatrist for two decades and a parent of two children in their early twenties. You are now parenting a generation of college students that have technological prowess and entrepreneurial skills, cultural diversity, and open-mindedness that surpass previous generations.[1] This generation also has many of the problems and pressures that started with the millennials and in some ways have worsened. Moreover, campus and community resources have not kept pace with college students' mental health needs. The college mental health crisis has become a perfect storm. Here are ten startling statistics:

1. One of four college students report having been diagnosed with or treated for a mental health disorder in the past year.[2] One psychiatrist estimates that one-half of college students have a mental health disorder, although not all of these students have been diagnosed.[3]

2. Anxiety and depression have been diagnosed in 17 percent and 14 percent of college students, respectively, in the previous year.[4]

3. One-third of college students binge drank in a two-week period.[5] In addition, there is a dangerous new trend on campuses called "drunkorexia," in which students will starve themselves or purge before drinking alcohol so they can get intoxicated more quickly.

4. Less than 40 percent of college students are academically ready for college.[6] Not surprisingly, only 40 percent of students graduate in four years or less.[7]

5. Financial pressure continues to climb. Student debt in 2016 topped $1.2 trillion, with seven of ten students owing on average $37,000.[8]

6. Students face new social pressures. They report greater loneliness and social disconnection, while at the same time feeling like they must portray their lives as perfect through social media.

7. Suicide rates have risen for young adults aged fifteen to twenty-four in the past fifteen years, according to the most recent Centers for Disease Control and Prevention report.[9] The suicide rate for men in this age group is three times that for women.

8. Sexual assault rates are at an all-time high, with one of four women having been assaulted by the time they graduate.[10]

9. Counseling centers cannot meet the needs of all students. The number of students visiting counseling centers has grown by 30 percent in the past six years, five times the increase in institutional enrollment.[11] Many counseling centers have limits on sessions, necessitating referral to the community.

10. Psychiatrists in this country are in short supply. Forty percent of colleges do not offer any psychiatry services on campus.[12] Finding a psychiatrist off campus can be challenging; I have received calls from parents all over the country—friends of friends and

readers of my articles—asking for referrals when their young adult children encounter long waitlists for psychiatrists.

In the face of this perfect storm, your college students need your support now more than ever. You can help your child identify problems and pressures early and assertively advocate for treatment if necessary. This will go a long way to promoting your child's safety and success. Remember the book *What to Expect When You're Expecting*? I and millions of other women read it cover to cover during our pregnancies. In a calm and empathetic way, the book takes you through some of the problems you might encounter during pregnancy and the ways you can handle these unexpected events. My book will inform you about "What to Expect When Your Child Goes to College," especially when the journey does not go exactly as planned.

The Campus Cure: A Parent's Guide to Mental Health and Wellness for College Students is a first aid guide to your child's emotional health, so you will be better prepared to handle a 3 a.m. distress call. With anecdotes and the latest scientific literature, this book will accomplish three goals: 1) increase your awareness of common mental health problems, pressures, and crises college students experience, 2) illustrate how you can support your child and collaborate with campus resources, and 3) provide stories of hope to parents who often feel alone and overwhelmed when their child experiences a mental health problem.

This book answers the many questions I have been asked over the years by parents of college students. Are antidepressants dangerous for young adults? Should my son be tested for ADHD? How do I know if my daughter is safe when she has mentioned she is suicidal? Parents are thirsting for knowledge on how to help their children who are confronting a mental health challenge. When I speak with parents of my patients, they are sometimes like a deer in headlights, shocked that their son or daughter is encountering a mental health issue that they know very little about. Often parents feel isolated and scared. This book provides the message that these problems are common and that their children can recover.

This book is divided into three sections: "Problems," "Pressures," and "Crises." The "Problems" section includes four chapters on the most common mental health problems students face: anxiety, depression, alcohol and drug abuse, and academic failure to thrive. Early recognition and treatment of these problems will prevent them from turning into crises. The "Pressures" section includes four chapters on stresses that have increased in the twenty-first century: loneliness, perfectionism, financial stress, and culture, sexuality, and gender challenges. The college landscape is now filled with pressures that increase the risk of mental health problems and crises. The "Crises" section has four chapters on topics that put your child's life at risk: suicidal behaviors, sexual assault, eating disorders, and psychosis. It is crucial that your child rapidly obtain medical, counseling, and psychiatry services for these problems.

I recommend you read every chapter. You might not think that your outgoing son could be lonely in college, but almost two-thirds of students report being very lonely at some point in the past year.[13] You might assume your easygoing daughter could handle the stress of college, not realizing that anxiety is the top mental health problem impacting college students. You might think your child would never feel suicidal, but one of ten college students seriously considered suicide in the previous year.[14] Perfectionism is a growing problem on campuses that can paralyze students; grades less than an A or B can lead to depression and anxiety. For some students, problems like anxiety, depression, loneliness, and alcohol abuse can occur all at once, while for others problems can emerge at different times during the college years.

Your awareness will help not only your child, but also his or her roommates and friends. Not every college student has a supportive and loving parent. You can be a guide for students who need an adult in their life. I've known many people to step in and mentor a young adult when a parent is not available to do this. The book is also for friends, grandparents, step-parents, ex-step-parents, aunts, and uncles. When a parent isn't there, it is a wonderful thing when someone else can step into that role.

Each chapter starts with a scenario, such as "your child has had such severe anxiety that she wants to leave school and come home," and then the question, "what would you do in this situation?" A vignette follows that will reveal how a parent guides his or her child toward recovery. You will learn how to recognize the problems, pressures, and crises as they uniquely present in the college population. In understandable and jargon-free language, evaluation and treatment options are reviewed that might include lifestyle changes, therapy, medication, and a medical evaluation. Most chapters explore how technologies like social media, texting, and online classes are impacting the mental health of today's college students. Each chapter ends with parent tips on dealing with the problem, a quick reference guide for parents who need immediate guidance.

This book will teach you how to be there for your child. Being there might be listening, saying "I understand, I've been there before." It could mean visiting your child for a weekend or a week to see how he or she is doing. It could also mean collaborating with mental health professionals on campus to facilitate treatment. It means knowing when and how to intervene if he or she is engaging in dangerous behaviors.

But how can I be there, you might wonder, when my child is legally an adult and I don't have access to educational, medical, and mental health records? What if my child does not inform me he or she is having a problem? These questions are answered throughout the book, but here is a snapshot of how to approach barriers to involvement.

1. *Let your child know you can handle any problem he or she presents to you and prove this statement by remaining calm during a crisis.* Students often have the best intentions by not telling you they failed a class or they have been feeling depressed. They feel they should handle things on their own or they don't want to burden you if you are under stress. Remind them that you are not there to take over, but to act as a mentor, guide, coach, and cheerleader.

2. *Ask your child for access to end-of-semester grades.* Your student may need to sign a Family Educational Rights and Privacy Act (FERPA) waiver form or take another step to allow you to directly view grades. Poor grades could be an indicator of an underlying problem: immaturity, a learning disability, undiagnosed attention deficit disorder, depression, or substance abuse. You can encourage your child to connect with campus resources to diagnose and treat the problem.

3. *Ask that your child inform you if he or she is seeing a therapist or psychiatrist, and request that he or she sign a release of information form if you feel it is important for you to speak with the mental health care provider.* It's a good idea for you to have phone contact or a meeting with a psychiatrist if your child expe-

riences severe depression, suicidal behaviors, psychosis, or a substance abuse problem. I always recommend contact if your child has had a recent psychiatric hospitalization. You can offer support and encourage your child to seek help if his or her symptoms escalate.

4. *Contact your child's university administration and mental health providers if you have immediate safety concerns.* You should do this whether your child has signed a release of information form or not, but it is better if he or she has signed the form. You can request to speak with your child's mental health provider and inform this provider of your concerns. If no release form is signed, the clinic provider may not be able to reveal that your child is getting care, but he or she can listen and take appropriate action.

As you read this, you might be wondering if I am asking you to be too involved. Will you be acting like a helicopter parent? I would answer a resounding "no." Every parent needs to foster independence and autonomy in their college-age children. But cutting the cord completely and letting your child be completely independent or "free range" in college is never a good idea. Each parent has to find his or her own balance between the extremes of detachment and micromanagement. Knowing your child's strengths and weaknesses will allow you to decide in which areas to stay involved and in which to step back.

One thing is certain: our college students still need guidance while their brains continue to develop. Neuroscience has taught us that our children's brains are going through rapid changes until they are about twenty-five or thirty years old. Legally college students are adults, but biologically and psychologically they are emerging adults.[15] The prefrontal cortex, known as the judgment and planning part of the brain, is not fully developed, while the limbic system, better known as the impulsive part of the brain, is going at full force. This impulsivity and novelty seeking might lead your child to experiment in good ways, like studying new subjects and making new friends, but also in bad ways, like trying drugs or abusing alcohol.

Several studies, in fact, demonstrate the benefits of parent involvement in the college years. A 2012 study showed college students who were more involved with their parents were more likely to have academic autonomy, better relationships, more career planning, and a healthier lifestyle.[16] Students still made their own decisions but turned to parents for advice. Other studies, which I will discuss in the book, showed appropriate parent involvement led to decreased drug and alcohol use as well as decreased suicidal thinking in college students and enhanced recovery from psychotic episodes. Organizations, from the National Alliance on Mental Illness to the JED Foundation, are supporting parent involvement for more serious mental health issues on campus.

When a parent recognizes a problem and encourages a college student to get help, it can make the difference between graduating and not graduating, between wellness and chronic illness. With three-quarters of mental illnesses beginning before age twenty-four, early treatment is crucial.[17]

You have tremendous power to make a difference in your child's life. This message was brought home to me when I attended my son's college graduation, which fittingly fell on Mother's Day. During the two-plus-hour ceremony, I had a chance to reflect on my son's college journey and think about his tremendous intellectual and emotional growth. I also spoke with other parents in the audience who were overjoyed at their children's accomplishments and also their own. As the president of the university said, the children could not have made it successfully through college without the love and support of their parents. He asked the students to give their parents a round of applause.

Here is a fact that seems to get lost in a sea of articles saying parents are too involved in their kids' lives: the college years can be a wonderful yet treacherous journey. As parents of college-age young adults, you have the passion and insight to help your child navigate through the rough waters he or she may encounter. This book will give you the knowledge and tools to overcome obstacles and fulfill every parent's dream for their child: health and happiness in the college years.

Part I

Problems

I

ANXIETY

The College Years Are Now the Age of Anxiety

The phone rings at 3 a.m. and you know it can't be good news. You hear your daughter's voice—she is breathing heavily.

"Mom, I think I'm having a heart attack."

Your daughter, Sara, a sophomore in college, tells you she is in the emergency room. She was studying late in the library when suddenly she could not catch her breath and had crushing chest pain. Feeling like she was going to pass out, she asked the librarian to call an ambulance. She starts to cry. "I've spent all of this week preparing for two tests tomorrow, and now I'm going to fail. And I'm upset because I just found out this guy I was seeing is hooking up with my roommate. I feel like my life is falling apart."

You listen to Sara sob from several hours' drive away. What would you do?

If you are a parent of a college student, you will get a call at some point late at night when your child's anxiety levels are sky high. For young adults today, the college years are truly the age of anxiety. Anxiety has surpassed depression as the most common mental health diagnosis in college students. Data from the spring of 2016 American College Health Survey tell the story of extreme anxiety on campus. One of six college students were diagnosed with or treated for an anxiety disorder in a twelve-month period. Three of five college students reported at least one episode of overwhelming anxiety and almost one of ten college students had panic attacks in the past year. In this landscape of anxiety, it is no surprise that one of four college students reported anxiety negatively impacted their academic performance.[1]

Anxiety has become the bread and butter of college mental health. It is now the top reason students visit college counseling centers, affecting 57 percent of students seen.[2] To help students better cope with anxiety, the center where I work offers several groups a year that teach mindfulness meditation techniques. In fact, my university celebrated its first Mindfulness Day last year and offered stress-reducing activities throughout campus.

WHY IS ANXIETY THE NEW NORM ON COLLEGE CAMPUSES?

Any student starting college would have some apprehension. He or she is away from parents and the structure they provide, taking challenging courses, meeting new people, and making his or her own decisions. But there is something different about today's college students. It's as if they are always swimming in a sea of anxiety.

At my own alma mater, Harvard University, pressure levels seem to have soared. When I went to my college reunion last year, I spoke with classmates whose children were currently students on campus. Their children were far more stressed out than we ever were. If we got a B, or even a C, we were still confident we would get a job or go to graduate school. We were less worried about finances. Our annual tuition, including room and board, was $11,000, a far cry from the $50,000 and more that students are now paying. Today, many students wonder if they will ever earn enough money to pay off their massive student loans. They fear for their economic future.

Finances, in fact, are the second most significant challenge that students face. Academics, not surprisingly, come first. When asked to endorse items that were traumatic or very difficult to handle in the past year, almost one-half of students endorsed academics and one-third finances. Intimate relationships, sleep problems, family problems, and career-related issues also caused significant stress in almost one-third of college students.[3]

What is shocking is that half of the students endorsed three or more items as traumatic or difficult to handle. Students are feeling overwhelmed by multiple pressures. As a parent, you can help your child contain, manage, and reduce anxiety when confronting these pressures. Here is the story of what one mother did when she received a distress call from her daughter.

SARA'S STORY: A TALE OF EXTREME ANXIETY

When Alice receives the 3 a.m. distress call from her daughter, Sara, she wakes up with a start and her heart races. Alice worries she herself is going to have a panic attack; she hasn't had one in years, but she takes a few slow, deep breaths just in case.

Sara starts crying, and Alice says, "I think you're having a panic attack, not a heart attack. I had my first panic attack in college too."

"This feels different, Mom, like I'm about to die. Here, speak with the nurse."

The nurse confirms Alice's view, telling her the medical work up did not reveal any heart or lung problems. "She can visit the campus counseling center for her treatment. Don't worry, she'll be fine." Should I drive up or not drive up to visit Sara, Alice wonders. She gets her answer later that morning.

Sara calls her again, pleading, "You need to come right away and get me. I want to go home. I don't feel well. My chest hurts and I can't eat. I tried to have breakfast but I threw up. I'm too anxious to leave my room." Alice cannot convince Sara to visit the campus counseling center. She cancels her work day and begins the three-hour drive to campus.

Alice finds her daughter in her dorm room with a packed suitcase, looking gaunt and tired. Sara tells Alice she has been skipping meals, too anxious to eat. Alice is tempted to take her home, but then says, "Before you decide to leave school, give treatment a chance. I took medication for anxiety when I was in college, and it made a big difference." Sara reluctantly agrees to go to the campus counseling center as long as her mother comes with her.

As the on-call psychiatrist that day, I meet with Sara and her mother in my office. Sara is anxious to the point of extreme discomfort, shifting in her chair, not making eye contact, looking like she is on the verge of tears. Despite her distress, I feel very hopeful; the presence of a caring parent who knows when her child needs help usually tells me this young adult will have the support she needs to recover.

Sara haltingly begins to talk. "I really don't want to be on medication, but my mother thinks it's a good idea. Last night was not my first panic attack. I've been having panic attacks a few times a week since the semester began, but somehow I powered my way through them. Last night was different. The chest pain was so bad, I thought I was having a heart attack. Maybe I should see a cardiologist."

I tell Sara she could see a cardiologist, but the emergency room doctors thought the pain was related to anxiety and stress. Was she feeling especially stressed out lately?

Sara bursts into tears. "I'm majoring in biomedical engineering, but I'm not sure I want to do this for the rest of my life. It's too much work now. I think my boyfriend broke up with me because I didn't have enough time to spend with him. I see my roommates partying on week-nights and I'm lucky if I have time to go out on a Saturday night. I've been so anxious lately it's hard to eat and sleep. Maybe I should just go home right now."

I acknowledge Sara's heavy workload as an engineering student, but I advise her not to make any changes in her major under the influence of extreme anxiety. In fact, Sara is getting all As and enjoys the material she is studying. Sara is feeling distressed but is not suicidal in any way. Sara decides to stick with her major a bit longer.

I tell Sara I want her to do cognitive behavioral therapy to learn how to decrease her anxiety, but I also recommend she take a daily medication because her anxiety is so high. I prescribe her sertraline, an antidepressant that is also helpful for anxiety. Sertraline is a selective serotonin reuptake inhibitor (SSRI), which works by raising serotonin levels in the brain. I start her on a low dose, as she is already nervous about taking medication. I explain that the effect of sertraline gradually increases with time.

Alice looks at me. "Since sertraline may not work right away, would you consider prescribing a medication like lorazepam? I remember lorazepam being helpful for me when I was in college." Although I prescribe lorazepam infrequently due to the risk of abuse on a college campus, I agree with her mother's suggestion. Sara has no history of substance abuse and would likely benefit from using it short term until the sertraline takes effect.

For the next month, Alice visits Sara every weekend, knowing Sara is still feeling shaky about staying in school. Her mother's calm and reassuring manner helps Sara give treatment time to work. Sara also checks in with her parents daily.

Over the next several months, she battles her anxiety with great determination, doing individual and group therapy to learn specific anxiety management techniques. She diligently practices these skills, using breathing techniques and meditation to prevent full-blown panic attacks. She continues to take sertraline, no longer needing lorazepam.

Sara allows herself time to pursue nonengineering activities, even if that means getting an occasional B instead of her usual A. Then Sara takes a big risk and does something that she has always dreamed of: she forms a small band with two other engineering students and they perform at local venues. Sara is the lead singer. After her performances, she hangs out with friends. Sara tells me she has a passion for music, and listening to music is the perfect antidote for anxiety.

About a year after her ER visit, Sara feels she is ready to taper off the sertraline. Sara, the frightened and trembling sophomore, is now a calm and confident junior. Our work together ends until she reappears in my office during her last semester of senior year.

"I don't know what to do," she says. "I've been offered my dream job, but it's far from where my parents live. What if I need their help?" I then ask Sara to review how far she has come in coping with her anxiety. As for her parents, she now sees them infrequently, sometimes forgetting to call them until her mother texts, "Haven't heard from you in a few days. Everything okay?" And everything is fine. Sara now sees that life's possibilities are open to her, and she is ready to pursue them.

Sara had one of the most severe cases of panic disorder I have seen, but through her hard work and family support, she also had one of the best recoveries. I don't know if Sara's road to recovery would have been as smooth without the support of her mother.

THE FIVE THINGS SARA'S MOTHER DOES RIGHT

Sara's mother:

1. *Recognizes the seriousness of Sara's symptoms and comes to her when she needs it the most.* Sara's anxiety paralyzes her to the point that she cannot take steps to help herself.
2. *Reveals her own struggles with anxiety.* Anxiety has a strong genetic component and tends to run in families. By telling Sara about her own challenges, she normalizes and destigmatizes Sara's experience of anxiety, which is common in the college years.
3. *Promotes medication, which may not be right for everyone but makes sense in this case, and therapy as tools to address Sara's anxiety.* I have spoken to many parents over the years who have doubts about the value of medication or therapy. Sara's mother, with her own history of anxiety, understands that sometimes it takes multiple tools to recover from severe distress.
4. *Remains hopeful and confident.* She could have allowed Sara to come home, which might have reduced anxiety for both mother and daughter in the short term, but instead offers Sara a plan for staying in school and addressing her symptoms.
5. *Provides follow-up support.* Even as she encourages Sara to stay in school, she makes extra visits and phone calls to help her. She tapers these contacts as Sara becomes more calm.

Sara's story is an example of extreme anxiety, but there are other kinds of anxiety that can be distressing to college students. How do you know when normal anxiety goes too far?

ANXIETY: AN ALARM THAT WON'T TURN OFF

What is anxiety? Healthy anxiety is a warning signal that we need to do something. For example, college students should have some anxiety at least a few days before a test. Their worry or sense of discomfort will motivate them to study.

Maladaptive anxiety is a signal that won't go away even as you take action to reduce your anxiety. It's like an alarm that won't turn off. In a full-blown panic attack, you could have a feeling of dread along with uncomfortable physical symptoms like a rapid heartbeat, a feeling of lightheadedness, rapid breathing, tunnel vision, tingling sensations, or nausea. Symptoms peak in about ten minutes and could last as long as thirty minutes.

A panic attack is the worst kind of anxiety because by the time it starts it is hard to stop. Certain parts of the brain, including the amygdala, become overactive, causing the sympathetic nervous system to set off a fight or flight reaction. Normally, the parasympathetic nervous system kicks in and acts like a brake to the high level of activation. With a panic attack, the brake does not get applied in time.

Anxiety comes in many forms. The following are different kinds of anxiety disorders that college students experience.

Panic Disorder

Sara's story gives us a good idea of what panic disorder is. It means someone has recurrent unexpected panic attacks followed by at least a month of fear of having another one. Some students who have panic disorder will stop going to class, not wanting to feel trapped in a lecture hall if a panic attack occurs. Many of my patients with panic disorder get so anxious that they get nauseous, and they can have trouble eating, like Sara did. The constant fear of having another panic attack can make it hard to concentrate in school, and grades can be impacted.

Social Anxiety Disorder

Think of terms like "shyness" and "performance anxiety." College students with social anxiety get stressed out in situations in which they feel they are being judged, like in a social setting or a lecture hall. They might have trouble speaking up in class or get so anxious during an exam that they forget the material and fail. They might also feel anxious at a party where they don't know anyone and turn to alcohol to feel more relaxed.

We all might get socially anxious at times, so when does social anxiety cross the line into becoming a disorder? When symptoms occur for more than six months, cause major distress, and interfere in day-to-day functioning. A student with social anxiety disorder might have trouble making friends because he or she is too anxious to talk to new people or his or her grades might decline because he or she gets paralyzing anxiety during exams.

Generalized Anxiety Disorder

College is the perfect breeding ground for generalized anxiety disorder. Students face constant deadlines, unclear expectations from professors, and pressure to succeed from parents. They may have difficulty sleeping, feel tired or irritable, have muscle tension, and have trouble concentrating. The anxiety never turns off—it's as if an alarm keeps ringing at a low level, reminding the student to study more, do better, and make more friends.

For the anxiety a student commonly experiences to be considered a disorder, the anxiety must be distressing and last for at least six months. It interferes with school, relationships, or both. Many of my patients with generalized anxiety disorder get irritable when they are anxious and may argue with a loved one. If your child is arguing with you, the underlying emotion might not be anger but anxiety.

DOES TECHNOLOGY TRIGGER ANXIETY?

In the previous section, I talked about anxiety as an alarm that won't turn off. Many of our technological devices are miniature alarms, constantly pinging, vibrating, and beeping to let us know we have received texts, e-mails, and Facebook posts. Are they sources of anxiety?

College students have told me about the impact of technology on their anxiety levels.

I was traveling in Europe this summer and visited some places without cell phone reception. I felt so much more relaxed without the constant texting. Sometimes I feel like my life would better if I didn't have a cell phone at all.

I was trying to fall asleep last night, but then I got a text from a woman I just broke up with. We texted back and forth for two hours, and I started to have a panic attack. I finally blocked her from texting, but then her roommates group texted me. I finally put my phone on do not disturb and went to sleep.

I've been extremely anxious the last two weeks and it's hard to sleep. I have group projects in two online classes and I can't get anyone to agree to a time when we can all chat online and discuss our parts. The project is due in three days and we haven't gotten anything done.

Technology can be very distracting and prevent us from being in the moment. I think mindfulness meditation techniques have become more popular in response to the constant distraction of technology. Mindfulness, one of the best treatments for anxiety, is the concept of being in the moment and paying attention to what is going on inside and around you in a nonjudgmental way.

Students tell me social media in general increases their stress level. They feel insecure when they see pictures of a student having fun at a party, going on a great trip, or getting a prized internship. They experience FOMO (fear of missing out) and walk around with a feeling that they are just not good enough. In chapter 6, I will review how the pursuit of perfection increases anxiety and other mental health issues.

Although new technologies can increase anxiety, there are many programs and apps that are designed to reduce anxiety. Some universities are using assisted online therapy, which combines online contact with therapists and online activities to reduce anxiety. There are also dozens of meditation and relaxation apps; you can look on the university's counseling center website for recommendations.

ANXIETY: YOU CAN FEEL IT IN YOUR GUT

"Every day I'm waking up with a stomachache."

"I'm going to the bathroom four times a day. What's wrong with me?"

Does your college student call you with gastrointestinal complaints? If so, you should also consider the role anxiety and stress may be playing in these problems. Many studies have linked anxiety to gastrointestinal pain, acid reflux, and irritable bowel syndrome. I get many referrals from primary care doctors who see patients for stomach pain related to stress and anxiety.

In Sara's story, we find she is too nauseous to eat. Several patients I see for the first time with acute anxiety have this complaint. Like Sara, they may have lost weight. Almost every patient I see with anxiety has some kind of gastrointestinal problem, including acid reflux, frequent or loose bowel movements, constipation, and discomfort from eating.

Many times, when students take SSRIs for their anxiety, their gastrointestinal symptoms improve. Some SSRIs can improve heartburn symptoms as well as irritable bowel symptoms like constipation and diarrhea. Occasionally SSRIs can cause nausea, a side effect managed by taking the medication with food.

If your child is having gastrointestinal problems, encourage him or her to be evaluated by a primary care doctor or gastroenterologist, and at the same time consider anxiety's role in these symptoms. Not every person can label what they are feeling as anxiety, but if they get sick or nauseous before every exam, they may be expressing anxiety through their gut.

ANXIETY HAS ITS SEASONS

Freshman Year

Is there anything more fraught with anxiety than saying goodbye to your daughter after you have helped move her into her freshman dorm? She has been connected to you for eighteen years, and now you are cutting the cord. I know my heart hurt when I left my daughter in her dorm room for the first time.

Freshman year can be an especially stressful time for you and your child. You don't know what the future holds, and she may be worried about keeping up with school work or making new friends. She may get her first C or F and feel overwhelmed. She may not know how to schedule an appointment with a doctor or get a prescription. And she may miss the comforts of home.

Parents generally visit and call more often during freshman year to ease the transition to college, and there is nothing wrong with this. If your child already has an anxiety disorder or develops one freshman year, these visits can help your child stay in the school rather than leave.

Sophomore Year

"I failed my chemistry and calculus classes. There is no way I can get into medical school. Now what will I do with my life?"

Your child starts college with certain hopes and dreams, but sometimes finds life does not go as planned. He might have imagined he would be a physician like his grandfather, and now he needs to change course. It is the middle of sophomore year and he has no idea what he wants to do with his life.

Many students have an identity crisis in college when they realize they have to change majors or career paths. Often students acknowledge they need to shift directions before their parents do, and parents may not want to accept this shift, seeing the future for their child in one way. The stress of changing paths and informing parents of their decision can cause major anxiety.

If your sophomore is not sure where he is heading, the best advice you can give him is to visit the campus career resource center. He can talk with counselors who can assess his interests and strengths and point him in a new direction. Once students find their passion, their anxiety levels will markedly decrease.

Junior Year

"How can I get everything done? I need to study for the LSATs, raise my GPA for my law school applications, and run a conference for the Law Society. I'm also in charge of my fraternity's rush. I don't even have time to sleep."

Junior year is crunch time, but you could call it crush time because students are weighed down by a sense of responsibility to get everything done, especially if they are applying to graduate school. Even when these students have time to sleep, they cannot fall asleep. Their minds race with the many tasks they need to complete.

At this point you can reassure your child that you are proud of all of his or her hard work and encourage him or her to prioritize his or her activities so he or she can get enough rest. I have seen students participate in too many clubs and volunteer hours to enhance graduate student applications, while their grades and standardized test scores suffer.

Senior Year

"I'm graduating a year ahead of my boyfriend, and I don't know if he'll want to stay committed to me once I leave town."

Senior year is the year of big decisions. Where will your child work? Will her relationship with her boyfriend last?

I see many seniors who don't feel ready to leave the college environment. They worry about how they will fit into their family's lives if they are moving back home to look for a job. They also worry about their social lives—how will they find friends if they are starting a job where most people are older than they are?

Lately, I see more seniors questioning their sexual identity. Are they gay, straight, or bisexual? They thought they'd know by now, but they're still unsure and feel anxious about their uncertainty. There are groups on many campuses where they can receive support from others who are struggling or have struggled with these issues.

Senior year is a great time for students to do group or individual therapy so they are not alone in their fears and anxieties. They can learn to accept that they have not resolved every issue they planned to address in college and they have many years to explore their identity.

WHAT HAPPENS IF YOU DON'T TREAT ANXIETY?

If a student has an anxiety disorder that goes untreated, the consequences could be serious and include academic struggles, substance abuse, and suicidal behavior. Two of three people in this country who have an anxiety disorder do not receive treatment, so parents should promote treatment to their children as a way to improve their lives and their academic performance. [4]

Academic Struggles

"I know the material, but when I go into the test, my heart races, I hyperventilate, and my mind goes blank."

"I'm so anxious all the time, I can't focus. When I am in the library I feel like pacing instead of sitting and studying."

Sometimes students get so anxious during a test they forget the material. Chronic anxiety impairs their concentration, so they can't learn the material they are studying or pay attention in class. If anxiety interferes with their sleep, they will not retain the material they reviewed that day or concentrate as well the next day.

Substance Abuse and Anxiety

Alcohol abuse, drug abuse, and anxiety are closely linked. In fact, 20 percent of people with anxiety have a drug or alcohol problem.[5] The link between anxiety and substance abuse is strong on college campuses because drugs and alcohol are readily available ways to cope with anxiety symptoms.

I have seen many students treat their anxiety with alcohol and drugs. Rather than call a parent after a panic attack caused them to fail an exam, they might go out that night and binge drink. Alcohol will temporarily reduce anxiety, but when it leaves their system, their anxiety rebounds to even higher levels.

For students with social anxiety, college can be a highly stressful place. Your child may be living in a dorm with two or three roommates; he may be going to house parties surrounded by people who are laughing and having fun, while he has no idea what to say. Your son may use alcohol to relax and be more open. Alcohol can become a daily habit for these students, the only way they can function.

Many students turn to marijuana to reduce anxiety. Studies have been inconsistent about marijuana's impact on anxiety, but I have seen students over the years who report anxiety attacks and emergency room visits after using marijuana. Because marijuana contains triple the amount of THC it did thirty years ago, it is more likely to cause anxiety in some people. Marijuana, with its negative impact on motivation and memory in college students, may ultimately increase anxiety when a student's academic performance declines.

If a student who uses alcohol and marijuana finds these substances are no longer helpful for anxiety, he or she may turn to hallucinogens like LSD, mushrooms, and ecstasy to achieve an alternative experience to his anxiety. The use of drugs to manage anxiety may lead to increased anxiety, depression, or even psychosis.

Anxiety and Suicidal Thinking

Anxiety disorders, particularly panic disorder, are associated with suicide attempts. One survey showed that of people who attempted suicide, over 70 percent had an anxiety disorder.[6]

Why is anxiety, and panic disorder in particular, associated with suicidal behavior? If you've ever had a panic attack, you know the answer to this question. My patients describe extreme discomfort when they are having a panic attack. Sometimes they will have nausea or vomiting. Panic attacks can be associated with pain and feeling like you are dying, as in Sara's case. A panic attack can make them miss an exam or need to leave class. The feeling of losing control is extremely uncomfortable.

If your child does have a panic disorder or another anxiety disorder, reassure him or her that there are excellent treatments for anxiety.

THE CAMPUS CURE FOR ANXIETY

As much as campus life increases anxiety, colleges now offer many opportunities to treat anxiety. Lifestyle changes are a good start to reduce stress levels. A medical evaluation can rule out physical causes of anxiety, like thyroid problems. Therapy and medications are also great tools for treating anxiety.

Lifestyle Changes

Is your child eating healthfully? Getting enough sleep? Healthful eating and a good night's sleep will promote a sense of well-being. Many college campuses have wellness coaches who will help your child with any sleep problems. Yoga and exercise classes, now widely available on or near campuses, can reduce anxiety. There are dozens of relaxation apps your child could find online.

Is your child using or abusing substances that can increase anxiety? Caffeine is a major culprit for anxiety, and I have seen many patients seeking treatment for anxiety walk into my office with a Venti Starbucks coffee or a Monster drink. Your anxious child might also be drinking alcoholic beverages and using drugs to reduce anxiety, but these substances will increase anxiety in the long run.

Is your child taking an ADHD medication that he has bought from other students to study longer? Tell him taking a stimulant when you don't have attention deficit disorder can increase anxiety. Whenever I see an anxious student, I ask if they are using nonprescribed stimulants. This short-term fix for a large workload will ultimately harm your child, increasing his risk for anxiety, an elevated heart rate, insomnia, high blood pressure, and seizures.

Does your child have effective ways to cope with stress? Many colleges now offer courses in stress management for credit. Encourage your child to sign up so she can learn valuable lessons to last a lifetime.

Medical Evaluation

If your child is having anxiety, a primary care doctor should evaluate for medical causes of anxiety, like thyroid disease or heart rhythm problems. Autoimmune disorders like lupus are associated with increased rates of anxiety disorders. Certain medications to treat asthma and inflammation can also cause anxiety.

The primary care doctor can also treat medical problems that tend to occur with anxiety, like the gastrointestinal problems I've mentioned. Anxious people are also more prone to back pain and headaches. Physical therapy for back pain and biofeedback or acupuncture for headaches can reduce your child's stress levels.

In Sara's story, I did not recommend she see a cardiologist, as her evaluation in the emergency room was normal. But sometimes I will refer patients who have anxiety to a cardiologist if they describe extremely high heart rates or irregular heart rhythms. A few of my patients have required daily treatment with a medication that slows their heart rate down.

Therapy

Cognitive behavioral therapy is truly the gold standard for anxiety disorder treatment. Therapists will help patients look at cognitive distortions that lead to anxiety. Catastrophizing is a common cognitive distortion among college students. They might think, "If I do badly on this test, I will never get into graduate school. And then I will never get a steady job or a house." People who are anxious tend to think the worst, and therapists will help them examine their irrational thoughts. Your child could reframe the thoughts by saying, "If I do badly on this test, I'll be disappointed. I'll reexamine my study methods and consider looking for a tutor or going to the professor's office hours."

These therapists will also teach anxiety lowering techniques like breathing and mindfulness. Certain breathing techniques can help your child slow his or her heart rate when anxiety takes hold. Mindfulness keeps your child focused on the moment, rather than stressing out about a big project that is due two months from now. People who are anxious are always worrying about the future, and I have seen freshmen who worry about being happy in their career when they are forty or fifty years old.

Many college counseling therapists employ cognitive behavioral therapy and also use psychodynamic therapies to look at conflicts and stressors that might be driving anxiety. Therapists can also take a problem-solving approach that links your child to appropriate campus resources. If your child struggles with anxiety about being away from home during freshman year, the therapist can help your child find activities on campus that will be fun and connect him or her with others. If your junior is anxious about his or her future after college, the therapist can help him or her explore his or her options and refer him or her to the career resource center.

Medication

How do you know if your child should consider medication for anxiety?

Let's say your daughter has an anxiety disorder. Her medical evaluation reveals no physical problems that could be causing anxiety. She has reduced her caffeine intake and does yoga. She is participating in therapy, but her anxiety gets so overwhelming that she cannot use the relaxation techniques the therapist taught her. She is always in distress and her grades are lower than they should be.

Your daughter should continue the positive changes she has made, but could also meet with a psychiatrist to see if medication is another tool for reducing anxiety. Many young people are hesitant to speak with a psychiatrist, but she is more likely to make an appointment with your encouragement. Meeting with a psychiatrist does not mean she must start medication; she could review her options and then make a decision.

Is there a time when you as a parent should strongly recommend medication? Sara's case is a good example. Sara feels unable to function or stay in school, and her anxiety is extreme enough to send her to the emergency room. If your child has anxiety so distressing that she is having suicidal thoughts, she should also consider medication.

Often depression goes hand in hand with anxiety, and if the symptoms are severe and include suicidal thoughts, a psychiatrist can help your child decide whether he or she would benefit from short-term treatment in a hospital, until he or she feels safe.

Several antidepressants reduce anxiety levels. Selective serotonin reuptake inhibitors like fluoxetine, sertraline, citalopram, escitalopram, and the norepinephrine serotonin reuptake inhibitor venlafaxine are very helpful for most anxiety disorders. The rate of improvement on these medications is gradual and varies from patient to patient. Patients will take these medications on a daily basis. After a year, a patient and his or her provider can consider discontinuing medication by tapering the medication slowly.[7] Some people will stay on these medications longer than a year. I write more about antidepressants in chapter 2.

Benzodiazepines like lorazepam and clonazepam can be used to treat anxiety in the short term, until the long-term medication has taken effect. We tend not to give benzodiazepines long term because people could develop dependence and might need higher doses to have the same effect. The prescription of benzodiazepines must be done carefully with anyone due to the potential for abuse.[8] College mental health psychiatrists are often especially careful, as college students have high rates of drug and alcohol use. For some of my patients who have occasional flare ups of anxiety, I might prescribe a limited number of pills of a benzodiazepine that they might take once every few weeks. I will not prescribe a benzodiazepine to students with drug and alcohol problems. In those instances, certain antihistamines and other nonaddictive medications can be used to treat anxiety.

FINAL TIPS FOR HELPING THE ANXIOUS COLLEGE STUDENT

1. *Stay calm.* If your child opens up to you and hears your voice rise with anxiety, he or she will hide his or her distress from you because he or she does not want to make you more anxious. Encourage him or her to take a deep breath, and you take a deep breath too. Listen and support your child.
2. *Don't add to the pressure on your child.* Your child wants to please you and live up to your expectations, but you might be encouraging a major or career that clashes with his or her personality or abilities. I'll talk more in chapter 4 about the balance between encouraging success and placing unrealistic expectations.
3. *Encourage your child to see a therapist and/or psychiatrist at the student counseling service.* Therapy will help your child learn skills to manage and prevent anxiety symptoms. If the anxiety is overwhelming, medication can help calm a student so he or she can engage in therapy.
4. *Promote lifestyle changes* that will reduce anxiety: exercise, yoga, meditation, adequate sleep, three meals a day, and avoidance of drugs.
5. *Visit your child* if he or she is overwhelmed by anxiety. You might join him or her for the first counseling center appointment or increase the frequency of your visits and phone calls until he or she feels better.

If your child has anxiety, know that help is available on campus. Once you link your child with the right resources, you can breathe a sigh of relief.

2

DEPRESSION

When College Is Not the Happiest Time in Life

"Dad, I'm too depressed to go to class."

You listen to your son, David, on the phone and wonder, could I be hearing this right? He's a senior in college, has a 3.8 GPA, and has already been accepted into law school. He has everything going for him.

You respond, "I don't understand. What happened?"

"I thought I could handle the breakup with Susan, but I can't."

David and Susan had planned to keep their relationship going even after David left for law school, but a month ago Susan changed her mind. Feeling like he lost the love of his life, David was devastated, spending most of his time in bed until he gave up on going to class altogether.

"I wasn't going to call you, but my roommate said he would if I didn't. I should have let you know sooner. I don't know what to do anymore."

Now what would you do?

College is supposed to be one of the happiest times in life, but eighteen to twenty-nine year olds experience the highest prevalence of depression compared with any other age group.[1] And depression rates continue to climb among college students, second only to anxiety as the most common problem seen in college counseling centers. According to the American College Health Association spring 2016 survey, 14 percent of college students were diagnosed with or treated for depression in the previous year. But not everyone with depression may be receiving treatment, as 37 percent of students reported feeling so depressed at some point in the previous year that it was difficult to function.[2] Only one of ten college students accesses care at his or her college counseling center, additional evidence that many distressed students are going without help.[3]

The consequences of untreated depression can be deadly. Suicide rates for young adults aged fifteen to twenty-four have steadily increased in the past fifteen years, and depression continues to be the most common cause of suicide.[4] Untreated clinical depression can take several months to reverse itself, so rapid treatment is essential to helping your child be safe. In the following vignette, one father takes extreme measures to address his son's depression.

THE TALE OF DAVID'S DEPRESSION

Ron convinces his son David to let him visit, and in a few hours, Ron is driving to see David. The next day, they come to my office.

David is as depressed as any student I have seen. Unshaven, with uncombed hair, he speaks slowly and softly, answering my questions while often looking down at his hands resting lifelessly in his lap. He barely eats the meals his roommate brings him. He is having trouble falling asleep at night and then sleeps for hours during the day. When I ask if he feels like hurting himself, he finally looks me in the eye.

"Lately I've been thinking it would be easier if I were hit by a car and died. Then this pain would end. I won't try to kill myself, because I don't want to hurt my dad, but if I don't feel better soon, I don't know what I'll do."

I'm concerned about David's safety. He is having suicidal thoughts and seems unable to take care of himself. Will treatment work quickly enough to bring David out of the danger zone? Medications can take one to two months to reach their full effect. Therapy can take even longer to promote change.

"David, sometimes the medicine doesn't work right away. And antidepressants can occasionally increase suicidal thinking in young adults. I recommend you go into the hospital where you can be safe while you start medication. I'm not going to force you to do this, but I think this would be best."

David's father has a different idea. "I'll stay with David to make sure he is safe. My job allows me to work remotely. If you can start him on medication now, I can encourage him to take care of himself and do his classwork so he can finish out the semester. If he feels worse, then we can consider the hospital."

Would David be safer staying with his father or admitting himself to the hospital? We review options, including David going home with his father, but David agrees to have his father stay with him, determined to finish out the semester. David will also take an antidepressant and see an off-campus therapist every week. I write a letter for our campus disability resource center so they will contact David's professors to request some extra time for him to complete his work.

We walk a tightrope with David for the next three weeks. He continues to have episodes of despair when he thinks he would be better off dead. At the same time, he also has times of improved mood and productivity. With his father's encouragement, he eats and sleeps regularly.

After a month of treatment, David turns the corner. Sitting in my office with his father, David smiles at me and says, "I still feel sad sometimes, but the episodes are not as deep or as frequent." He is looking forward to going home with his father and seeing his mother and younger sister for Thanksgiving. He'll come back on his own to finish out the semester, but his parents will keep checking in with him by phone. "My roommate and I are already planning out activities for our spring semester. We're going to the beach on the weekends and he's going to teach me how to surf, something I've always wanted to do. I can't believe I'll be graduating so soon."

I look at Ron, whose eyes tear up with joy and relief. I feel a sense of gratitude to this father, who was truly his son's lifeline.

WHEN COLLEGE STUDENTS MASK DEPRESSION

David is not alone in initially hiding his depression from his father. Many students will not tell their parents if they are feeling down. In my office, students offer many different explanations for why they wear a mask of happiness in front of their parents when they are hurting inside.

"I'm an adult now. I should be able to handle my problems on my own."

"My mother will just get worried and overreact. That will make me feel worse."

"My father is already depressed. If he hears how badly I'm doing, he might become suicidal."

Every day in my office, I witness the fallout of hidden and untreated depression. Failing grades. Poor self-care. Self-destructive behaviors. Rapid treatment can be critical to success and even survival. But what if your child is suffering in silence? How would you know if he or she is depressed? You may need to explore more deeply with your child his or her feelings, thoughts, and behaviors. Knowing the signs and symptoms of depression can help.

DEPRESSION: CARRYING THE WEIGHT OF THE WORLD

"It's like walking through molasses."

"A big sack of problems is always weighing down on my shoulders."

"I see the world through a fog."

My patients use many metaphors to describe the pain of depression, a biological and psychological condition that involves a two-week or longer period of symptoms that could include a down mood, inability to enjoy activities, poor concentration, irritability, fatigue, eating too much or too little, and suicidal thoughts or behaviors. Depressed college students may push through their pain, only seeking help when their grades decline or they find it hard to get out of bed. Some students go in and out of depression and others can stay in a chronic state of low mood.

If your son is not telling you he is depressed but sounds down when you speak with him on the phone, ask outright if he is feeling depressed. Ask about how he is doing in school, how he is sleeping, and how he is eating. Even if he does not admit to being depressed, you can encourage a visit to a campus therapist who can evaluate him. If there is a family history of depression, be open about it and emphasize the importance of treatment. Most importantly, you can tell him that depression is common among college students and that there is strength, not weakness, in seeking help.

If you are worried your depressed daughter is suicidal, ask about it. There are no perfect words for this, but you can tell her that sometimes people who are depressed feel like hurting or even killing themselves. Does she ever feel this way? Asking about suicide in a calm and non-judgmental way will allow her to tell you how she is really feeling, so you can get her the help she needs.

WHY ARE COLLEGE STUDENTS MORE DEPRESSED NOW?

The increased rates of depression in college may reflect the fact that depression has been starting at younger ages in general over the last fifty years. Dr. Peter Gray offers theories for this increase in depression in his article "The Decline of Play and Rise in Children's Mental Disorders."[5] Children have less control over their lives in general as there is more structure and less free play; this loss of control can be associated with feelings of depression. Furthermore, our culture puts an emphasis on materialism and external signs of success; people feel more compelled to impress others than to set their own personal goals and feel good about their achievements.

Loneliness and lack of social support may also contribute to college student depression. Lack of social connection across wide populations has been shown to increase the risk of depression. In my office, I have heard many students talk about their sense of loneliness and social isolation while living in a freshman dorm with dozens of other students. Whereas my generation lived in dorms where we did not own cell phones and we propped open our doors so we were constantly interacting with other students, this generation relates to others less through face-to-face contact and more through social media. Students may have to work harder to make connections on campus, but they can. Chapter 5 will show how you can help your child defeat loneliness.

Every day, I'm reminded that financial pressures may be driving some increased rates of depression. Recently I saw a young woman who was depressed and learned she did not have money for food or health insurance. I scheduled an appointment with a campus social worker who could help her get her basic needs met. Part of her depression stemmed from academic troubles she was facing and the recent loss of a scholarship. In general, studies have linked bad economic times to depression, and as a Floridian living in the epicenter of the 2008 housing collapse, I have seen many students struggle to support themselves when parents lose houses or jobs. Chapter 8 will describe how you can help your child cope with financial pressures.

DOES TECHNOLOGY CAUSE DEPRESSION OR DOES DEPRESSION LEAD TO MORE TECHNOLOGY USE?

Years ago, I remember calling a father with some very bad news. "I recommend you bring your son home. He is severely depressed. He's been involved with a role-playing video game for fourteen hours a day and is failing his classes." This young man's sleep and meal schedule had vanished, replaced by a virtual reality.

Did the video games cause his depression or did the depression lead him to play video games? I think he got into a vicious cycle in which video games relieved some of his sadness, but his obsession with the game worsened his depression. Playing video games activates the reward pathway of the brain, making them addictive to some individuals.

Over the years, I have seen several patients, mostly male, spend so much time on video games that they were failing a class. If you have a son who is depressed, you should ask him if gaming is impacting his depression. Reducing his time playing online games may improve his mood as well as his grades.

On the other hand, some of my patients tell me video games help relieve their stress and improve their mood. One patient has made friends through an online game whom he subsequently met in person. Another plays a video game that helps her set goals to relieve her depression. In fact, there are many apps to address depressive symptoms.

Social media is another form of technology that can affect mood, and one study showed that increased social media use was associated with increased levels of depression in adults.[6] Again, it is hard to assign cause and effect. People who are more depressed may be inclined to check their social media sites more often. On the other hand, some people will use social media sites to connect with people with similar problems and get support.

How much time is your college student spending on social media? I want my patients to spend more time studying and socializing and less time pointing and clicking. As a parent, the little control you have over your child's technology use in high school is gone now that your child is in college. Nonetheless, you can ask your child in a curious and non-judgmental way how he thinks video games or social media are impacting his mood.

Depression has of course existed long before the rise of the Internet, video games, and social media. The treatments for depression, on the other hand, have evolved greatly over the past century, with numerous medications and psychotherapies providing avenues for recovery. How do you know which treatment to choose?

DOES MY COLLEGE STUDENT NEED THERAPY, MEDICATION, OR BOTH?

During my psychiatry training, we would often treat depression with psychotherapy first and turn to medication if the therapy did not work. Now the pendulum has swung the other way, and someone might be given a medication for depression before trying therapy. What is the best way to defeat depression?

Studies looking at depression treatments offer some general recommendations. If your child has severe depression, a combination of medication and therapy will best promote recovery. A combination will help in mild to moderate depression as well, but in these cases, your child should talk with his or her mental health provider and express his or her preference because patient preference influences outcome.[7] I have had patients who only want medication treatment for depression and others who want therapy. Some want both.

If your child's depressive symptoms go away, how long should he or she continue therapy or medication? If this is your child's first episode of depression, he or she should stay on medication for about nine months to a year and then work with his or her psychiatrist to slowly taper the antidepressant. Some students, though, prefer to stay on medication longer, or they may wait until a less stressful time like the summer to taper and stop their medications. As for therapy, continuing treatment can be beneficial in terms of preventing the recurrence of depressive symptoms.

Do you have a strong preference for therapy or medication for your child? I have found that most parents are open to their children trying different treatments for depression. But other parents have concerns about their children taking antidepressants. Parent concerns increased in 2004 when the FDA issued a black box warning on antidepressants advising that children and adolescents up to age twenty-five have an increased risk of suicidal thoughts and behaviors when taking antide-pressants. Later reviews showed the risk was statistically significant only in those under age eighteen. Furthermore, the study this warning is based on does not indicate an increased risk of completed suicide, and more recent studies suggest that the benefits of antidepressants in ado-lescents outweigh the risks.[8] In my experience, many college students greatly benefit from antidepressant medication.

Nonetheless, patients, even those over twenty-five years old, can have unexpected reactions to medications. When prescribing antide-pressants, I discuss the risk of suicidal thoughts with my patients be-cause this risk increases when the student first starts taking the medica-tion. I advise my patients: "If you get suicidal thoughts when you start the medication, you can stop the medication and let me or another health care provider know. This could be a side effect of the medica-tion." I meet with patients more frequently at the beginning of treat-ment to check for side effects. I also encourage students to let their parents know they are starting an antidepressant so they can provide extra support if their child is having any problems with the medication.

If you have any concerns about your child starting antidepressants, you should request he or she sign a release of information form so you can speak with his or her provider to discuss the pros and cons of medication. Ideally you, your child, and the provider can agree on a course of action. Your opinion makes a big difference about whether your child will continue on antidepressants or not. I've had patients go home for vacation and stop medication because they think their parents will disapprove only for them to have a relapse in depression.

If your college student has a more severe form of depression with suicidal thoughts, I will encourage him or her to sign a release of infor-mation form so I can let you know he or she is starting medication and what the risks are. When you talk with him or her, you can be alert for negative reactions to medication and encourage him or her to inform his or her doctor.

How will you and your child know whether to pursue therapy, medication, or both to treat depression? Your child should be able to make an appointment at a campus counseling center where a therapist will "triage" or assess what his or her needs are. If treatment begins with therapy, there are many effective ones to choose from.

THE POWER OF THERAPY

I once treated a young woman for depression who felt worse on every antidepressant she tried. I added medications like atypical antipsychotics to augment the effects of the antidepressant, but this did not work. Mood stabilizers, which sometimes help depressed people feel better, also did not help. At one point she was suicidal and was hospitalized. When she returned to school on a combination of medication, she was depressed once again. I knew I had to do something different and sent her to a therapist off campus who could see her weekly. She went reluctantly, and slowly but surely this therapist built up trust with her to the point that she was willing to engage in cognitive behavioral therapy. Whereas before she tended to catastrophize every disappointment, she could now see that a B grade or a friend turning down a lunch invitation was not the end of the world. I was eventually able to taper her off medication, and she continued therapy until graduation.

Connecting with the right therapist is essential, and studies show that treatment outcomes improve when there is a good fit between a therapist and a patient. As for the kind of therapy that is helpful, cognitive behavioral therapy has the best outcomes. This therapy addresses cognitive distortions that lead to negative thoughts and encourages behaviors like meditation and exercise that improve mood. Interpersonal therapy focuses on bereavement, role transitions, and communication problems that contribute to depression and might help a student who is coping with a relationship breakup or the death of a loved one. Psychodynamic therapy increases insight into how previous relationships influence current relationships, allowing a student who gets into tempestuous relationships to break the pattern.

What about group therapy for your depressed college student? Mindfulness-based cognitive behavioral group therapy has been shown to be an effective treatment for depression. I have had patients do groups like this with profoundly positive results. Campus counseling centers offer a wide variety of groups, but if the depression is more severe, it is best to start with individual counseling.

THE POWER OF PROZAC (AND OTHER ANTIDEPRESSANTS)

"I'm reaching the point of no return."

I recently saw a young man who for many years had tried to address his depressive symptoms through therapy. He would do well for a while and then his depression would come back, along with suicidal feelings. He felt himself crossing a line this time and was worried he would act on these feelings and try to kill himself. He wanted to start antidepressant medication as soon as possible. Within a week of starting medication, his mood improved greatly. A pre-med student, he felt less pressure about school and did not despair as he used to when he got anything less than an A.

Antidepressant medication may lift the heaviness of depression that weighs your child down, allowing him or her to engage in therapy. These medications alter your brain biology, raising levels of neurotransmitters that improve mood. Fluoxetine (Prozac), the first modern antidepressant, raises serotonin levels. Bupropion raises norepinephrine and dopamine levels. Venlafaxine raises levels of serotonin and norepinephrine. Medications like fluoxetine that raise serotonin levels are the first line of treatment for depression.

These medications have other very positive effects on the brain. They decrease inflammation, which is found to be increased in some cases of depression. They increase the levels of brain-derived neurotrophic factor (BDNF), improving communication between neurons in the brain. Finally, they turn off the chronic stress response, which tends to elevate corticosteroid levels.

Antidepressants can also have side effects, particularly when your child starts them. For the first few days, he or she may get nausea, headaches, and some gastrointestinal discomfort. If these side effects don't go way, he or she should let his or her psychiatrist know. Sometimes your child may need to try a few different medications before he or she finds the one that works.

If your child starts antidepressants, he or she should meet with the psychiatrist in the first few weeks to decide if he or she is on the right dose and also check in about side effects. Appointments can be spread out once a dose is established and he or she is feeling better.

Some patients feel better after a few days of medication. When this happens, I am pleased, because usually that means the patient is going to have a good response to medication. Some responses are more gradual, and if there is not enough improvement, your child and the psychiatrist will add another medication to augment the effects of antidepressants or change the medication.

How do I know which medication to choose? I will take a family history, and if a family member had a positive response to a certain medication, I might choose that one. As I said in chapter 1, it helps for you to be open about your own history of mental health issues and which medications worked. I also look at the unique profile of the medication and try to match it to the symptoms a patient is experiencing. If someone is very anxious, along with being depressed, I might prescribe sertraline, which will help with anxiety and depressive symptoms. If someone is very tired all the time, I might prescribe bupropion, which tends to be activating.

Once my daughter asked me to describe how I choose antidepressants, and she said it sounds like trial and error. While we use clinical reasoning, there is still too much guesswork. Ideally we could use more precise methods like genetic testing to help us select antidepressants. In fact, there is testing available that will tell you how a patient will metabolize medications and even how he or she might respond to certain antidepressants. Unfortunately, this test can be very costly and most insurance companies will not cover it. Some students qualify for a discount on the test. I look forward to the day when we offer personalized medicine or targeted treatment, with genetic testing and brain scanning helping us pick the most effective antidepressants for all patients. If your child is having trouble finding the right antidepressant for him or her, consider paying for genetic testing, while seeing if there is a discount or coupon for it.

WHEN DEPRESSION IS NOT JUST DEPRESSION

Depression usually does not travel alone and often partners with anxiety as much as 50 percent of the time.[9] In my practice, the majority of patients I see for depression have some form of anxiety disorder. These disorders may have the same root cause: a lack of serotonin, norepinephrine, or dopamine. As stated in chapter 1, many of the medications used to treat depression are also used to treat anxiety.

What if your child tells you, "Mom, I've been really depressed. Now I feel like my professors are hacking my computer and I keep hearing voices inside my head telling me I'm worthless and my life is not worth living." If your child has delusions or hallucinations along with depression, he or she may have a psychotic depression, putting him or her at increased risk for self-harm. A psychiatrist should rapidly evaluate him or her and the three of you should talk, by speaker phone if necessary, to determine the best course of action. Ideally, he or she can be treated as an outpatient with medication (an antidepressant and antipsychotic) as well as with therapy. If safety is a factor, a short-term hospitalization can be helpful. With timely treatment, students can achieve excellent recoveries. You can read more about psychosis in chapter 12.

Sometimes what starts out as a depressive episode can blossom into bipolar disorder. I remember starting a patient on fluoxetine for depression right before he went home for spring break. His mother called me five days later, saying her son was not sleeping and was running around the neighborhood. Fluoxetine had induced a manic episode, an infrequent occurrence, but a risk whenever someone starts an antidepressant. We stopped the antidepressant and the young man was fine for a while, but then went on to develop bipolar disorder, with manic or hypomanic episodes alternating with depressive ones.

Bipolar disorder occurs infrequently in college students, affecting under 2 percent of the college population.[10] Usually someone has a few depressive episodes before going on to have a manic episode. In a person prone to bipolar I disorder, an antidepressant can actually induce a manic episode, all the more reason for a psychiatrist to follow up with a patient within a few weeks after starting him or her on an antidepressant medication. Bipolar I disorder requires treatment with a mood stabilizer; antidepressants should never be the sole treatment for someone with bipolar I disorder. You can read more about bipolar disorder in chapter 12.

Now you know how therapy and medication can help your depressed child. They are two parts of a five-point plan to put your child on a path to recovery.

A FIVE-POINT PLAN FOR DEFEATING DEPRESSION

Wellness activities, a medical evaluation, therapy, medication, and the disability resource center are wonderful recovery tools for the depressed college student.

1. Wellness Activities

Exercise can reduce symptoms of mild depression, boosting levels of serotonin, dopamine, norepinephrine, and endorphins. Most colleges now have fitness centers with a wide array of classes. Some of my patients find Zumba or yoga give their moods a lift. *Avoiding alcohol and drugs can also improve your child's mood.* Alcohol is a brain depressant and will bring your child down if he or she is already depressed. I have also seen marijuana, LSD, and cocaine exacerbate depression. If your child is depressed and using drugs or drinking excessively, he or she may need a specialized program called a dual diagnosis program to address these problems.

2. Medical Evaluation

If your child has not had a recent physical, he or she should get one. Medical causes of depression may need to be eliminated, like anemia and thyroid problems. I have seen some students whose depression started with the onset of mononucleosis. The primary care provider may decide to order labs to rule out these problems.

Sleep disorders can also cause depression. When I have seen students with excessive sleepiness, I send them to a sleep clinic for evaluation. I have had patients with both sleep apnea and narcolepsy who had remarkable recoveries from depression after their sleep disorder was treated. Unfortunately, many insurance plans, especially student plans, will not pay for sleep studies. I encourage parents to help cover the costs, as untreated sleep problems can greatly interfere with a student's ability to function in school and in life.

3. Therapy

You have encouraged your depressed daughter to see a therapist, and she has finally called the campus counseling center to make an appointment. It happens to be midterms. She reports back to you, "Mom, there's a month wait for a therapy appointment. What am I supposed to do until then?"

Unfortunately, as more students access therapy without a matching increase in resources, wait times have increased. Some students are referred out right away to community providers because campus counseling appointments are full. You should talk with your daughter and decide if you feel this is an urgent issue. If she is eating or sleeping poorly, having suicidal thoughts, and missing class, she should be seen quickly. She can usually access the counseling center on-call system on a weekday and meet with someone. But speaking with someone on campus does not guarantee ongoing treatment. *Keep in touch with your child until you know she has obtained ongoing services.* If she needs to get services off campus, the counseling center may have a case manager help her get an appointment in the community. The counseling center website may have a list of resources.

Whether she has on-campus or off-campus therapy, consistency is important. In the early stages of depression, she may need weekly appointments. With time, visits could be spaced apart. When she is feeling better, she may benefit from monthly appointments for a check in or "tune up." For some of my patients whom I see every month or two for medication management, I have done supportive therapy that includes focusing on strengths, problem solving, and being aware of emotions and how they impact thoughts and behaviors.

4. Medication

Getting antidepressants may be the most challenging problem your daughter may face in treating her depression. Four of ten colleges do not offer psychiatry services, and those that do may have a waitlist.[11] If there is too long a wait on campus, your child could ask for a referral to an off-campus psychiatrist. A case manager might help her find an appointment, but if not, I recommend you get on the phone and help her find one. A depressed college student may not have enough energy to pursue care herself.

If your child gets medication on campus, she may work with a psychiatrist, a psychiatric nurse practitioner, or a primary care doctor. Some students will start with a primary care doctor but transfer to a psychiatrist if they don't respond to treatment. With our growing national shortage of psychiatrists, primary care doctors prescribe the majority of antidepressants in the general population.

5. The Campus Disability Resource Center

"Dad, I just started treatment for depression but it's taking time to work. I'm having trouble concentrating and even motivating myself. If I don't feel better soon, I may have to take the rest of the semester off."

The campus disability resource center will help your child by coaching him in school work and allowing some initial flexibility in deadlines. The counselor at the center might also encourage your child to drop a class to reduce his academic stress. Most people recognize that people don't recover from depression right away. If your child cannot keep up with the work at all, he may need to medically withdraw from the semester and come back the next semester. He should meet with the disability resource center when he gets back so academic coaching can continue.

To be able to use the disability resource center, your child will need a note from a mental health care provider; these letters should document the diagnoses and the accommodations that are recommended.

WHAT IF YOUR CHILD IS HOSPITALIZED FOR DEPRESSION?

If your depressed college student feels like hurting herself and she cannot be safe, she will be encouraged to admit herself to a psychiatric hospital. Most people will go into the hospital voluntarily, but occasionally students are involuntarily hospitalized. Involuntary hospitalization is a controversial area, and many newspaper articles and news reports have quoted college students who feel they were unfairly hospitalized.

I try to avoid involuntary hospitalization as much as possible and will work with patients to create a safety plan that involves friends or family, while giving medication and therapy a chance to work. If family or friends are unavailable, it would be ideal to provide someone additional support through a peer respite, a residence run by people who have experienced mental illness. A peer respite has recently opened in our area and soon will have a residential component, something that will greatly assist our community.

My patients who enter a hospital voluntarily generally report a positive experience, benefiting from individual therapy, group therapy, and starting medication. If your child goes into the hospital, it is essential that you physically come to meet with your child and the treatment team to come up with the best plan after she is discharged from the hospital. It could be going home for treatment or staying in school with fewer classes and pursuing treatment on campus. Many dean of students offices have case managers that you and your child can talk with to devise the best plan for school, whether she stays in school this semester or comes back next semester. If she goes home, the case manager can also help you with the medical withdrawal process, which may allow a tuition refund.

The key to this situation is working with involved parties as a team so you and your child can come up with a plan that will keep her safe and promote academic success. If she chooses to take a semester off, don't worry. She can still excel. I have worked with many students who were hospitalized for depression, took a semester off, and completed college, going on to careers in health care, law, engineering, and education. College students are remarkably resilient.

FINAL TIPS FOR HELPING YOUR COLLEGE STUDENT COMBAT DEPRESSION

1. *Stay calm and hopeful if your child says he or she is depressed.* If you become upset, he or she will shut down and not turn to you for help.

2. *Encourage your child to pursue a comprehensive evaluation and treatment plan.* A healthy lifestyle, a medical evaluation, therapy, and psychiatry could help your child recover from depression.

3. *Provide ongoing support through phone calls and visits.* Family support is an important part of depression and reduces the risk of suicide in college students.

4. *Connect your child with the campus disability resource center.* The disability resource center can provide academic coaching as well as accommodations to help your child succeed.

5. *Consider other options if the depression worsens.* Your child's safety is more important than finishing out a semester. Sometimes leaving school, going home, or entering a hospital will allow your child to recover and return to school more ready to deal with academic stress. Work as a team with your child and his or her therapist, psychiatrist, and dean of students representative to make a decision.

We think of college as the best time of our lives, but for some college students, it can be their first time facing an episode of depression. With treatment, your child can develop the tools to fight his or her way out of the darkness of depression into the light of recovery.

3

SUBSTANCE USE DISORDERS

Should You Just Say No When It Comes to Drugs and Alcohol?

Your daughter, Dani, turns twenty-one years old today. You call her at school to wish her a happy birthday. Because you've heard rumors that some students celebrate their twenty-first birthday by taking twenty-one shots of alcohol, you warn her to be careful.

"C'mon, Dad, I'm over binge drinking. That was so freshman year."

Three weeks later, you receive a phone call around lunchtime. It's a nurse in the emergency room who was given permission by Dani to speak with you. The nurse informs you that the campus police brought Dani in the night before, after she was found running around campus shouting that someone was chasing after her. You learn that since her birthday, Dani has been drinking alcohol daily and smoking marijuana multiple times a day. The previous night she used cocaine, triggering her paranoia. Dani eventually fell asleep in the emergency room, and when she woke up her psychotic symptoms had subsided. The nurse gives Dani the phone.

"Sorry, Dad. I know you told me to be careful. I'll never use cocaine or other hard drugs again. I'll cut back to using marijuana once a day, and save drinking for the weekends. I'm fine now. I'm going to go back to the dorm."

You tell Dani that you are driving up today to check on her. She says that isn't necessary. "Don't worry, Dad. I've got this under control."

What would you do?

Preventing substance use disorders in your college student or treating them if they happen is one of the toughest challenges a parent can face. You may be the last person to learn your child has a substance use disorder, and may only find out if he or she ends up in the emergency room—that is, if your child agrees to notify you. Often your child won't tell you, knowing you will be upset or try to get him or her to stop using drugs or alcohol. His or her friends might notice concerning behaviors, but your child may have sworn them to secrecy. The university may or may not tell you if your child's drug problem comes to their attention. I've found that each university has different policies regarding contacting parents about campus drug or alcohol violations. Under the Family Educational Rights and Privacy Act (FERPA), university administrators can tell you your child has a drug or alcohol problem if the "behavior is an articulable and significant threat to the health or safety of a student."[1] They have the option to notify you, but not the legal requirement.

What if your child is seeing a psychiatrist for an alcohol- or substance-related problem? Will the psychiatrist inform you of your child's ongoing drug use? Under the Health Insurance Portability and Accountability Act (HIPAA), a psychiatrist cannot contact you without your child's consent unless "the disclosure is necessary to prevent a serious and imminent threat to the health or safety of the patient or others."[2] Surprisingly, most of the time when I am working with a student who has a substance use problem, he or she will allow me to speak with a parent right away. However, occasionally a student won't agree to let me talk with his or her parents, and my hands are tied if he or she is not in immediate danger of harming him- or herself. But I know the longer a student abuses drugs or alcohol, the higher the risk of harm. Being a parent myself and not being able to advise a parent to intervene is one situation that can keep me up at night.

Often these parents suspect drug use by their child's behavior, but they don't know what to do. They are caring and loving. They may not have allowed their child to use drugs in high school, and they would be concerned about their child's behavior if they knew the extent of the problem. I hope this chapter will help parents recognize the symptoms of substance abuse early on and know where to access help.

Unfortunately, substance use disorders continue to be a major problem on college campuses and in college-aged adults in general. Substance use disorders, according to the *Diagnostic and Statistical Manual of Mental Disorders* (DSM-5), include problematic uses of substances that lead to distress and impairment in functioning. The term "substance use disorder" encompasses a wide range of behaviors, from daily use to binge use. The previous edition of the diagnostic manual, the DSM-IV, made a clear divide between substance abuse, which might mean less frequent but still harmful use, and substance dependence, which means daily heavy use that is associated with physiologic dependence and withdrawal. "Substance use disorder" might be a better term to describe the spectrum of behaviors we see in clinical practice. Most college students are not daily users of substances and fall into the abuse rather than dependence category.

Alcohol use disorder causes the most suffering on college campuses, but quite a few other drugs contribute to academic problems and emotional distress as well. Here are the latest statistics on alcohol and drug use:

- Nearly two-thirds of college students drank in the past month, and one-third of college students binge drank in the past two weeks.[3] Alcohol is associated with nearly 2,000 college student deaths, 700,000 assaults, and 100,000 sexual assaults per year.[4]
- At some point in a thirty-day period, 18.6 percent of students used marijuana and 10 percent used other drugs.[5]
- In a thirty-day period, 1 percent of students used alcohol and 2.7 percent used marijuana on a daily basis.[6]
- Within the past year, many students used prescription drugs not prescribed to them: 6.5 percent used stimulants, 5 percent used painkillers, and 3 percent used sedatives like alprazolam.[7]
- Of those students who took nonprescribed stimulants like the ADHD medications amphetamine/dextroamphetamine and methylphenidate, most took them to enhance studying, while some took them to get high.[8] Stimulants taken in greater than recommended doses can lead to high blood pressure, insomnia, anxiety, seizures, and psychosis.
- Other drugs of abuse on college campuses include LSD, mushrooms, cough syrup (dextromethorphan), and cocaine.

- The rate of campus substance use disorders is high. Almost one of four college students meet criteria for substance abuse or dependence.[9]

One class of drugs that has been of growing concern on college campuses is opioids, which includes drugs like oxycodone, hydrocodone, and heroin.[10] While completing this book, I read newspaper reports of increasing opioid overdoses among college students. They have not escaped the national opioid epidemic that killed over 33,000 people in 2015.[11] If abuse of these drugs occurs, comprehensive treatment is essential due to a high risk of overdose. Many students, though not abusing these drugs, are still impacted by the opioid epidemic in this country. I have had patients experience the devastating loss of a close friend to an opioid overdose.

Many students, like Dani, will experiment with a combination of drugs, often with disastrous consequences.

DANI'S DRUG WAR

Gabriel wants to see his daughter, Dani, after her visit to the emergency room, but he also thinks he should respect her wishes not to come. Dani agrees to speak with him every day. He's concerned about Dani's plan to continue smoking marijuana and drinking after her recent emergency room visit, but can he really tell her to stop? Besides, Gabriel smoked marijuana during the first year of college without a problem. Like Dani said, if she stays away from the hard drugs, she should be okay.

One month later, Gabriel gets a call from Dani's roommate. "You've got to come take Dani home. She's been smoking marijuana multiple times a day, and has missed most of her classes. She seems depressed and paranoid much of the time. She's been binge drinking and doing other drugs on weekends. A few days ago, she took two hits of LSD and started shouting, accusing us of planning to hurt her. Now she's saying she's too depressed to get out of bed, and we're afraid to leave her alone."

Gabriel's heart sinks. He wishes he had gone up to see her the first time she had a bad reaction to drugs. He should have convinced Dani to meet with a substance abuse counselor. Now she is in serious trouble. Gabriel gets on the phone with Dani and convinces her to go to the campus counseling center. There a counselor arranges for her to meet with a psychiatrist in the afternoon. If Gabriel leaves now, he can get to campus in time for the appointment.

That afternoon, I meet with Dani and Gabriel. Dani's face is expressionless, and she describes feeling empty and sad. She is not suicidal or experiencing any psychotic symptoms. She hasn't had any marijuana or alcohol since the LSD incident. She said that over the past month she had increased her marijuana use to fight her depression, but she only felt worse. She took LSD, hoping it would lift her mood, but experienced a sense of detachment instead. "I hate the way I feel. I know I need to stay away from drugs and alcohol, but I'm afraid of how I'll feel if I stop taking them for good."

Gabriel puts his hand on Dani's shoulder and tells her, "I want you to come home, Dani, where you can go to an outpatient rehab program near our house. You can work in my office until you feel more stable, and if you can stay sober, I'm fine with you going back to school."

Dani becomes tearful. "But I hate to leave my friends now. Can't I just go to the campus counseling center for treatment? It's almost the end of the fall semester, and I'll have a fresh start in a few weeks."

After Dani and I review her history of drug use, I tell Dani, "You tried to reduce your drug and alcohol use after your emergency room visit last month, but it didn't work, despite your best efforts. I agree with your father about going home and attending outpatient rehab; you need more resources than our campus can offer you to battle your drug problem. This problem is not your fault; some people are genetically prone to having drug and alcohol problems, and you might be one of these people. However, at this point you need to make choices that will keep you healthy and safe. Drugs and alcohol are especially problematic for you because you've already had a few episodes of paranoia on drugs and you've become significantly depressed. If you keep using drugs and alcohol, your depression and psychosis could become long lasting. A rehab program is the best place for you to recover from your substance-related problems. Individual and group therapy are essential in helping you maintain sobriety. The program also offers family therapy for your father to participate in. Today, I'll prescribe an antidepressant to help with the depression. In the rehab program, you can see a psychiatrist who can evaluate your response to medication and make any necessary changes."

Dani goes home with Gabriel and participates in the outpatient rehab program. She meets other people her age struggling with addiction and mood problems. She finds that the support from individual and group therapy lifts her mood, and she soon stops craving drugs. She continues taking her antidepressant, realizing that she was using drugs to self-medicate feelings of depression.

Dani returns in the summer semester and meets regularly with the campus AA group. She also sees an addiction specialist who helps her strengthen her coping skills so she does not turn to drugs in times of distress. She is committed to her sobriety. We meet every few months; she wants to continue the antidepressant, which helps her feel "normal," like her old self. Dani is totally different than when I first saw her, wearing a lively expression and talking about the many campus activities she is involved in.

Gabriel is thrilled by his daughter's progress. He is taking a different approach to teaching Dani's younger brother about the dangers of drug use. He talks with Dani's brother frankly about the problems Dani faced, urging him not to try drugs in the future. If he does drink, he needs to avoid binge drinking. Dani's brother says, "Don't worry, Dad. I'll be careful."

In Dani's drug war, Dani's father does not initially appreciate the dangers of her drug and alcohol use. He looks at his own benign experience with marijuana and alcohol, not understanding that Dani has taken her use to the extreme and added other drugs into the mix. With marijuana now containing triple the THC (tetrahydrocannabinol) than it did two decades ago, today's marijuana is a much more potent drug.[12] Dani's father has witnessed firsthand what research is showing: drugs are especially damaging to the still-developing adolescent brain.

THIS IS THE ADOLESCENT BRAIN ON DRUGS

Most parents will encourage their children to stop all drug and alcohol use when their children face problems with abuse and addiction, especially if they have associated mental health problems like depression or psychosis. However, sometimes I will call parents, with their child's permission, to discuss treatment for their child's substance abuse problem, and I will get other responses.

"This binge drinking is just a phase. He'll outgrow it. A lot of college students do this."

"She might be doing drugs, but she's doing well in school. Why should I worry?"

"I've been smoking marijuana every day for years without a problem. I don't see a problem with my son smoking."

I will explain to these parents that the adolescent brain is especially vulnerable to the toxic effects of alcohol and drugs because the brain is undergoing major changes until age twenty-five. A review of several studies shows how the use of alcohol and drugs can negatively impact adolescent brain maturation.[13] Normally, the adolescent brain is finishing development of the prefrontal cortex—the planning, decision-making, and judgment part of the brain. The adolescent brain is also improving efficiency by 1) removing or pruning unnecessary connections between individual neurons and 2) increasing white matter, which enhances communication between different parts of the brain. In adolescents, heavy alcohol use can decrease the volume of the prefrontal cortex and the hippocampus, the memory region of the brain. Alcohol can also decrease white matter in the brain. Marijuana has been shown to disrupt both white matter development and the pruning process. Alcohol and marijuana can impair brain function and efficiency.

What are the real-world outcomes of these brain effects? Heavy alcohol and heavy marijuana use both have negative impacts on memory, attention, and school performance.[14] One study showed that college students who frequently used marijuana skipped classes more often, had lower GPAs, and took longer to graduate than other students.[15] I have worked with many students who excel academically as freshmen despite drug and alcohol use, only to face academic struggles as upperclassmen when their substance use continues or escalates. They may get by and graduate, but without a job or graduate school admission. They seem to have lost their drive to make plans for the future.

I have reviewed how excessive drug and alcohol use can interfere with brain maturation and academic growth. However, when it comes to psychological growth, the impact can be just as profound. One major problem with regular drug use is that it prevents college students from developing healthy coping skills for the academic stress, heartbreak, and loss that they may experience. They may choose to drink or use drugs when they are stressed out rather than exercise, talk with friends, meditate, or watch a Netflix series. When they don't develop solid coping skills, they are more likely to experience depression and anxiety disorders.

Often substance use disorders and mental health disorders occur around the same time, first appearing during the adolescent years, something most college mental health psychiatrists can attest to.[16] Substance abuse can exacerbate mental health disorders and interfere with medication prescribed for treatment. In Dani's story, her depressive symptoms emerged before alcohol and drug use; the substances she took to feel better only exacerbated her symptoms. Marijuana, cocaine, and LSD were all factors in her paranoia and psychotic episodes. In chapter 12, I'll discuss how these and other drugs can cause or exacerbate psychosis. If your child is having any mental health disorder, it is best for him or her to abstain from any type of drug use. Ideally, he or she will avoid alcohol, but if your child does drink, he or she should keep alcohol intake to a minimum. If your child is experiencing both a mental health disorder and a substance use disorder, he or she may benefit from a dual diagnosis treatment program.

PREVENTION OF SUBSTANCE ABUSE IN COLLEGE STUDENTS: FOCUS ON FRESHMEN

"There's nothing a parent can do to stop a college student from using drugs."

One father of a college student made this statement after reading an article I wrote about drug abuse prevention. As a parent, he is correct that we can't have complete control over what our child does in college. I've seen parents teach their children not to use drugs, only to have these children go on to have substance abuse problems. Nonetheless, he is wrong to think we have absolutely no control. Studies show that parents have influence over their college student's lifestyles, meaning they can impact their child's use of drugs and alcohol.[17] Because freshmen are particularly vulnerable to substance abuse, interventions should be done early on.

Parents can reduce their college freshman's drinking if they start communicating about alcohol with their children as early as senior year of high school and continue through freshman year of college, according to a 2014 study by Turrisi and Ray.[18] Three parent factors are crucial: approval, accessibility, and monitoring. Students will drink less if they know their parents disapprove of excessive drinking, are available to talk with them when needed, and will be asking them about where they are going and what they are doing. Another study showed that if students perceived their parents had a limit on the number of alcoholic beverages one should consume, students internalized this limit and drank less in college.[19]

Teach your child about the dangers of binge drinking: five or more drinks for a man and four or more drinks for a woman in a two-hour period.[20] Encourage a far lower amount. It is generally recommended that women not have more than one drink per day and men not have more than two drinks.[21] Advise them not to drink on an empty stomach; some students are doing this more often and using other eating disorder behaviors to accelerate intoxication, something I'll write more about in chapter 11.

Marijuana is a controversial subject, as many people—especially college students—favor legalization. Parents should certainly discourage daily use based on the negative effects I have described. For my patients, I recommend completely avoiding marijuana use. With marijuana, it is hard to know if there is a safe amount, as a study of college students showed that even smoking once a week caused disruptions to the nucleus accumbens and amygdala, the motivation and emotion centers of the brain.[22] The last thing you want to see in your college student is a disruption in motivation. Your child might also fall into the small percentage of people who are at risk for becoming psychotic after using marijuana. Having seen many students with distressing psychotic experiences related to marijuana, I'd rather they not take a chance. As for other drugs, including nonprescribed ADHD medications, cocaine, LSD, and mushrooms, parents should oppose their use. The harm of these drugs far outweighs any perceived benefit. For more parenting information about alcohol and drug abuse, go to the websites for the National Institute of Drug Abuse (https://www.drugabuse.gov/parents-educators) and College Drinking Prevention (https://www.collegedrinkingprevention.gov).

Of course, your efforts to educate your children about substance abuse should start earlier than the college years. As a psychiatrist, I taught my children early on about the dangers of drug and alcohol abuse. Most psychiatrists I know who work with college students have set firm limits about substance use with their children because we've seen the devastation of drug abuse firsthand. The Partnership for Drug-Free Kids provides some specific ways to talk to teenagers about substance abuse, including using teachable moments.[23] If your child brings up an incident about a friend who used drugs, if you read a story on your newsfeed about addiction, or if you have a relative who has experienced a drug problem, these are opportunities to talk about the risk of drug use.

The longer you can keep your child away from drug and alcohol exposure, the less likely he or she is to have a substance use disorder.[24] The adolescent brain is particularly vulnerable to addiction. In answer to the question "can you just say no when it comes to drugs and alcohol?" there is a lot more to do than just say no. Education, involvement, and positive parenting will all reduce the risk for substance abuse. But questions may still arise, like: What if our best efforts do not keep our children away from drugs and alcohol abuse? How would we recognize if our children are using drugs?

RECOGNIZING SUBSTANCE USE DISORDERS IN THE COLLEGE STUDENT

There are several signs that may help you recognize if your college student is having a drug or alcohol problem, including mood swings, sleep changes, social isolation, and weight loss.[25] Here are some of the signs of substance abuse I see in college students; when these signs occur, parents should take steps to get their children help.

A *drop in grades*: When students use drugs or drink heavily, they may initially manage to do well in school. However, the substance abuse will eventually catch up with them as their motivation decreases over time. They may oversleep and miss class or have trouble concentrating. I urge all parents to review end-of-semester grades to see if their children are experiencing any emotional or substance abuse problems. In chapter 4, I'll talk about how to have access to these grades.

Mood disturbances: I often see students who are experiencing depression or irritability related to drug abuse. If you become aware of these mood changes, ask your child what is stressing him or her out and if he or she ever uses drugs or alcohol to cope. Whatever the cause of these mood swings, you should encourage your child to meet with a therapist and request that your child sign a release of information form so you can speak with the therapist. Tell your child you are there to help and that you want to talk with the therapist about the changes you have noticed.

Increased spending: Some students will spend a great deal of money on drugs. If your child is frequently asking you to send money, you need to question why. For the first few years of college, I encourage you to monitor how your child is spending money by having access to his or her online bank accounts. I'll talk more about the importance of financial monitoring in chapter 8.

School discipline problems or legal problems: If your child faces school discipline or legal trouble due to drug or alcohol use, take this seriously. Your child might minimize the problem, but always be clear about your concerns. Encourage your child to be evaluated by a counselor.

Let's say your child has signs of a substance-related problem, but she is still denying it. You can call the campus counseling center and ask to speak to the on-call provider to make them aware of your concerns. You can ask them if she is already seeing a counselor at the counseling center. They cannot say whether your daughter is receiving treatment unless your daughter has signed a release of information form. However, the information you provide is likely to be given to a counselor if one is seeing your child. Whether or not your daughter is a client at the counseling center, the counselor can give you general advice on how to help your child and provide you with additional resources.

What if you become aware of concerning information? Your daughter's friend tells you your daughter is prescribed a stimulant for ADHD by a campus psychiatrist, but she is abusing it and getting psychotic when she takes high doses. You can call the campus mental health services and say it is urgent that you speak with her psychiatrist. Even if your daughter has not signed a release of information form, the psychiatrist can listen to your concerns and take action to keep your daughter safe.

If you suspect escalating substance abuse and are worried about your child's safety, you can call the dean of students office. Colleges generally have a help line where a person can advise you of the next steps to be taken. A resident advisor or a campus police officer can do a well-being check. If your child lives off campus, you might try to get in touch with his or her roommates or you can ask the police to check on him or her.

SUBSTANCE ABUSE TREATMENT IS A FAMILY AFFAIR

What should you do if you know your child has a substance use disorder?

Call the college counseling center to see what resources are available on campus to promote recovery and encourage your child to pursue treatment. Many schools now offer collegiate recovery centers or programs that could include AA meetings, sober living dorms, and alcohol-free social events.[26] The university where I work offers a range of services for alcohol and drug issues on campus. For students with more serious substance abuse problems, a comprehensive recovery program nearby offers both inpatient and outpatient services with therapists and board certified addiction specialist physicians and psychiatrists. One part of comprehensive care is to have a physical examination and laboratory work with a primary care doctor. Drugs and alcohol can negatively impact your child's physical health.

If students are caught on campus engaging in underage drinking, drug use, or destructive or dangerous behaviors related to substance use, they might face a variety of consequences that include mandatory treatment. Parents might be notified. Students might be forced to take classes through the college's health promotions office and mandated to attend counseling. For more serious offenses, they might even be required to undergo urine drug screens as a condition of staying in school.

What if your child has a substance abuse problem and won't seek help? He might be failing his classes because he is drinking every night. He might have spent the night in the hospital for alcohol poisoning. He might be smoking marijuana even though he is having psychotic episodes. You know your child's life is at risk, but you feel powerless to help.

The first step is to let your child know you're concerned about the way he is using substances. State the specific behaviors you have witnessed that worry you. Do this in a nonjudgmental and loving way. Tell your child you want him to get help for his problem. Say you care about his emotional and physical health. He may say that his friends are using the same drugs, but point out they may not be having the same consequences. Some people are biologically more prone to experiencing problems with drugs and alcohol than others, just like some people are more prone to high blood pressure or depression. Make it clear to your child that you are willing to help him find treatment to get him healthy again.

The second step is to sit down with your child and an addiction specialist to formulate a plan. The campus may have an addiction specialist for your child to speak to free of charge, but you might need to seek someone off campus. It's important for you and your child to understand each other's expectations. You should expect that your child will pursue treatment with a substance abuse specialist. Your child may expect you to keep providing financial support as before, but you may want to handle money differently so you are not sending money to enable a drug habit. If you have been sending money for rent, pay this directly. Keep a close eye on finances.

What if your child says he will stop using drugs or alcohol on his own and will not see a counselor? He says he wants you to trust him. In consultation with an addiction specialist, you will have to decide how to handle this. These decisions are not easy. If the specialist recommends outpatient treatment or inpatient rehab, you can present this choice to your child: he will pursue treatment and continue receiving your financial support or he will forgo treatment and support himself financially. This choice may be what motivates him to get help.

I have found that many parents are hesitant to stop financial support out of fear that their child will cut off contact with them, or that their child will become distraught and hurt him- or herself. Because these situations are very complex, I always recommend ongoing consultations with an addiction specialist or meeting with family support groups like Alcoholics Anonymous and Narcotics Anonymous for advice.

Whatever you do, do not blame yourself. Addiction is a complex illness with strong biological and social components; peer influences are powerful. It can be helpful to apply the serenity prayer from Alcoholics

Anonymous to parenting: Grant me the serenity to accept the things I cannot change; courage to change the things I can; and wisdom to know the difference.

FINAL TIPS

You are on the front lines of preventing drug abuse from middle school onward. You are the first responder if substance use gets out of control. Here are tips to promote wellness and recovery in your child.

1. *Practice positive parenting.* The most important step you can take to prevent drug abuse is to have a warm and loving relationship with your child. You will be far more effective offering guidelines to your child if you have a comfortable communication style.
2. *Start a conversation about drugs and alcohol early on and continue throughout college.* Your child cares what you think and wants to meet your expectations. Have a discussion that is loving and educational.
3. *Set limits on drug and alcohol use.* Studies show that parents setting limits on alcohol use in college can significantly reduce alcohol consumption in their child. Be empowered to promote positive behaviors for your child's current and future wellness.
4. *Approach drug use as a health issue, not a moral issue.* Tell your child you are concerned about the harm substance use is doing to his or her brain and body. Remember that addiction is a disease, not a deficit in character.
5. *Work with an addiction specialist to promote recovery in your child.* Consult with as many people as you need—professionals and family support groups—until you are confident you have the right tools to help your child.

I have seen many people with drug and alcohol problems overcome these issues and graduate with bright futures. Wanting to do well in school and live up to your expectations can be two motivations for recovery. With your love and support, you can encourage your child to begin his or her journey to health and wellness.

4

ACADEMIC FAILURE TO THRIVE

Attention Deficit Disorder and Other Ailments

Your son, Alan, is home for the December break of his sophomore year, and you ask about his grades. He says, "I did pretty well, you know, As and Bs." Normally an energetic person who can't sit still, he's been sleeping for the last few days and looks depressed. When you ask him if he's okay, he says everything's fine. At the end of the vacation he comes to you with a tense and guilty expression on his face. "I didn't want to tell you this, but I got 3 Cs and a D this semester. I'm already on academic probation, and I hope I don't get kicked out of school."

You are shocked to hear this. Alan has been telling you he has been doing well since freshman year, but now you know this is not true. You ask him what happened, and he says he doesn't know.

What would you do?

Parents have different fears when they bring their children to college. Some have major concerns about whether their child will succeed academically, while others are more worried about safe choices when it comes to drugs and sex. Whether your child was a great or average student in high school, you should be alert to academic problems early on in his or her college career.

In the college setting, academic failure is a common and costly problem. Less than 40 percent of college students are academically ready for college.[1] Not surprisingly, only 40 percent of students graduate in four years or less; 60 percent graduate in six years or less.[2] Those who never graduate may be burdened with college loan debt that could take decades to pay off. They may bear the emotional costs of not developing a sense of self-sufficiency and accomplishment.

With so much at stake, college students rate academics as the biggest stressor they face. Almost one of two college students report academics were traumatic or very difficult to handle in the past year.[3] Many colleges are now making efforts to reduce the stress and increase rates of graduation in four years. They are requiring students to meet with advisors more regularly so students fulfill their major and elective requirements.[4] But there is still great variation from college to college and course to course regarding interventions for academic struggles. In some schools, a professor will contact a student if he or she has missed a class or failed an exam, whereas in other schools a student might not attend class for much of the semester and no one will reach out to him or her. You should encourage your child to choose a school that will provide the level of academic guidance and support his or her personality requires.

Will the school notify you if your child is struggling academically? The answer is no, even if you are paying tuition. Under FERPA, the school will not call you, as your child is legally an adult. The school has the option of calling you for other reasons, like if there is a health or safety emergency or if he or she has violated a drug or alcohol policy.[5] Academic ailments do not fall under these categories. But even under FERPA there are ways you can have access to the end-of-semester grades. I'll talk more about that later. The bottom line is that you will want to be aware of your child's academic progress so you can offer support and make suggestions.

You might wonder if I am asking you to helicopter your child academically. I am in no way suggesting you call every day to check on a test grade or call a professor to challenge a grade. Later in this chapter, I will outline some dos and don'ts for your involvement. One study that followed parents and children for four years showed benefits of parents being involved in college students' lives.[6] Parent contact and suggestions—but not decision making for the students—allowed for greater academic autonomy and more time spent in career planning. In this study, most parents decreased involvement as time went on. But letting go completely can be an unwise move, as the following story shows.

ALAN'S ACADEMIC ODYSSEY

Robin and her husband sit down with Alan to talk about what's been going on in college. Robin, a psychologist, feels upset with herself. How did she miss that Alan was struggling in school? At the same time, she is determined to help Alan get to the bottom of the problem. Alan has always wanted to be an architect, but his dreams are at risk of being crushed by his poor academic performance.

"Mom and Dad, I don't know how this happened. I barely had to study first semester and still got As and Bs. But some of the material was a repeat of what I learned in high school, so it wasn't that hard. Second semester, I bombed and was about to fail two classes, so I dropped them, and got Cs in the two other classes. I put in the time to study, but I didn't know how to organize myself. I could not sit still and absorb the material I needed to learn. I didn't want to worry you and told myself if I tried harder, my grades would get better. But this semester was even worse, and I couldn't keep up with the material. I feel frustrated that I can't figure out how to do better in school. This has never happened to me before."

As Robin listens, she recalls how hard it was for Alan to sit still in high school. It was especially hard for him to read an entire book for English classes, so he would often read summaries, and he still ended up with As. Everything came easily to him. He always had so much energy—running track and doing multiple community service projects. With his energy and difficulty focusing on tasks like reading that he did not enjoy, she wondered if he had ADHD. But he always did well in school, so she never pursued an evaluation.

Robin presents her theory as to why Alan is struggling academically, and Alan replies, "I've been wondering if I have ADHD too. Maybe I should get an evaluation. I don't really want to take medication, but at this point I know I need help."

Robin arranges for Alan to have an evaluation with a psychologist before he returns to school. He undergoes psychological testing that includes a variety of intelligence, achievement, and skills tests. Robin is also asked to complete forms about Alan's current and past behaviors. The testing is consistent with ADHD, and Alan brings the report back to school.

When I meet with Alan at the campus counseling center, he is hopeful that he has found an answer to his academic problems. He does fidget a great deal in his seat, and he sometimes interrupts me as he is so eager to express his ideas. I agree that medication is a great idea for Alan, and that after he completes a physical exam and lab work, I will prescribe amphetamine/dextroamphetamine (Adderall) to help him focus better. Once I say this, Alan stands up to leave as if the appointment is over. "Let's talk about a few more things before we wrap up, Alan." Alan takes a seat, and I say, "Medication is only one part of the treatment for ADHD. I want you to register at the disability resource center on campus so you can get coaching. It's important you meet with someone on a weekly basis to make sure you are staying on track academically. The resource center also offers groups with other students so you can learn techniques to manage your ADHD symptoms." Alan agrees with this plan, and says, "Oh, before I forget. My mother is in the waiting room and wanted to come in for the last few minutes of the session."

Alan brings his mother back to my office. Robin is glad I'll be working with Alan, but expresses some concern about stimulant medication like amphetamine/dextroamphetamine. Will he get addicted to the medication? Robin's father was an alcoholic. I tell Robin that I will stay within standard doses of medication and meet with Alan on a regular basis to see how he is doing. The large majority of students I see do not misuse or take too much of their stimulants. Furthermore, the state has a drug database that lists all prescriptions that are filled for controlled substances. I check that database each time I prescribe a stimulant and would know if Alan was filling prescriptions of a stimulant from another doctor.

"Don't worry, Mom. I don't even like taking Tylenol. I'll take the medication correctly."

Alan meets with the disability resource center coach and learns study techniques. He takes his medication as prescribed. Alan is now able to sit for longer times to study, absorb the material better, and not make careless mistakes on tests. His turnaround in grades is significant, and he does well for the first few months of the semester. But midway through, he comes into my office with some concerns. "I'm starting to fall behind. I'm not sure what to do. What if I fail and have to leave?" I am struck by his pessimism and ask what has changed since I last saw him.

"I've been spending too much time playing video games with a friend who goes to another school. It's a great way for us to get together, and I plan to spend thirty minutes, but before I know it, three hours have passed." I tell Alan that I see many people with ADHD get caught up in video games and that it might be a good idea for him to take a break completely. He agrees to go socialize by running or working out with a friend every day. Alan also decides to bring his game system home for spring break and leave it there. He finishes the semester with As and Bs.

Alan's academic turnaround is dramatic. Robin's encouragement of an evaluation and treatment for ADHD sets Alan on a new academic course. If Robin had known about her son's grades sooner, she could have expedited the process. Your involvement as a parent can prevent academic problems from lingering and growing. Knowing how your child is doing academically from the start can change the course of your child's college career.

TAKE YOUR CHILD'S ACADEMIC TEMPERATURE BY CHECKING SEMESTER GRADES

"A parent shouldn't have to see a college student's grades for each semester. You should be able to trust what your child tells you."

One father expressed this sentiment to me when I presented my thoughts about parents checking semester grades. His views may apply to many college students, but all too often I have seen Alan's story play out. Students might be doing poorly for several semesters before their parents have any idea they are in academic trouble. Some students get by at first because they can drop a certain number of classes before a deadline. If they have a mental health problem, they can go through a system of medically withdrawing from a class or the whole semester without an academic penalty. Parents might not even know they have medically withdrawn from the semester while they continue to live near the school. I've seen students go through this process a few times without their parents knowing.

In the past, a parent might know sooner if a student were struggling academically. My college grades were mailed to my parents' home, and I automatically assumed my parents would view them. I had no problem with this. Now end-of-semester grades are generally not sent home but are displayed electronically on a school portal. Under FERPA, you cannot have access to your child's grades without his or her permission, except if your child is a dependent for tax purposes. In the end, you or your child might need to fill out an online or paper form so you can access grades. Each university has its own system for setting this up.

I strongly recommend you and your child take the steps required so you can check your child's end-of-semester grades. These grades give the most accurate measure of your child's academic temperature and will let you know if your child's GPA needs intensive care. Freshman and sophomore years are the critical times to assess how your child is adjusting to school, but senior year can also have its bumps and detours, so consider checking grades until your child has that diploma in hand. Some students perform worse academically during senior year as graduation looms and they have no idea what they want to do with their lives. They stare at their homework, frozen in fear and unable to act in the face of an unknown future.

A few years ago, a news story about a missing Penn State student brought the academic difficulties seniors can face and their alarming consequences home.[7] The student's parents came to his graduation in May, but he was missing. They discovered he had dropped out of college in the fall, but had told them he was still in school. Fortunately, the parents found him a few days later, safe and sound, but the outcome for this family could have been devastating.

If your child is withholding his or her academic struggles from you, he or she is not intending to hurt you. Like Alan, college-age children believe they should be able to solve a problem on their own without burdening their parents. They may also be ashamed that they are not living up to your expectations. Most of the time, they feel great relief when they finally open up to their parents. However, because they may not keep you in the academic loop, check their grades online. Follow the famous Ronald Reagan maxim, "Trust, but verify."

DON'T MAKE GRADES THE ONLY MEASURE OF SUCCESS

While I've made a big deal about checking end-of-semester grades, take care not to give the message that your child's self-worth should be based primarily on grades. Your goal in viewing grades should be to see how your student is progressing academically and emotionally, giving you the opportunity to offer suggestions and support.

Do not check your child's grades daily; students have told me parents' constantly checking grades increases their level of anxiety, which can hinder performance. One study showed parental overinvolvement in academics, with frequent phone calls and reminders to get things done, was correlated with poorer college performance.[8]

On the other hand, when you do speak with your child, you can ask how classes are going and listen for any signs of trouble. At that point you can suggest the use of campus resources as I will describe shortly. I preemptively encouraged both of my children to get tutoring in subjects in which they had weak high school preparation even before they had any difficulty in the course. Planning ahead had a positive impact on their academic experience.

While advising your child about using campus resources, you should not call a professor or teaching assistant about your child's grades. If your child believes he or she has been graded unfairly, he or she can talk with the professor or pursue other routes to appeal the professor's decision.

What grades are normal and what should you be worried about? That is a hard question to answer, as some schools have grade inflation and most students do well; other schools might grade more harshly, and Cs and Bs the first semester of freshman year are not unexpected. I would advise parents to encourage students to meet with an advisor or professor for any grade below a B to evaluate what went wrong and what can be improved next semester.

If you're not sure if your child is progressing well, you can call the dean of students office and ask for an administrator from their parents and family programs. A specialist in that office could give you general advice. You could also ask your child about speaking with his or her academic advisor. I'll write more about this later in the chapter.

Ask your child to do the best that he or she can in school, but not at the cost of sleep or time with friends. Do not take the tiger mom approach of demanding straight As. If your child is taking an overly perfectionistic approach to college and not leaving any room for a grade less than an A, he or she may face a greater risk for depression or suicidal behaviors. Chapter 6 will review the harm of perfectionism that goes too far. Remember, it's better to take a holistic approach to your child's college career and encourage both academic and social growth.

USE GRADES TO DIAGNOSE AND TREAT ACADEMIC AILMENTS

Why do some college students thrive academically while others fail?

This is a topic that it is being investigated more and more, with interesting results. Some studies have found two key ingredients to academic success: grit and social belonging.[9] Grit could be another term for persistence or resilience. It means working hard in the face of obstacles or failure. Social belonging means someone feels he or she is a part of the campus and has connections both to college personnel and other students. Feeling disconnected from campus is associated with lower grades, as well as worse mental and physical health.

As a parent, you can encourage grit by staying calm if your child reports doing poorly on a test. Take a solution-based approach to the problem. Describe a challenge you faced and how your hard work paid off. You can also encourage making social connections as a way to improve academic health. Suggest your child go to office hours and get to know a professor. He or she can form a study group in a class that is challenging. Suggest your student attend an on-campus concert or movie so he or she can have a break from studying and prevent burnout. You can read more about how to combat social disconnection and loneliness in chapter 5.

The 2016 American College Health Association Survey examined more specific factors that impact academic success. Mental health issues topped the list. When asked what interferes with academic performance, one of three students endorsed stress, one of four anxiety, one of five sleep difficulties, and one of seven depression. Other top factors affecting more than one of ten students included work, sickness, concern about family or friends, and Internet use or computer games.[10] Other problems that interfere with school work include immaturity and lack of readiness for college, an inadequate academic foundation, ADHD or learning disabilities, substance abuse, and a major life stressor such as a breakup or family illness.

Given the myriad causes of academic problems, where would you begin in diagnosing and treating your child's academic problems? Ask your child straight out what he or she thinks is getting in the way. He or she might admit to feeling depressed or anxious, and you can encourage him or her to get the help he or she needs. But if you are still not sure, encourage your student to take the following steps.

First Steps

- Visit his or her professor as well as his or her academic advisor for suggestions.
- Use the campus tutoring center or writing center. Use off-campus tutoring services if his or her needs are not being met.
- Visit a campus resource that teaches study skills. Health promotions departments and/or counseling centers will offer individual or group counseling in these skills.
- Go to a success coach on campus or hire an off-campus coach to get more structure and support.
- Search for other causes if these first steps do not help.

Digging Deeper

- Meet with a counselor or psychiatrist on campus to see if there is a mental health issue like depression, anxiety, or substance abuse interfering with his or her academic performance. Treat any mental health issues with therapy and/or medication.
- Work with a therapist to learn how to better cope with academic stress.
- Undergo psychological testing to see if he or she has ADHD, a learning disability, or another mental health disorder interfering with school work.

Working with the Disability Resource Center

- Register with the campus disability resource center if he or she has a medical or mental health problem that interferes with his or her school work. Your child will need to provide a letter of documentation from his or her health care provider. Disability resource centers offer accommodations for people with ADHD and other mental health issues.
- Use accommodations tailored to his or her specific problem. People with ADHD and learning disabilities might request a quiet testing center, extra time for tests, and coaching.
- Ask the disability resource center to reduce the number of required credits if he or she feels he or she needs to move at a slower pace. I have seen people with ADHD, depression, anxiety, and other challenges reduce their course load and still graduate successfully, even going on to graduate school.

If your student continues to struggle, it's a great idea for both of you to have a group meeting with the relevant college personnel, including advisors and mental health professionals. You can set up a plan for success. If your child can't meet the goals of this plan, it may make sense for him or her to take some time off from school to work on the skills that will allow him or her to flourish academically when he or she returns.

ACADEMIC PROBLEMS CAN BE INTERTWINED WITH MENTAL HEALTH ISSUES

As the American College Health Survey shows, mental health problems are a major cause of academic problems. Most likely your child is capable of doing the work at the college to which he or she was accepted, but mental health problems create all kinds of complications. Here are some scenarios I have seen over the years.

Analise started out as an all-A student majoring in biology with a plan to go to PA (physician's assistant) school. She started smoking marijuana every day because she felt anxious, and for a few years marijuana relieved her anxiety. But during her junior year she just could not keep up with work and switched majors. During her senior year, she started feeling very depressed and got Bs and Cs. She graduated on time, but made no plans after graduation and returned home.

Janelle did well during her first year of school, but at the beginning of sophomore year, her best friend died of cancer. Janelle's parents wanted her to take time off, but she said she would be fine. She spent time studying but just could not absorb any material. She felt depressed all the time and could barely get out of bed. After failing her classes that fall, she applied for a medical withdrawal from her courses. Her parents wanted her to stay home for the spring semester to fully recover from her depression while they provided emotional support. Instead Janelle returned to school, taking an antidepressant her primary care doctor prescribed. She said she did not need to see a therapist. Soon she was again overwhelmed by sadness and failing classes; she decided to return home.

Treating any underlying mental health or substance abuse issue is a major key to academic success. I've seen too many students with serious mental health issues have difficulty coping with academic stress. Then they fail, thus exacerbating their mental health problem. They get into a vicious cycle of depression and academic failure. For more serious mental health issues, it can be better to take time off and pursue treatment before attempting to do school work.

ADHD is a mental health issue that impacts 5.1 percent of college students.[11] Some bright students like Alan come to school with undiagnosed ADHD. They can get by on brains in high school, only to be overwhelmed by the challenges of college. If your child is diagnosed with ADHD, comprehensive treatment can dramatically change the trajectory of his or her career. Unfortunately, the diagnosis and treatment of ADHD are ripe with controversy.

ADHD AND CAMPUS CONTROVERSIES

Several years ago, I attended a meeting on my campus during which a counselor proposed that psychiatrists not treat ADHD on campus. Administrators were concerned about national reports of stimulant abuse on campus and did not want campus psychiatrists to become part of the problem by prescribing stimulants to students. Ultimately, we psychiatrists continued to prescribe medications for ADHD, while taking measures to ensure our students are not abusing the drugs we prescribe them. We have strict guidelines, including having students undergo psychological testing to ensure the ADHD diagnosis is accurate and urine drug screens to ensure they are not abusing substances. We generally do not prescribe stimulants to people who have a history of substance abuse. Furthermore, many states now have prescription databases that would show if a student was getting a stimulant from another doctor, preventing you from giving additional medication that might be used for abuse or profit. In fact, only a small minority of people with ADHD abuse their stimulants. The bigger problem is that they could be sharing it with or selling it to another student. In fact, most of the students who misuse or abuse amphetamine/dextoamphetamine obtain it from a friend who is prescribed it for ADHD.[12] If your child is receiving a stimulant for ADHD, ensure that he or she keeps it in a secure place and never gives it to friends. The medication could cause harm to his or her friend, as I discussed in chapter 3. Furthermore, giving a stimulant to a friend is illegal. These medications are highly regulated by the government due to their risk of abuse.

When taken properly, stimulants as well as nonstimulant medication for ADHD can have a profoundly positive effect on a student's academic career, as Alan's story shows. I can think of dozens of students I've treated for ADHD who greatly benefited, while only a few students have misused these medications. There are nonstimulant medications one can prescribe to someone with ADHD who may have a history of substance abuse. ADHD medications generally work by increasing levels of norepinephrine and dopamine in the brain.

What is ADHD, or attention-deficit/hyperactivity disorder? It is an array of symptoms that impact concentration in a society that requires absorption of increasing amounts of information and sitting for long periods of time to work on cognitive tasks. ADHD, inattentive type, includes symptoms of difficulty sustaining attention in class, making careless mistakes on homework, difficulties organizing work, and being distracted easily. ADHD, hyperactivity type/impulsivity type, includes symptoms like difficulty sitting still, fidgeting with hands, talking excessively, and interrupting conversations. Some people may have ADHD combined type, displaying both inattention and hyperactivity.[13] These may sound like common characteristics of adolescents, but a good diagnostic interview will evaluate for these and other symptoms. Psychological testing can confirm the diagnosis.

The book *Delivered from Distraction* by Edward Hallowell and John Ratey is a must read for anyone with ADHD and those who love them.[14] Both authors are physicians who have ADHD and have run innovative treatment programs for ADHD. They view ADHD as a combination of traits and behaviors that have many good, but some negative, aspects. These traits can be managed and channeled in ways that can lead to great success, and they discuss ways to achieve this. People with ADHD are often creative people who think outside the box. This book offers practical tips for living with ADHD that range from exercise, to regular sleep, to healthful eating. Cognitive behavioral therapy and medication can provide great benefits. Having the right people in your life to coach and encourage you is essential.

I've reviewed the way grades can help diagnose mental health problems like ADHD and lead to interventions to get a student back on track academically. But there are also preventive measures you can take to promote academic health. Encouraging your child to find a major that is right for him or her, work with an advisor that understands him or her, and use technology appropriately can promote academic success.

MAJOR DECISIONS

Janet comes from a home of perfectionists. Her mother is a biology professor, her father a lawyer, and her brother an engineering graduate student. Janet comes to college majoring in biology and pursuing pre-med requirements, believing this is what her parents expect. After all, her mother always tells her she would make a great doctor.

When Janet takes biology her first semester of freshman year, she has a sinking feeling that she does not belong in this class or this major. The professor moves too quickly through material that does not even interest her. She tells her parents she is considering dropping the class after nearly failing her first test, but her mother encourages her to stick with it.

Her mother starts providing tutoring every night by Skype. Janet wants to visit the tutoring center on campus, but she thinks she will upset her mother if she rejects her help. Janet feels more demoralized as her mother tutors her, especially when her mother says, "I don't understand how you don't get this concept."

Janet does even worse on the second test and realizes she needs to drop the class or she will fail. She meets with her advisor to discuss options. Her advisor asks, "What classes are you liking right now?" Janet tells her she loves her children's literature class, and she is considering becoming an elementary school teacher. She changes her major to education.

Janet waits a few days to call her parents, worried they will be angry about her change of plans. When she tells her mother the news, her mother responds in a way that surprises her. "I'm glad you're going to pursue what you like. I always worried you were majoring in biology just to please me."

Children feel a great deal of pressure to live up to their parents' expectations. They often make assumptions about what parents want and are relieved to find parents are open to other possibilities.

My children both asked my husband and me for advice about majors. We looked at the choices together and they decided. They both switched majors during their freshman years, consistent with studies that show that students change their majors over 50 percent of the time.[15] Expect that your child might try on two or three different hats until he or she finds the one that suits him or her. Most schools have dozens of majors to choose from, and college is the best time in life to explore different interests.

Should your child choose a major that leads directly to employment? As a psychiatrist, I want my patients to pursue a major that they enjoy, that they have aptitude for, and that will allow them to grow as a person. As a parent, I want all of the above and for my children to have employment after college if they do not go to graduate school.

The best advice I can give is *encourage your child to meet with an advisor in the career resource center by the middle of sophomore year.* The career resource center advisor might guide the student to a potential job connected to his or her major or suggest classes that will provide useful job skills post-graduation. You can still be an anthropology major and take business management classes, if you think you might want to go into a business field.

ADVISOR ANGST

Lisa, an excellent math and science student in high school, enters college determined to become a dentist. When she meets with her advisor during orientation, he registers her for four classes that include calculus and chemistry to fulfill her pre-dental requirements. She asks about delaying calculus until the next semester because she feels her high school math classes were inadequate. She does not want to be overwhelmed during her first semester, but he says it's better to get the classes over with.

After two weeks of school, Lisa is overwhelmed by massive amounts of material she must learn in chemistry and calculus. She has no time to do extracurricular activities, let alone sleep.

She meets with her advisor and explains that she cannot keep up with both of these classes together. Her advisor's response is, "If you are going to be a dentist, you better learn to work hard." He recommends she continue with her current schedule.

After another two weeks, she realizes she is never going to pass both classes, even with the tutoring she is receiving. She calls her mother crying, and her mother remembers learning at parent orientation that the dean of students office has success coaches who can advise freshmen struggling with academic or social issues. On her mother's advice, Lisa meets with a success coach the next day.

When Lisa walks into the office filled with photographs and comfortable furniture, she feels immediate relief. After bringing her a cup of tea, the coach asks Lisa about herself and how she is adjusting to school. Lisa describes her struggles in the two courses, and the coach encourages her to drop one of the classes. The coach explains that for some students the combination of calculus and chemistry is too much. To fulfill her pre-dental requirements, she can take a class in the summer. The coach also gives Lisa the name of a different advisor who might better meet her needs.

Having a good advisor is crucial to a student's academic experience. A good advisor understands your child's strengths as well as weaknesses and will guide your child to take classes that are challenging without being overwhelming.

I've met savvy advisors who may know something about the quality of a student's high school and have a knack for placing students in just the right classes. Smart advisors also know the learning style of their advisees and recommend professors who are a good match. Great advisors go beyond the academics and understand the nuances of your child's personality, promoting college as a way to grow academically as well as socially.

It is hard to know if your child is matched with the right advisor when he or she begins school. You as a parent may not be able to judge the appropriateness of the classes recommended by the advisor until your child starts the classes. Fortunately, most schools have a drop/add period that allows students to switch classes early in the semester if a class is too challenging.

The advisor also has a major role in ensuring your child graduates on time. The advisor should know the major and general education requirements inside and out and set a goal for graduation in four years, unless the student wants to extend his or her stay for special circumstances like the completion of a double major or pre-med requirements. I recently heard the story of a junior who found out mid-semester that he would need to take extra classes every term and attend summer school to graduate on time. He and the advisor had misunderstood the requirements of a major that was new to the school. This kind of mistake can be a costly one.

If you feel the advisor is detracting from rather than enhancing your child's college experience, you should recommend a switch to someone who will provide a positive, fresh approach.

As Lisa's story illustrates, many campuses have personnel like success coaches or case managers with a social work background and a firm knowledge of the academic world. They will help students look at classes, majors, and themselves as people to see what fits. In other words, they look at your child as a whole person and help him or her determine how his or her academic and personal goals can mesh.

How involved should you as a parent be in the whole advising relationship? The culture of most schools will vary on this issue. Most parents assume there will be no involvement, as I did before my children went off to college. My own children surprised me with a request for some parental participation, so I followed their lead. I sat in with my daughter and her advisor as she picked her classes for the first time, trying not to say too much while offering a few opinions. My son's college provided the opportunity for parents to meet with their child's academic advisor during fall family weekends, and my son encouraged me to join in the meetings for his first three years of college. In the end, though, my children and their advisors were the chief decision makers and I mostly listened. I did appreciate the opportunity to better understand my children's advising experience.

As parents, you want your children to have an excellent relationship with his or her advisor so they can work as a team to chart a positive academic course. Your role as a parent in that relationship should be minimal and based on your child's request.

THE IMPACT OF CHANGING TECHNOLOGIES ON ACADEMIC SUCCESS

The delivery of knowledge is happening in new and innovative ways, as colleges offer coursework online rather than in a classroom setting. Throughout the country, students can follow a traditional route by taking classes on campus, take all online classes, or do a combination of both. As this technology is relatively new, it remains to be seen how it impacts the learning experience. Anecdotally, I can report that most students want some classes with face-to-face contact. Whether or not these technologies enhance the learning experience, they may be contributing to increasing levels of social anxiety and loneliness on campus. In chapter 5, I'll write more about the importance of students finding ways to increase face-to-face contact when online classes, social media, and cell phones are keeping them apart.

Of course, in the academic world there are incredible benefits to new technologies. Whereas past generations of college students had to go to a library to access information for projects or papers, today's college students have information at their fingertips through the Internet. They can create incredible multimedia presentations. They have a level of knowledge about software, social media, and spreadsheet design that makes them excellent candidates for internships and jobs.

However, there is a dark side to this technological wizardry. I hear it often in my office. While a student is trying to write a paper, he gets a group text, a news alert, an Instagram post, or a Facebook message. Students may get caught up in the world of the Internet, playing online games for hours before realizing it is 1 a.m. and they haven't completed their homework assignment. It is no surprise that one of ten college students reports the Internet or computers were negatively impacting his or her academic performance.[16]

Students are able to block some forms of media on their computers so they can complete their school work. You can ask your child if he or she ever struggles with Internet distractions while he or she is trying to study. Encourage your child to be mindful of study time and try to focus on the task at hand. Ironically, new technologies are being used to fight the distraction of current technologies. At two recent national meetings on college mental health, I saw several vendors promoting apps that enhance student wellness, academic success, and organization. I have not explored these applications, but there may be something to them. Let's hope that this brave new world of technology can be used to harness your child's academic potential.

FINAL TIPS: A TOP TEN LIST OF DOS AND DON'TS FOR PARENTAL ACADEMIC INVOLVEMENT

1. *Do check your child's grades at the end of every semester.*
2. *Don't check your child's every test grade.*
3. *Do encourage your child to obtain tutoring early in the semester if he or she is having trouble with a class.*
4. *Do recommend your child visit the campus counseling center if mental health issues are interfering with school.*
5. *Don't call your child's professor and complain about a grade.* Do encourage your child to talk with the appropriate campus advocates if he or she believes he or she is being graded unfairly.
6. *Don't pick your child's major, but if asked for advice, sit with your child and the online catalog and brainstorm the possibilities.*
7. *Don't force your child into a career that he or she has neither aptitude for nor interest in.* There are jobs in fields other than medicine, law, and engineering!
8. *Do encourage your child to go to the career resource center by his or her sophomore year* to explore what jobs he or she might pursue in the future based on his or her academic interests.
9. *Do encourage your child to meet with his or her academic advisor on a regular basis.*

10. *Do encourage your child to change advisors if he or she is repeatedly given bad advice.*

You can promote your child's academic progress by having reasonable expectations about grades, encouraging your child to choose the major that suits him or her, and suggesting your child find the advisor that works best with him or her. If your student is struggling academically, he or she may have underlying mental health issues that need to be addressed. Ensure that your child is connecting with the campus resources to promote academic wellness.

Part II

Pressures

5

LONELINESS

The Importance of Social Belonging in College Success

You're visiting your son, Hunter, on a Friday afternoon in October during freshman parents' weekend. The trees are lush with fall foliage and music blares from the open windows of the residence halls. As you walk with Hunter to his dorm room and ask about school, he mumbles a response, staring blankly ahead. It's hard for you to read what he is thinking. Is he annoyed with you? Overtired? Not feeling well? You go up to his room and notice he has not hung the poster you sent him last month. His roommate barely acknowledges either one of you. Through-out the weekend, you and your son go to different activities, but he seems sad and does not speak with other students. On Sunday, when it comes time for you to leave, Hunter looks at you and says, "I don't belong here. I have no friends. I want to go home with you."

What would you do?

Loneliness is a common and concerning phenomenon on college campuses. A study showed one of four students felt very lonely in the previous two weeks and almost two-thirds felt very lonely at some point in the past year.[1] It's strange to think that you could feel lonely on a campus of five hundred or five thousand students, but it happens all the time.

What is loneliness? It's the perception that your social needs are not being met. A student may outwardly appear to have many friends, but inwardly feel extremely lonely, like he or she cannot open up and be his or her true self. Loneliness is a normal part of the human experience, but you don't want it to become a chronic condition. Learning how to connect with others is a crucial developmental task of emerging adulthood. Forging social networks and strong relationships will lead to a more satisfying and safe college experience.

THE DANGERS OF LONELINESS

When I see a new patient in my office, I always ask about his or her social support system. Do you have someone you can call when you have a problem? Do you have trustworthy friends you can talk freely with? Have you told your father you're feeling depressed? If the answer is "no" to these questions, a warning bell goes off inside my head: this student's loneliness needs to be addressed, just as much as his or her depression, anxiety, or other problems. Why? *Because solid relationships are essential to your college student's academic success, mental health, and physical well-being.*

Researchers have found that social support and social belonging improve college students' GPA, motivation, and graduation rates.[2] Several colleges have developed programs, particularly for minority and first-generation students, that promote social belonging. In some programs, upperclassmen mentor freshmen and talk about how they overcame their college struggles. Chapter 7 reviews how campuses are making efforts to give culturally diverse groups a greater sense of belonging.

Creating healthy connections promotes emotional wellness. Talking with a friend or parent is a key way to deal with the problems and pressures of the college years. Without strong social connections, adults in general have increased rates of depression, psychosis, and suicide.[3] College freshmen without a solid support system are more likely to have suicidal thoughts.[4]

It makes sense that loneliness harms emotional health, but did you know that loneliness is hazardous to your college student's physical health? Some studies have found elevated blood pressures, increased blood sugar levels, and worse responses to the flu vaccine in young adults who battle loneliness.[5] Lonely people in general tend to eat less healthfully, exercise less frequently, sleep restlessly, and turn to alcohol and drugs more often.[6] In people of all ages, loneliness and social isolation can even increase the risk of death by 30 percent.[7] To paraphrase an old Barbra Streisand song, people need people.

Freshman year is a critical time for making connections and getting comfortable on campus. But making meaningful friendships can be a challenge for some young adults suddenly on their own in a place where they may not know anyone. When social expectations are not met, it can be a frightening time for you and your child.

HUNTER, THE HOMESICK FRESHMAN

Hunter's plea to return home is the last thing James, his father, expected to hear at the close of freshman parents' weekend. Hunter did not seem happy over the weekend, but don't all freshmen go through ups and downs? Besides, during their daily phone calls since school began, Hunter had said everything is fine, he is getting along well with his roommate, he is making friends.

But everything has not been fine. Sitting at a local coffee shop off campus, Hunter tells his father what has really been happening.

"I thought college would be a fresh start. In high school, I felt lonely, like no one liked me. It was hard to talk with my classmates. In college, I assumed I would become friends with students who shared my interest in robotics and engineering. But then the first week of school turned out to be the opposite of everything I expected. My roommate ignored me when I spoke to him. When I went to the cafeteria and sat at a table, trying to start a conversation, the other students barely acknowledged me. In lecture halls, people texted on their phones before and after class, never making eye contact with me even though I was sitting right next to them.

"I finally stopped trying to make friends. I was too embarrassed to tell you the truth. Now I feel depressed, like a social failure. I'm afraid to start conversations with my classmates. Every time I open my mouth to talk, my heart beats quickly and it's hard to catch my breath. Maybe my life will never get better. I think I should go home for now and transfer to another school next semester."

Hunter's eyes are watering as he tries to hold back the tears. James gets up and hugs him.

"It sounds like you've been really disappointed with your experience. I'm glad you could tell me what's been going on. I know you feel miserable now and you want to leave school, but I'd like you to talk to someone at the campus counseling center before you make that final decision. The counselor might be able to suggest some ways you can feel more comfortable on campus. I'll stay in town for an extra day and I'll go with you to the first appointment."

The next morning, Hunter and James meet with the on-call counselor. Hunter talks about his loneliness and social anxiety. He also admits he sometimes thinks about suicide as a way to escape his pain. He would never go through with it because he does not want to hurt his father, and suicide is against his religious beliefs. He says, "I've never felt this depressed and anxious before."

The therapist tells Hunter, "We'll work together and do therapy to address your loneliness and social anxiety. But I also want you to meet with one of our psychiatrists. You're describing significant symptoms of depression and anxiety. If these symptoms get overwhelming, it could be hard for you to take steps to be more social. The psychiatrist can recommend treatment for your symptoms, which could include medication."

The therapist describes a phenomenon college mental health professionals often see. Loneliness can contribute to depression and anxiety, and students become too depressed and anxious to take the necessary steps to fight loneliness. Loneliness grows, keeping the cycle going. Treating the depression and anxiety with therapy, medication, or both can break the cycle.

The therapist invites me into the session with Hunter and James. Hunter is extremely shy, sometimes glancing at the door as if he'd like to escape. With tears in his eyes and a tremulous voice, he describes his sadness, anxiety, loneliness, sleep problems, concentration difficulties, poor appetite, and suicidal thoughts. Hunter's grades have begun to slip and he has missed some classes. Hunter has several symptoms consistent with social anxiety disorder as well as depression. Some of his symptoms began in high school and blossomed in college under the stress of extreme loneliness.

I tell Hunter, "I recommend you take medication, an SSRI like citalopram or sertraline. This will treat both your anxiety and depression."

James jumps in. "But shouldn't therapy be enough to work? Hunter has never done therapy. He might have a very positive response."

I tell Hunter and James that he could try therapy alone, but medication is usually recommended when depression and anxiety become this serious. Medication also tends to work more quickly than therapy and can help therapy be more effective. To stay in school, he may need a more rapid response.

Hunter, James, the therapist, and I discuss the best course of action. Should Hunter go home and get treatment there? Do therapy on campus? Try medication? In the end, Hunter decides to start therapy on campus. He agrees to meet with me in a week, after he does some more research on medication on websites I have provided. Hunter's father will visit every few weeks until Hunter feels more secure.

A week later, Hunter comes to my office, saying he had to leave class a few times because his anxiety was so strong. Hunter decides to start medication, and over the semester, his anxiety and depression lessen. He speaks up more often in class and joins a study group for one of his courses.

When Hunter returns for the spring semester, taking new classes with different professors and students, loneliness again overwhelms him. He calls James one night, wondering if he should transfer schools after all. "Join the robotics club. Call me afterwards to let me know how the first meeting goes," James tells him. Hunter reluctantly joins the club and immediately connects with the other students. By the end of the semester, he is elected vice president.

During his sophomore year, Hunter starts attending a local church every week with other students and forms a small group of friends. He still feels shy when he meets new people outside of his activities, but is not distressed by this. He realizes some people are more introverted than others, and he accepts that about himself. By the end of his sophomore year, Hunter is no longer on medication and is glad he remained in school.

Anxiety returns to Hunter in his junior year when he is interviewing for summer internships. He tells James, "I'm afraid that when I apply for jobs, the companies will see me as socially awkward. I'm already uncomfortable leading group projects in school. How will I ever become a project manager in a job?" James suggests Hunter work on his social skills by participating in group therapy at the counseling center.

Hunter signs up for a group, dreading the first meeting. How will he open up to other students about his anxiety and vulnerability? But right away he feels accepted by the other students and actively participates in group discussions. He offers advice to freshmen in the group who struggle with loneliness. Outside of the group, he begins to make new friends beyond his engineering and church circles. He no longer judges or questions himself when he talks in class. Throughout all of this, Hunter talks to James daily. His father will be a touchstone in his life for many years to come.

James is a wonderful guide on Hunter's journey to form social connections. James takes several steps to help him adjust to college life.

- He visits during freshman family weekend, a great time to check in with a child and to assess his or her social health. Most colleges have a freshman family weekend in the fall during which parents can attend activities and lectures with students.
- He understands his son is in distress and offers additional support, but also gives him room to grow and work with campus resources like the counseling center.
- He encourages his son to join clubs, a great way for students with mutual interests to connect.
- He maintains increased contact through visits and phone calls and reduces campus visits over time. He continues daily phone calls, typical of many parents and college students.

Some students like Hunter, who are more focused on academics and tend to be shy, develop social skills later than others. College students develop socially and academically at different rates. Remind your child to focus on what is positive in his or her life, like academics and clubs. Social networks can take time to build.

What If Your College Student Won't Open Up?

What if Hunter's story took a different turn? The family weekend is coming to a close, and Hunter says everything is fine, even though he looks lonely and unhappy. James is about to leave, suspecting his son is miserable. James could say, "It may be hard for you to talk with me about what is bothering you, but there is a counseling center on campus where you can meet with someone who works with a lot of other fresh-men and might know how to help. You don't have to tell me what you talk about, but just let me know that you've met with someone."

James could also make some suggestions I offer later in this chapter to increase social connections on campus. He can visit Hunter in a few weeks to see if he is feeling better. If James is really worried about Hunter and doesn't know what to do, he can call the campus counseling center and ask for advice, telling the counselor specifically what he has observed that is of concern. James can also call the dean of students office, who can provide information or suggestions on how to help. In chapter 9, I cover in greater depth the steps you can take if your child is in distress and you have safety concerns.

Freshman year may be the loneliest time for students, and changes in technology may explain why.

SOCIAL MEDIA: A SOCIAL DISCONNECT?

Freshman year is the time to forge friendships that will help your child weather the storms of the college years. But a study of freshmen re-vealed a disturbing trend. Students in 2014 spent far less time engaging in face-to-face contact than they did in 1987, and far more time using online social networks.[8] My freshman patients tell me the dorms are not as social as they expected. It seems like people sit behind closed doors texting or posting, reluctant to connect with those living in the same hallway or even with their roommates.

Another barrier to building social connections is online classes. Many students initially like the idea of online classes, giving them great-er flexibility in their schedule and the ability to work from home. They don't have to deal with parking or transportation challenges on campus. Some of these students come to dislike online classes because they feel less and less a part of campus life. They miss interacting with other students.

Many mental health professionals feel the rapid growth of new tech-nologies has had a negative impact on social skills development. Some young adults don't seem to have the social skills or awareness previous generations had. They may not know how to look someone in the eye or carry on a conversation. When students have fewer opportunities to practice their social skills, their anxiety may rise in social situations, fueling the increase in social anxiety we are seeing on college campuses.

We cannot turn back the clock on technology, but we can be more mindful of how technology impacts our children. We should encourage more face-to-face contact, which is so valuable to social health.

TRIGGERS FOR LONELINESS

While loneliness can strike freshmen hard, there are other vulnerable times in the college years. For Juliana, college became an especially lonely place.

"My girlfriend moved out. The loneliness is unbearable."

Juliana enters my office during the summer before her fifth and final year of college. She is taking an extra year to graduate because she failed several classes during her freshman year. When we first met at the end of freshman year, I prescribed medication to treat her depression, and her academic performance improved during her sophomore year. After her mood was stable for about nine months, she tapered and stopped her medication. Around that time, she also met her girlfriend. They lived together until two weeks ago, when her girlfriend broke up with her.

Distraught, tears running down her face, Juliana is now so depressed and lonely that she stopped attending her summer classes and doing school work. She either sleeps or watches YouTube videos to kill time. Compounding her loneliness, her friends have graduated or are away interning for the summer. Her support network is currently unavailable.

Of greatest concern is that Juliana is experiencing suicidal thoughts for the first time. I encourage her to restart the antidepressant that had worked for her before and talk with a therapist. Juliana allows me to call her mother, who lives only an hour away. Using the speaker phone, the three of us discuss a plan to help Juliana through this difficult period.

Her mother comes to stay with her for a few days until she feels better and maintains contact with her throughout the summer. This plan helps Juliana feel more supported until she can get more involved in campus activities and classes in the fall.

Juliana's story reveals the trifecta of loneliness triggers: *a relationship breakup, summer, and senior year.*

Relationship breakups are some of the major causes of loneliness in college students. First love can make your child hyperfocused on his or her partner, causing him or her to lose contact with friends. Students on the receiving end of the breakup may have few people to turn to. In addition, if your child is prone to depression or low self-esteem, the breakup can be especially painful.

Summer can also be a time of increased loneliness. Some students may stay in their college town, taking classes or working, while many will go home or pursue internships. Clubs that normally meet are no longer active. Students must make more of an effort to stay in touch with friends. Some of my patients have had recurrences of depression or anxiety during the summer semesters and restart medications that they had discontinued.

Senior year can be a time of struggle, as students realize they will leave their secure nest surrounded by friends their own age. If they are unsure of their post-college plans, they can feel even more disconnected. For students like Juliana who take more than four years to finish school, senior year can be a particularly tough time. When their friends graduate, they may feel left behind.

If your child is encountering loneliness triggers, ask questions and make statements that help him or her talk about his or her feelings.

Breakup: *I remember my first breakup in college. That was tough. Tell me how you're feeling. Is there anything I can do to help?*

Summer: *How do you like being at school during the summer? It must be nice to have smaller classes and get around campus more easily. Does it sometimes get too quiet?*

Senior year: *I liked senior year of college because there was less work. But I also felt lonely sometimes. All my friends were preparing for their next step in life. I felt like we were drifting apart. What has it been like for you?*

Breakups, summer, and senior year can be times of loneliness. Some groups of students are also more prone to loneliness.

GROUPS AT RISK FOR LONELINESS AND SOCIAL ISOLATION

Students with Social Anxiety Disorder

As discussed in chapter 1, social anxiety disorder is the psychiatric term for someone who has exaggerated fears of social situations. They tend to misinterpret people's reactions to them and feel they are being judged in a negative manner. They are very self-conscious, and social interactions can produce intense anxiety. Meeting new people, doing a presentation in class, or speaking on the phone can be very difficult. People with social anxiety can become isolated and lonely, even if they want to be around others. Social anxiety is defined as a disorder in which the symptoms cause great distress or interfere with one's functioning. Hunter's social anxiety disorder makes it much harder for him to connect with other freshmen and even participate in class, causing him significant distress and a desire to leave school.

The good news is that there are many effective treatments for social anxiety disorder, including individual and group therapy, as well as medication. If your child has social anxiety disorder, encourage him or her to meet with a mental health professional to determine the most effective treatment.

I encourage students with social anxiety disorder to consider doing group therapy. It is a great way to try out new social interactions and get feedback about how you come across. Your child can also provide feedback and support to others, which improves mood by enhancing a sense of altruism. Group members realize they are not alone in experiencing anxiety. For the past few years, as a co-leader of a therapy group called Understanding Self and Others, I have seen the power of group therapy to reduce loneliness and anxiety. Students with social anxiety often feel less anxious by the end of the group. They feel more comfortable meeting new people and opening up with friends.

If you think your child has social anxiety disorder, encourage him or her to seek professional help. I have seen people with this problem make dramatic recoveries.

Students with Autism

Autism is an umbrella term for many syndromes, but it includes basic problems with social communication. People with autism may misinterpret other people's verbal or body language or express themselves in unusual ways. They often make poor eye contact and use extremely blunt language. People with autism are present on campus now more than ever.[9]

These students may lack an awareness of how their words affect others, criticizing a professor for making a mistake by exclaiming "that was a stupid thing to say." A professor on the receiving end of this comment might send the student to the dean of students office for disruptive behavior. People with autism can also have misunderstandings in the dorm. A student with autism might say, "I'd like to throw my computer at you" when he or she is angry at a roommate. He or she might be expressing how he or she feels in the moment, but has no intention of throwing the computer. Nonetheless, school administrators might refer him or her to the campus counseling center for a safety evaluation.

With all these communication challenges, some people with autism prefer to be alone. But too much social isolation is as harmful as loneliness. For example, one young man who spends the majority of his time playing video games becomes more isolated from classmates, increasing his depression and suicidal thoughts. His depression finally lifts when he joins an animal rescue society, bonding with a group of caring people. For many students I've seen who are on the autism spectrum, having a few friends and some positive social interactions greatly improves mood.

If your college student has autism, encourage him or her to connect with a therapist at the campus counseling center in case misunderstandings arise because you cannot negotiate issues for your child as you did in high school. Counselors can offer support and advocate for your child as he or she adjusts to school.

You should also evaluate your child's readiness to attend a college far from home, as your child might need more support than the campus can provide. If the student is ready to move away, you should explore what resources each campus offers. Important factors in your decision should include access to a counseling center, psychiatrist, and disability resource center. A psychiatrist can provide medication because many people with autism have depression and anxiety. The disability resource center can offer academic coaching for students who may have relied on their parents for structure in high school and other accommodations students might need.

International Students

A study of international students in the United States produced some concerning findings about social interactions. Nearly 40 percent of international students reported not making friends with American students; the figure was even higher for students from Asia, who may struggle with English more than students from Spanish-speaking countries. [10]

College administrators, aware that language and cultural differences may make it difficult for international students to connect with others on campus, offer avenues for these students to increase social interactions and obtain social support. The campus international center provides assistance in adjusting to campus life. Many counseling centers offer support groups for international students, even in their native tongues. My own campus has a mentoring program to pair an American student with an international student who may be struggling with a new language. Some schools have case managers in their dean of students office who work with international students and their families. Most students do adjust, but some need additional campus support.

If you are a parent of an international student, you are an essential figure in his or her campus adjustment. My patients who are international students often keep in close touch with their families as they adjust to a new language and a new culture, and I applaud this. Skype and other apps allow these students to speak with their parents daily for free.

Even if you communicate every day, your child may not want to tell you when loneliness becomes extreme. He or she may not want to stress you out, feeling you have sacrificed a great deal to allow him or her to attend school far away from home. Let him or her know you are there to support him or her and help resolve any dilemmas that might arise.

I sometimes encourage my patients who are international students to request their parents visit for additional support. One student felt so disconnected from his professors and other students that he was about to leave his program. He decided to stay after his mother visited from Pakistan for a month, cooking his favorite foods and giving him a sense of belonging. This reassurance allowed him to reach out to others in his program and make a few friends.

As international parents, you can help with your child's social adjustment by keeping in touch with your child, visiting if needed, and encouraging use of the international student center and counseling center support groups.

THE CAMPUS CURE FOR LONELINESS

You can be the critical link to cure your child's loneliness. While you bridge the loneliness gap with your support, you can encourage the use of campus resources to promote social health. Good *social interactions, social support, and social skills* are essential to defeat loneliness.[11] Fortunately, colleges offer many resources to promote a sense of belonging. Encourage your child to do the following.

Increase Social Interactions

- Take face-to-face classes and avoid taking all online classes.
- Arrive to class early and get to know the person sitting next to you.
- Schedule study time with a friend.
- Eat lunch with a friend at least once a week.
- Participate in one or two clubs each semester. It may take three or four tries to find the organization that fits. It does not have to be a competitive organization like debate team or model United Nations. Over the years I have seen students enjoy clubs involving Frisbee, board games, hiking, camping, and star gazing. Fraternities and sororities can provide many opportunities for social interactions. Volunteer work is also a great way to connect with others and build up self-worth.

Build Social Support and a Sense of Belonging on Campus

- Go to a professor's office hours to ask questions and deepen your knowledge of the material.
- Meet with your advisor on a regular basis to get advice about your major and keep track of your academic requirements. If this advisor is not a great fit, ask for a new one.
- Let your friends or family know if you are having a problem; don't try to handle everything on your own.
- Set a goal to have two good friends by the end of the academic year. Find friends who will accept you for who you are and support you when you are feeling vulnerable. A few close friends, even without a large social network, can greatly reduce loneliness.
- Meet with a success coach or case manager in the dean of students office if you are still not meeting people on campus. They can provide support and recommend campus activities that suit your personality.
- Go to your campus counseling center if your sense of loneliness is getting overwhelming. The counselor will give you the support you need while you brainstorm ways to connect with others.

Improve Social Skills

- Make small talk when you go to the supermarket, convenience store, or restaurant. This is a great way to practice conversation because most people in customer service are well trained to put you at ease.
- Speak up in at least one class every day.
- Join a campus therapy group that focuses on improving social skills.
- Read a book about improving social skills. *The Shyness and Social Anxiety Workbook* is an excellent self-help book that teaches social skills like making good eye contact, using body language effectively, and knowing how to make small talk. [12]

LONELINESS: SHOULD THEY STAY OR SHOULD THEY GO?

What if your child has made every effort but just can't seem to connect with students or professors on campus?

While the large majority of students who describe extreme loneliness feel connected by the end of freshman or sophomore year, some students never achieve a sense of belonging on campus. They may have participated in therapy, joined clubs, and created a group of friends, but they continue to feel disconnected. They tell you they want to transfer to another school. You don't know what to say. On the one hand, you want them to keep trying and "tough it out." On the other hand, you are concerned about their mental well-being, especially if they are being treated for depression or have had any suicidal thoughts. Do you encourage them to stay in school or transfer?

Sometimes transferring or taking time off is the best thing for your child's safety and well-being. But if you're not sure what the best answer is, schedule a meeting with you, your son or daughter, and his or her current support network that might include a case manager in the dean of students office, a counselor, a psychiatrist, or an advisor. Sometimes these discussions can be conducted via phone if you are unable to attend a session in person.

If your child transfers to a different school or takes time off, don't be disheartened. Your son or daughter is not giving up; he or she is trying something different to improve his or her situation. When students I work with are considering leaving school, we explore ways to help them get connected. If they leave in the end, I am fully supportive. The most important thing is your child's health and happiness, and if transferring schools is what it takes, so be it.

ARE WE LIVING IN A LONELY WORLD?

Loneliness is not just a problem on college campuses; it is epidemic in our culture. As much as 15 to 30 percent of people are chronically lonely.[13] I believe we are living in a lonely world instead of the material world that Madonna so popularly sang about. Are you rushing through your days? Eating meals alone? Caught up in helping your children and parents instead of making social connections of your own?

Parents, you can model making your social health a priority even in a culture that seems to move 24/7. Sit down and have a quiet dinner with your spouse or friends, putting the phone aside. Make time for your friends and call them when you are having a rough day. Likewise, reach out to your friends if you know they are having a difficult time.

Make some new friends. Between work and family, we get stuck in our routines, but it can be fun to expand your social circle with someone new. Brighten up someone's day with small talk; it could develop into something more meaningful, and even if it doesn't, it may enhance someone's day, including your own. Recently, I was on an airport shuttle filled with people who, along with me, had attended a meeting on college administration. When I asked people how they liked the meeting, conversations sprang up about the meeting seminars, their jobs, and their destinations. It was a great way to learn about others and connect on our ride to the airport.

FINAL TIPS FOR HELPING THE LONELY COLLEGE STUDENT

1. *Remind your child that loneliness is a problem many college students struggle with and that it does not mean there is something wrong with him or her.*
2. *Loneliness is a problem that can usually be solved by increasing social interactions, strengthening social support, and improving social skills.*
3. *Use campus resources to cure loneliness: clubs and sports, success coaches, academic advisors, case managers, the counseling center, and the disability resource center.*
4. *Encourage your child to set three goals to improve his or her social health.*
5. *Stay in touch with your child during lonely times until he or she is feeling more connected to others.*
6. *Encourage your child to reach out to someone else who might be lonely.* This will help create a more supportive, connected campus community.

"No man is an island entire of itself," wrote John Donne in 1624. Poets recognized the power of social connection long before science proved its health benefits. Many great songs like "Eleanor Rigby" and "You've Got a Friend" talk about the universal problem of loneliness and the benefits of social connection. You can be there as a cheerleader if your child encounters roadblocks or rejection on the path to making friends. Once your child finds his or her place in the campus community, you'll feel a sense of satisfaction and joy.

6

PERFECTIONISM

The Dangers of Duck Syndrome

Your daughter, Paulina, is home for winter break. It's her junior year and she is exceptionally tired, sleeping almost all the time. When she is not sleeping, she is studying for the MCAT, the medical school admission test, scheduled for April. You want to take her to the doctor because she is so tired, but she explains the source of her fatigue. "Mom, I can only sleep three hours a night during the school week. It's the only way I can get my work done, do research, and volunteer at the hospital. My pre-med advisor says I must do all that, and get all As in my science classes, if I want to get into medical school."

You tell her she is doing too much and something's got to give. Then she explains, "Mom, because I got a B on the biochemistry midterm, I had to make sure I ended the semester with an A. Otherwise, I'll feel like I've failed."

What would you say?

Your daughter may be suffering from an ailment that seems to be plaguing college students at high rates—extreme perfectionism, also known as "duck syndrome." Duck syndrome is a term first used at Stanford to describe students who feel like they must appear perfectly together on the outside no matter how stressed they feel on the inside, like ducks that appear to effortlessly glide on water while paddling furiously below the surface. Students are under increasing pressure to maintain a façade of perfection—receiving high grades, having a busy social life, and looking great, all while appearing calm and collected.

Many students I see in my office are afflicted with dangerous levels of perfectionism. The university where I work is the state's flagship university, meaning students come in with high SAT scores and are often at the top of their high school classes. Whereas work might have come easily to them in high school, they are taking challenging college classes where they could get a C or even an F. I have seen some perfectionists respond to disappointment in extreme ways. One extreme could be like Paulina's, doing everything and more than is expected of her, sacrificing sleep for the sake of stellar grades. The opposite extreme could be defeat, knowing you are never going to get all As and deciding to give up altogether. Both responses to pressure can lead to despair and depression.

Are we seeing higher levels of perfectionism on college campuses than in the past? In searching the literature, I was hard-pressed to find a study measuring rates of perfectionism in college students. At the same time, I found news reports citing perfectionism as a concerning and dangerous trend on campus. A 2015 *New York Times* article titled "Suicide on Campus and the Pressure of Perfection" cited examples of students who attempted suicide or took their own lives while suffering from high levels of perfectionism.[1] The article mentioned a cluster of suicides at the University of Pennsylvania that led to the formation of a task force to examine mental health on the campus. This task force identified a concerning but all too common view held by students that one has to be perfect academically and socially. Perfectionism was a hot topic at the 2017 annual meeting of the American College Counseling Association, where large numbers of members attended a talk on "Radically Open DBT (RO-DBT): Treating Over-Thinking and the Plight of Perfectionism in College Students."[2]

Perfectionism is bad for your mental health, increasing the risk of suicide. Over half of people who died by suicide had high rates of perfectionistic traits and a fear of failure, according to two studies in which friends and family of the deceased were interviewed.[3] Furthermore, perfectionists tend to have higher rates of depression, anxiety, and eating disorders than the general population.[4]

Perfectionism is a trap, a goal with built-in failure. By definition, perfectionism is the need to be or appear perfect.[5] However, we can never do everything perfectly. People who are perfectionists are constantly criticizing themselves, failing to live up to their constant need to succeed. Some psychologists are encouraging people to use the phrase "pursuit of excellence" rather than "perfectionism" to describe a healthier approach to school and work.[6] In the next story, Paulina's own perfectionism is magnified by the external demands and pressures of pre-med requirements. Paulina is forced to reevaluate whether her perfectionism is as productive as she thinks, especially when it leads to a recurrence of past mental health problems.

PAULINA'S PERFECTIONISM

Anna does not know how to help Paulina. It may be true that Paulina has to study hard and participate in activities to get into medical school, but does that mean she cannot sleep? One night, worried about Paulina and unable to sleep herself, she goes into the kitchen and is shocked to find Paulina scrubbing the interior of the refrigerator. This is something Paulina used to do in high school; she would stay up until all hours cleaning the kitchen, especially when she was feeling anxious. Paulina was diagnosed with obsessive compulsive disorder and started medication. Her symptoms diminished and then disappeared. Paulina was tapered off her medication before going to college and seemed to be doing well. Anna wondered, was Paulina having a recurrence of obsessive compulsive disorder (OCD)? Were OCD symptoms contributing to her lack of sleep?

Anna tells Paulina she'd like her to meet with a campus psychiatrist when she gets back to school. Maybe she needs to restart medication for OCD.

"I'm fine, Mom. Cleaning is not the worst problem. I'll meet with the psychiatrist if it makes you happy, but I really don't want to take medication again."

Paulina keeps her promise and meets with me at the counseling center soon after winter break. She sits in the chair and smiles politely, explaining that she's had a return of obsessive compulsive symptoms and her mother thinks she needs treatment. As we're talking, she periodically looks at her phone. I ask her what she is checking, and she tells me the microbiology professor will be posting test grades any minute;

she needs to know her grade. At one point, she gets tears in her eyes. She says, "I got a B on the first test. Now I'll have to study harder, but I'm running out of time. I'm barely sleeping."

I ask Paulina to describe a typical day for me, and I learn that studying is not the only thing getting in the way of her sleep. She lives in constant fear that she will get sick and not be able to do her school work, so she cleans her apartment for one hour before she leaves for school and two hours every night. She says her roommates participate in housekeeping, but they are not thorough enough, and she cleans up after them. Her roommates are getting annoyed with her, and all this cleaning is keeping her up at night.

Paulina sighs. "I thought I was ready for that test, but now I'm so tired I can't even think straight. I think my OCD symptoms are catching up with me. I could get much more sleep if I wasn't cleaning all the time. I need to do something about it. But I don't want to take medication. Is there anything else you can suggest?"

I tell Paulina that we have an excellent cognitive behavioral treatment program for OCD at a nearby outpatient clinic. Paulina has never tried therapy for the OCD and is open to the idea. I also tell Paulina that I'm concerned about her level of perfectionism. When she tells me that her pre-med advisor says she needs to get all As in her science classes to get into medical school, I tell Paulina, "There are plenty of good doctors who got into medical school without all As. You're looking at one of them." I encourage Paulina to work with the therapist on putting less pressure on herself because her high stress levels most likely contributed to a recurrence of her OCD symptoms.

In a few months, Paulina and I meet again to review her progress and decide whether medication should be added to her treatment. Paulina is doing extremely well and does not need medication at this time. Since starting the program, Paulina has pulled back from cleaning constantly and allows her roommates to clean, even if they do not do it perfectly.

Paulina tells me that when her OCD symptoms improved, her therapist was also able to focus on Paulina's perfectionism, the feeling that she had to do everything and more to get into medical school, whatever the risks to her health and sleep. She has decided to focus on her research project and is holding off on volunteering until the summer, when she has more time. Most importantly, Paulina is allowing herself the time to get a full night's sleep. She has also joined the campus outdoor adventure club and every few weeks is trying new activities like tubing, kayaking, and hiking. She loves being outdoors and doing an activity that is not about getting into medical school but is just about fun. Paulina smiles genuinely and leans back in the chair, far more relaxed than when I first saw her. And she doesn't once check her phone for her latest grades.

Paulina's mother Anna is instrumental in being a catalyst to get her to acknowledge her OCD symptoms and to pursue treatment. Although the treatment Paulina's mother recommends—medication—is not what Paulina wants to use in the end, her meeting with me is one step toward the therapy that effectively treats her OCD as well as her perfectionism.

Although most people with perfectionism do not have OCD, many people with OCD have high levels of perfectionism, like Paulina.[7] Both perfectionism and OCD are about trying to control the environment around you to reduce anxiety. Realizing we cannot control everything, and sometimes going with the flow of things, can be a huge relief.

A FEW WORDS ABOUT OBSESSIVE COMPULSIVE DISORDER IN COLLEGE STUDENTS

Do you worry you've left the stove on and check that it is off two or three times before going to bed? Do you save stacks of old magazines in case you might want an article in the future? Many of us have some obsessions and compulsions; this does not mean we have obsessive compulsive disorder. To meet criteria for a disorder, these obsessions and compulsions must take up at least one hour a day or cause serious distress or dysfunction.[8] OCD can emerge during the college years, with the average age of onset of nineteen years old. More than 2 percent of college students report being diagnosed with or treated for obsessive compulsive disorder.[9]

College students can have a variety of OCD symptoms. They might have an obsession centered on a fear of germs. The resulting compulsion is hand washing, sometimes up to twenty times a day, to reduce this fear. If they don't have access to a sink, their anxiety can skyrocket and turn into a panic attack. College students might also have an obsessive fear about an intruder entering their house or apartment. They might check the locks on the doors and windows multiple times before leaving the house, arriving late to class.

College students might have OCD behaviors about their school work. They might feel compelled to watch video recordings of each class three times, even though they've picked up most of the information after one viewing. They cannot begin studying until everything is lined up perfectly on their desk, their chair in the same exact spot, just the right distance from the desk. They may spend half an hour getting everything right; otherwise, they will be too anxious to focus. The behavior turns into a ritual before each study session. These obsessions and compulsions can take up huge amounts of time, interfering with the timely completion of school work.

Fortunately, treatment for obsessive compulsive disorder is highly effective. Both cognitive behavioral therapy and antidepressants that raise serotonin levels (SSRIs) will reduce OCD symptoms. Studies show that therapy can be just as if not more effective than medication, so I will always encourage my patients who have OCD to pursue therapy.[10] Some people prefer treatment with medication, especially if they have other mental health problems like depression or an anxiety disorder.

If your child has OCD, encourage him or her to see a therapist who provides cognitive behavioral therapy focused on OCD. OCD treatment includes something called exposure and response prevention. In this kind of treatment, a therapist might expose a patient to a feared situation—for a student obsessed with orderliness, this could mean sitting with the therapist and doing homework with papers scattered on a table. The anxiety levels might initially increase but then lessen as the patient gets used to this circumstance. Therapists will teach patients relaxation techniques to use in the face of feared situations.

WHAT IS SOCIAL MEDIA'S ROLE IN THE PRESSURE TO BE PERFECT?

Social media is taking the pressure to be perfect to new levels for college students.[11] Students describe to me the pressure to display the perfect life on Facebook, Instagram, and Snapchat. They post selfies, sometimes photoshopped, and want to see if they can get the most likes.

Their self-esteem can be shattered if they do not feel they are popular enough online or if others critique them.

When they read other people's posts, they feel like a lesser being, not good enough in comparison. A friend might have been hired for the internship that he or she was vying for, another friend may have a great spring break planned with several friends, someone else may have a fabulous study abroad program. However, what others post may only be half of the story. Sadly, the *New York Times* article mentioned earlier also described depressed students using positive images on social media to hide their distress from family and friends. If your child is preoccupied with social media and what others are doing, encourage him or her to get offline and have meaningful face-to-face encounters with other students. Encourage him or her to focus on his or her successes and what he or she needs to do to meet future goals.

While social media may add pressure to college students to appear perfect, there may be additional factors driving perfectionism. After all, perfectionism has been a problem even before the debut of Facebook in 2004 and the popularity of cell phone selfies. I believe economic anxiety and financial fears may be fueling much of the perfectionism we are seeing. In chapter 8, I write at length about how many parents and students worry that the American Dream is over, believing children will be financially worse off than their parents. Student debt is skyrocketing, and the job market continues to go through upheavals. Early on, parents are more concerned about children getting into the best preschool, magnet school, private school, and college to ensure a more secure financial future. Students are under extra pressure to do great in school, get the best internships, and have the perfect job or graduate school lined up after graduation. Students fear a failing grade could be failure for life.

THE END OF PERFECTIONISM: FIGHTING PERFECTIONISM ONE DAY AT A TIME

I recently found an antiperfectionism message in the least likely of places, a *Wall Street Journal* article about the 2016 Olympic gymnastics gold medal–winner Simone Biles.[12] Ms. Biles practiced hard, but also had balance in her life. She lived at home instead of going away to training camps, went on family vacations, and attended friends' birthday parties. Whereas other coaches talked about striving for "perfection," Biles's coach talked about competing "from a place of joy."

I feel like college students have lost some of that sense of joy in their education. Is there a way to get that back? Can we teach our children to strive and achieve while loving what they are learning? Lately I've been hearing about two different therapy approaches that address perfectionism in college students.

The first, self-compassion, is an approach used in individual and group therapy that emphasizes three elements: self-kindness, common humanity, and mindfulness.[13] Self-kindness means talking to yourself as you would a friend, without constant criticism and judgment. Common humanity means recognizing that we all make mistakes and have failures; this idea makes us less judgmental of ourselves and feel less alone. Mindfulness means being in the moment and not overemphasizing the negative aspects of one's life.

Another approach that I've previously mentioned, radically open dialectical behavior therapy, looks at perfectionism as a trait in people who tend to be anxious about novel experiences, fearing failure. They may have an overcontrolled way of thinking, a more rigid way of doing things and relating to others, putting them at increased risk for anxiety disorders, depression, and anorexia. Radically open DBT group therapy teaches openness, flexibility, and social connectedness. Participants have opportunities to practice more relaxed body language, engage in novel activities, learn how to identify and express emotions, give and receive constructive feedback, and practice self-compassion.[14] It takes a lot of courage for a perfectionist to engage in any group therapy, but the act of doing this can create much more flexibility in relating to others.

When I work with highly perfectionistic students, I will apply concepts from the self-compassion and radical openness approaches; you as parents can use these ideas as well when you are talking with your child. If the students are being destructively self-critical, always berating themselves, I ask them to speak to themselves as they would a friend. They would never berate or put down a friend about a poor grade the way they criticize themselves. I urge students to try to be in the moment and experience what they are doing today, rather than always thinking about where they will be five years from now. I encourage them to engage in a club unrelated to their major, to take time for friends, to do an outdoor activity, and to not base their self-worth entirely on their grades. I ask them about what they enjoy learning in classes and which professors they relate to. I want a student to see him- or herself as a whole person, not someone whose sole purpose in life is to produce good grades, gain acceptance to the best graduate school, and get a great job. As one student said to me, he is more than his grades. Realizing that helped free him from the trap of perfectionism.

FINAL TIPS FOR DEFEATING PERFECTIONISM

Here are additional steps you can take to help your college student avoid the destructive effects of perfectionism.

1. *Reveal a time you failed at something, how you felt, and what you did to cope.* You may have started out in college majoring in engineering, but an F in Physics 2 put you on a different course and now you are enjoying working in urban planning and sustainability for your local community.
2. *Reduce any extra pressure you are putting on your child.* You might be urging him or her to become a pharmacist, but if he or she is neither enjoying nor excelling in his or her science classes, he or she should change paths. Be realistic about strengths and weaknesses and likes and dislikes. Set reasonable standards for the grades you expect, but don't constantly ask him or her about test scores, as I discussed in chapter 4.
3. *Refer him or her to campus resources if perfectionism is causing academic or mental health problems.* Tutors, advisors, career resource center counselors, and mental health professionals are available for help and advice.
4. *Teach your child that health comes before perfection.* Sleep should not be sacrificed for the sake of academics. If your child cannot keep up with his or her work load, he or she should use campus resources to improve his or her efficiency or adjust his or her schedule. Hunger should not be ignored for the sake of being thin or studying longer. Adequate sleep and meals are necessary for both academic success and emotional wellness.

5. *Practice self-compassion as a parent.* Much of parenting is on the job training, and we are all bound to make mistakes. Aim for excellence, while forgiving yourself for failure. Open up to your closest friends if you are struggling, and you will find you are not alone. I hope this book will help you see that many parents have children with problems and pressures, and with your help and their resilience, these students can recover.

In my residency training, we studied the concept of the "good enough mother" espoused by pediatrician Donald Winnicott in 1953. The idea is that we have to be good enough to meet our children's needs, but we cannot be perfect. Some professionals have applied the principle of being good enough rather than perfect to the computer and health care industries, aiming for standards and excellence, but knowing we cannot be everything to our patients, our customers, and our children.[15] Teach your child to avoid the trap of trying to be Superman or Superwoman and to instead pursue realistic, health-sustaining goals.

7

CULTURE, SEXUALITY, AND GENDER CHALLENGES

A Time to Heal

One reason I love working with college students is that they generally accept people who are different from themselves. They judge each other by their kindness and trustworthiness, not by their race, ethnicity, sexual orientation, or gender identity. Colleges create an atmosphere of inclusivity by offering groups and resources for people of multiple backgrounds. Over my two decades of working as a college psychiatrist, I have watched the student body grow more diverse.

At the same time, there have been recent incidents on campuses nationwide that have challenged the peace of campus life. Racist and anti-Semitic posters and e-mails have sprung up at colleges, largely delivered by outside hate groups.[1] Many of my patients who are part of racial and ethnic minorities feel they need to watch their backs more closely. My patients from the LGBTQ (lesbian, gay, bisexual, transgender, and queer) community are especially worried as they watch states battle over bathroom bills and transgender rights. Students in the majority worry about their minority friends who are feeling stressed out. Students in the minority have always had to deal with prejudice, but this is an especially stressful time for them.

I encourage every parent to read this chapter, whether or not your child is part of a racial, ethnic, sexual, or gender minority group. You might be able to help a child of a friend or a friend of your child's.

People who are part of any minority group have always faced higher rates of stress due to overt and subtle prejudices. They also face unique mental health challenges.[2] They need love and support now more than ever.

CULTURE

Gabriela's Gift

You are very proud of your daughter, Gabriela, who has gotten a full scholarship to a state school where she is going to be pre-med. You had come to the United States from Peru so your daughter could have the educational opportunities you never had.

One day she calls you and says she just left the psychiatrist's office and is thinking about taking medication for depression. How is that possible? She always seemed happy when you were together. You tell her to just call you when she feels down. She doesn't need medication.

But you are really upset when she tells you she is no longer pre-med because she failed chemistry last semester. You feel a mixture of sadness and frustration. You ask, why didn't you tell me any of this before? She says, I didn't want to let you and the family down. Then Gabriela says, "The truth is, I just feel like an imposter in college. I don't feel like I belong." Then she tells you she has to get to class and hangs up the phone. What would you do?

Academic Challenges: Imposter Syndrome

First-generation students, Hispanic students, and nonwhite students can at times suffer from imposter syndrome.[3] They may not feel like they belong at college, either because their parents did not go to college or because they do not see many people like themselves on the faculty. While minority student enrollment has increased, the minority faculty representation has not changed at the same rate. The student body is 58 percent white, 17 percent Hispanic, 14 percent black, and 7 percent Asian.[4] The faculty, on the other hand, is 78 percent white, 4 percent Hispanic, 6 percent black, and 10 percent Asian.[5]

Some of the first-generation and minority students I've worked with use the term "imposter syndrome," aware of feeling like they don't belong. They may feel like giving up, not believing they can get through college like other students. If you as parents did not go to college, it's important that you provide extra encouragement to your child when he or she faces an obstacle. Encourage him or her to use campus resources—the tutoring center, the dean of students office, or the counseling center—if he or she is struggling academically. Some campus health promotions offices have individual coaching in study skills. Many campuses have mentoring programs or groups for first-generation or minority students. Encourage your child to attend. He or she might want to join a group representing your cultural background to achieve a greater sense of belonging on campus. In chapter 4, I wrote about the importance of social belonging in promoting academic success. Finding some friends with similar backgrounds or cultural values can give students a feeling of being at home.

Mental Health Challenges

Of great concern is that black, Hispanic, and Asian students are less likely to seek help for serious mental health concerns, including suicidal ideation, than white students, with cost and stigma being barriers to treatment.[6] Many minority groups mistrust health care systems due to well-documented incidents of medical mistreatment in our country's past. Several groups are trying to decrease stigma against mental health treatment in minority communities. The Steve Fund (stevefund.org) is an organization devoted to promoting the emotional well-being of students of color on university campuses. This organization was started by the family of a young man of color who died by suicide. The Steve Fund website provides information for parents on ways to promote academic and emotional wellness.

In my own practice, I'm glad to see more students of all backgrounds seeking treatment for common mental health issues. I'll usually ask what their cultural beliefs are about therapy and medication for mental health issues. Is there stigma in their home community about taking antidepressants? Some students I see have delayed starting medication for more serious mental health issues because they worry how their family will view it.

I've even had patients abruptly stop medication when they go home for the summer to parents who might come from a country or culture that does not support taking psychiatric medication. If you take medication, you are considered "crazy." Students are afraid of their parents' reaction if they bring up the subject of taking medication. I ask all parents to keep an open mind and learn as much as they can about treatment. In fact, if a patient tells me his or her parent objects to medication, I will always offer to speak with a parent. I have access to translator services if there is a language difference. In my practice, I want to provide enough education for parents so they can support the steps their child is taking to get help.

Gabriela's Gift, Round 2

You call Gabriela back that evening and tell her you thought about what she said and you support whatever she decides. You tell her that she has a gift in science and you support her giving chemistry another go if she wants to. You tell her she can go to the professor's office hours or the campus tutoring center. But if she is happier not being pre-med, you support that too.

You also tell her you don't know a lot about depression or taking medication for it, but you are willing to learn. If it's okay with Gabriela, you'd like to speak with the psychiatrist and ask a few questions.

"Whatever problems you have, Gabriela, I'm there for you. I'm so proud of you being in college."

Final Tips for Cultural Challenges

1. *Understand the new college culture your child is in.* Ask him or her about college life. Be an anthropologist and explorer.
2. *Tell your child about what your culture teaches about resilience and hope.* Let him or her know how you overcame failures and obstacles.
3. *Encourage your child to use campus resources to succeed, including tutoring, the dean of students office, and the counseling center.* If he or she fails a test or a class, it is not the end of the world.

4. *Let your child find the academic path that works for him or her, even when it is not exactly what you dreamed.*
5. *Be open to mental health treatment.* Study websites like WebMD (http://www.webmd.com) and Mayo Clinic (http://www.mayoclinic.org) to learn about therapy and medication treatments for common mental health problems.

SEXUALITY

Thomas's Quest

Your son, Thomas, is a senior and is supposed to be applying for jobs, but he seems stuck, like he is down. He broke up with this girlfriend six months ago, so you are wondering if that is the cause. When he is home for winter break, you ask him to sit with you and tell you what is bothering him. He says, "I've been seeing a therapist because I've been feeling depressed lately. I've been wondering if I am gay or bisexual for the last year, and I don't know what to do about it. I didn't want to tell you because I thought you would be against my being gay."

What would you say?

The Spectrum of Sexuality on Campuses

You might be shocked if your son, who has always dated women, now says he might be gay or bisexual. In fact, he may not fit neatly into any particular category and may lean toward being bisexual at one point of his life and gay at another point. Sexuality may be more fluid than we realize. College students are more flexible in their views of sexuality and are using a wider range of terms to describe sexuality. Pansexual is a term that is growing in popularity to describe being open to loving anyone, whatever their gender or sexuality.[7]

One survey showed the diversity of college student sexual preferences. While the majority of college students—80.4 percent—described themselves as heterosexual, the other 19.6 percent revealed a wide diversity in sexual orientation. Six percent identified as asexual, 5.5 percent as bisexual, 1.8 percent as gay, 1.1 percent as lesbian, and 1.5

percent as pansexual. The rest (3.7 percent) described themselves as queer, same gender loving, questioning, or another identity.[8]

Academic and Mental Health Challenges

"My father is completely accepting of my being a lesbian. When I came out to him, he said he already knew."

"My mother doesn't want to have anything to do with me. She can't understand why I am gay."

While there is greater societal acceptance of different kinds of sexuality, people who are part of the sexual minority still face high levels of prejudice growing up. The prejudice can come from students, teachers, and family members. I'm going to use the term "sexual minority students" to describe students who are lesbian, gay, bisexual, or another nonheterosexual category. Rejection from a family member can be a particularly painful event.

Parental rejection can cause great emotional harm. A study of twenty-one to twenty-five year olds who were gay, lesbian, or bisexual showed that those who experienced little or no rejection from family regarding their sexual orientation were much less likely to become depressed, attempt suicide, use drugs, and have unprotected sex compared with those who experienced higher levels of rejection.[9] In my work with college students who have diverse sexual orientations, I see the benefits of parent acceptance as well as the harm of rejection.

In general, sexual minority students experience higher rates of anxiety, depression, and suicidal thoughts. They are also more likely to abuse drugs and alcohol.[10] A survey of college freshmen showed that LGBTQ students experience higher rates of depression and feeling overwhelmed than sexual and gender majority students.[11] LGBTQ college students report greater problems with cognitive functioning and their role as a student, most likely as a result of the stress and mental health problems they are experiencing.[12]

Your unconditional love, whatever your child's sexuality is or becomes, is critical to his or her well-being. Suggesting your child seek out support from the office of diversity or LGBTQ resource center can be very beneficial to his or her own self-acceptance and sense of well-being. Encouraging him or her to seek mental health services if he or she is feeling stressed is essential.

Thomas's Quest, Round 2

You tell Thomas you are surprised by hearing he might be gay or bisexual, but you are fully supportive of his sexuality. "I never want you to feel like you can't tell me what is going on in your life. It's hard when you feel you hide your true self from your family. I'll always support and love you." You tell him you are glad he is seeing a therapist for his depression, and you want him to call you if he is ever feeling low.

It may be hard to know what to say if your child talks to you about his sexuality, especially if you grew up in a culture that was less accepting of sexual minority lifestyles. Here are some tips to support your child.

Final Tips for Sexuality Challenges

1. *Listen to what your child says and respond in a nonjudgmental tone.* Ask questions if you don't understand something, but don't say, "Are you sure this is a real thing?" Tell your child you're glad he or she felt comfortable enough to open up to you.
2. *Show support and acceptance of your child even if you are struggling with your feelings.* You may have concerns your child will be discriminated against or shunned by others. You can get more information about how to help your child by joining your local chapter of Parents, Families, and Friends of Lesbians and Gays (PFLAG) (https://www.pflag.org).
3. *Promote safe sex, just as you would if your child were heterosexual.* Encourage condom use to prevent sexually transmitted diseases (STDs). If your child is in a monogamous relationship, recommend testing for STDs before unprotected sex occurs.
4. *Encourage your child to get support from campus resources if he or she is feeling alone or facing rejection from peers.* Joining a campus support group for lesbian, gay, and bisexual (LGB) students can lead to a greater sense of social belonging.
5. *Recommend your child visit the campus counseling center if he or she is experiencing symptoms of depression, anxiety, or substance abuse.* College students are remarkably resilient, and timely treatment will accelerate their recovery.

GENDER

Jessa's Journey

One day you receive a phone call from your son, Jesse. He sounds nervous on the phone and you ask him what's wrong.

"Nothing's wrong. I've just got big news that's really going to surprise you. I've been thinking about my gender lately, and I'm not sure where I stand. Sometimes I feel more like a woman than a man, and I'll put makeup on. Other days I feel more masculine. But lately the feminine side seems to be taking over. I'm comfortable with that. I've met other students who are gender fluid or gender questioning. I don't know where this is going, but for now, I'd like you to call me Jessa."

You are shocked to hear this. You have always been open-minded when it comes to people having different genders or sexualities. But you've always seen Jesse as your son. How will you get used to Jessa as your daughter? And is this something that is going to stay or change?

A GENDER REVOLUTION?

Gender is a hot topic on campus and in the country right now. College students now view gender in a far different way than my generation did. This change in view is affecting everything from dorm living arrangements to the language we use for gender. Just as in sexuality, young adults are more likely to see gender on a spectrum rather than in clearly defined categories. Half of people aged eighteen to thirty-four believe that gender is a spectrum and that some people fall outside conventional categories of male and female.[13]

Men and women are moving out of typical gender constructs. Men are becoming nurses and women are joining the military. But sometimes their behaviors conflict with how their parents expect them to act. A female student tells me, "My mother is upset with me for moving in with my boyfriend before marriage." A male student says, "My father thinks I'm not muscular or manly enough and he is always telling me to lift weights." Students are struggling to accept themselves when their and their parents' values collide.

While college students see gender on a spectrum, the majority of college students—96.9 percent—describe themselves as identifying with their sex at birth.[14] In other words, a person who is designated female at birth continues to identify as female. Just over 3 percent describe themselves as nonbinary. Nonbinary in this survey means students are either transgender or their current gender is not consistent with how they were assigned at birth. Nationally, researchers estimate that about 1 percent of the adolescent population is transgender.[15]

What does being transgender mean? Definitions can vary from one organization to the next. Many consider transgender an umbrella term for people who do not identify and/or express themselves as the sex they were assigned at birth. This could include people who were designated male at birth and identify as female, who were designated female at birth and identify as male, or who don't identify as either gender.[16] A transgender man is someone who was designated female at birth but identifies as male. *Gender fluid* describes people whose gender identity and expression could vary from day to day.[17]

Being transgender is not new to this country and in fact is part of many cultures throughout the world. Some cultures are fully accepting of genders that fall outside of what is typically male or female and have names for other genders. Gender is incredibly complex, emerging from a combination of chromosomes, hormones, physical characteristics, psychology, and culture. Brain studies have shown some differences between transgender and nontransgender people, but the results have been inconsistent.[18]

Mental Health and Academic Challenges

College students who are transgender have about double the rate of depression and anxiety compared to other college students. They have thought about suicide at triple the rate of other college students.[19] They may be more vulnerable to these mental health issues because they are more likely to be bullied in middle school and high school or face rejection from family and friends. Transgender individuals also have much higher rates of eating disorders.[20] They have four times the rate of diagnoses of anorexia and bulimia than other college students. They also use diet pills, laxatives, and purging for weight control at a higher rate than other students. There are a variety of possibilities as to why transgender students have higher rates of eating disorders and eating disordered behaviors. Stress and struggles with body image may contribute to the high rate of eating disorders. In chapter 11, I'll write more about how parents can help children who have eating disorders. If your child is transgender, it is worthwhile to ask if he or she ever copes with stress by engaging in eating disordered behaviors.

Colleges continue to work out details on how to create a welcoming and inclusive environment for all students on the gender spectrum, with many schools offering new housing options, LGBTQ resource centers, and support groups. Colleges and national organizations are offering training for mental health professionals to better help students who are transgender. Some colleges have medical providers who have special training in providing hormone treatment for students who are transgender.

If your college student comes out as transgender, you may feel shocked or overwhelmed. You may be concerned about prejudice against your child. You may also worry about different aspects of transition. Will your child dress as the gender he or she identifies with, take hormones, have surgery? Each transgender individual may follow a different path, going through few or all aspects of transition. Some studies have shown hormone therapy for transgender people results in mental health benefits, with improved psychological functioning and less anxiety and depression.[21]

In Jessa's situation, she is not sure where she stands. She may dress differently but is not planning on any medical treatments at this moment. Coming out as gender questioning in a college environment has been a safe and supportive experience for her.

Your support of Jessa is critical because mental health issues occur with increased frequency in college students who are transgender.

Jessa, Round 2

You take a deep breath and tell Jesse, no, Jessa, that you are surprised by this news and it's taking you time to process it. You say you support her choices.

"This isn't a choice, Mom, this is just the way I am."

You tell Jessa that you are going to read more about gender and you would love to come up to school to talk with her about it.

"I'm busy this weekend, but how about next weekend?"

"Great, Jessa. But I just want to ask if you are feeling okay about his. It's such a big change, and I don't know how your friends are reacting to this news."

"Everyone's great, Mom. I'm part of a transgender support group on campus, so I'm learning from everyone. But it's really no problem."

You hang up the phone and realize Jessa sounds happier than she has in a while. But you're still feeling overwhelmed. You decide to follow Jessa's lead and join a local family support group through PFLAG, a gay and transgender advocacy group. You know you will always love Jessa, and with time you will be comfortable with wherever Jessa lies on the gender spectrum.

SEVEN TIPS FOR PARENTS WHEN IT COMES TO COLLEGE STUDENT GENDER

1. *Be prepared for your child to move outside of typical gender constructs and be on a gender spectrum.*
2. *Understand that gender is increasingly fluid in young adults.*
3. *Maintain a loving and positive attitude.* Your child is closely watching your response and may be less likely to communicate with you if he or she feels rejected.
4. *If you are feeling overwhelmed, talk with a therapist or find support through PFLAG (https://www.pflag.org), an organization for the LGBTQ community and their families.*
5. *Ask your child what pronoun he or she wants you to use.* Some will want the pronoun for the gender they identify with, while others will want another word. Some students prefer the pronouns they and their instead of he/she or his/her.
6. *Help your child navigate through insurance challenges and be an advocate.* Many college insurance plans offer coverage for transition-related medical treatments.
7. *Encourage your child to see a campus therapist or a psychiatrist if he or she is struggling with mental health issues.*

Cultural, sexual, and gender minority students may face some unique academic and mental health challenges on college campuses. At the same time, colleges often have resources for students, and students form their own groups to feel more at home. College, in fact, is generally a very supportive environment if you are minority. If your child is part of a minority group, be aware of academic challenges early on and encourage him or her to seek help. Encourage your children to seek care with their campus mental health services if they are under increasing stress. Your belief in their ability to succeed and your unconditional love are critical factors in their academic and emotional wellness.

8

FINANCIAL STRESS

Debt Bubbles, Depression, and Health Care Blues

It's April and you're looking forward to your daughter, Maria, coming home from college in a month. Although you've missed her this year, you're proud of her hard work. She's studying pre-pharmacy at a competitive university. You're glad she followed your advice and picked a career with financial stability. As a real estate developer, you suffered a big financial hit during the Great Recession. You're now working in a real estate office and living paycheck to paycheck.

You're surprised when Maria calls you, sobbing. "If I don't get all As on my finals, I may lose my scholarship and have to drop out of school." Maria's scholarship covers tuition, housing, and living expenses, something you cannot afford right now.

You feel your stomach drop. "What do you mean? I thought you did well the first semester and you're doing well now."

"I didn't want to worry you, but I was on academic probation last semester, and my grades aren't much better this semester. In the fall, I spent way too much money going out with people in my dorm and buying clothes online. I loaned my roommate money that she never paid back. Because I was running out of money and had credit card debt, I took a waitressing job to pay my expenses, but I couldn't get enough sleep or get my course work done. I was devastated when I saw my fall semester grades and was determined to do better this spring. I cut my spending and reduced my work hours. But I've been feeling so depressed that I can't concentrate even when I have time to study. What should I do?"

What would you tell your daughter?

Before 2008, I rarely asked my patients how finances impacted them, and now I ask all the time. From huge student loans, to scholarships jeopardized by poor grades, to costly health insurance and medications, students need your help managing their finances now more than ever.

What is your parenting style when it comes to finances? Do you take a hands-off approach, trusting your child will make the right decision and come to you with a problem? Do you helicopter, monitoring every expenditure your child makes, and letting him or her know if you feel he or she is overspending? Many factors may influence your style, including your own financial health. Whether you are well off or struggling, it is critical you provide guidance to your child before he or she veers off into dangerous financial waters. Many eighteen or nineteen year olds cannot handle complex financial decisions or appreciate the long-term consequences of their financial choices. In addition, since the Great Recession of 2008, your college student is under more financial pressure than ever.

COLLEGE STUDENTS NEED FINANCIAL FIRST AID

Every day in my office, I hear about financial fears.

"I'm really worried about getting a job after finishing school. I have many friends that recently graduated who are now living at home and working part time."

"I don't think I'll ever make as much money as my parents did, and then I'll feel like a failure."

"The medication you prescribed is helping me a lot, but the price just went up and I can't afford it anymore. I don't want to ask my parents for help—they are already under financial pressure—so maybe I should stop taking the medication."

Whether you are wealthy, middle class, or financially struggling, your college student most likely has financial concerns. Finances are second only to academics as a leading cause of stress in college students, with one of three students reporting finances were traumatic or very difficult to handle.[1]

I have seen more and more students face extreme financial struggles, wondering if their financial aid will come in on time to pay for their textbooks, rent, and food. I have referred students to our school food bank when they cannot afford to eat. Our university also has emergency loans for students facing specific financial hardships. If your child is struggling, he or she may not tell you. He or she may be embarrassed or want to avoid putting financial pressure on you. Will he or she be able to pay for medication or the costs of seeing a therapist off campus? Health insurance and health care costs are a major stressor, topics I will cover later in this chapter.

Students tell me they are under extreme pressure to do well academically, feeling like their economic futures rest on their ability to secure their place in the best graduate school or company. They believe there is no room for error. Even their summers must be perfectly choreographed. Students are applying earlier and earlier, often during the fall semester, for prestigious summer internships. Will they get that perfect position in a top bank, social media company, or engineering firm? Students see these internships as a stepping stone to a great job after graduation. After submitting resumes and cover letters, they go through multiple interviews—for a summer job! Most people of my generation never felt this kind of pressure.

Why are the students so worried about their financial future? Is it because they see the reality of the post-recession economy? More young adults are living at home. And when they do have jobs, they feel their American Dream slipping away. Since the 1970s, the percentage of thirty year olds earning more than their parents has declined from just over 90 percent to around 50 percent.[2] If the trend continues, your child's living standards could be lower than what he or she grew up with.

Of equal concern is that the job market continues to be in upheaval as the nature of work and jobs evolves. A *Wall Street Journal* article aptly called "The End of Employees" describes the trend of companies hiring part-time contractors or consultants rather than full-time employees. This practice gives the company more flexibility in adjusting work force size depending on the economy, hiring during profitable times but then letting employees go when the economy slows.[3] This method offers little security to the consultant, who may not have a stable source of income or access to affordable health insurance. I've heard many young adults voice concern about affording health insurance in the future.

Student debt may be adding to your child's insecurity about his or her financial future. Student debt topped $1.2 trillion in 2016, with seven of ten students owing on average $37,000.[4] If your child goes to graduate school, his or her total debt could top $100,000. Many parents are helping their children pay for college, but more students are taking out loans as costs continue to rise.

If your child relies on scholarships and loans to be in school, he or she is under tremendous pressure to do well. One bad semester can jeopardize his or her ability to continue receiving financial aid. He or she may not want to stress you out if there is a problem and only turn to you when the problem becomes a crisis.

In "Maria's Financial Meltdown," Maria's financial decisions put her on a path to depression, while her father learns that staying involved in Maria's finances is vital to her financial, physical, and emotional health.

MARIA'S FINANCIAL MELTDOWN

When Alex hears his daughter Maria sobbing on the phone, he is too bone tired to get upset. He has been showing houses all day and did not make one sale. He isn't sure if he will be able to pay his rent this month, and now Maria is at risk of losing her scholarship. How did this happen? Maria was always so dependable and responsible. Alex takes a deep breath and tells Maria, "Honey, we've been through tough times before. We'll get through this. Now slow down, let's talk about what happened, and we'll come up with a plan."

Maria calms down once she hears her father's voice. He has always been her rock. It's just been the two of them since her mother died when she was four. Maria agrees to try to get some sleep tonight and meet with her scholarship advisor tomorrow to explain her situation. Maria also agrees to visit the campus counseling center because she is constantly tearful and tired.

The next day, Maria's scholarship advisor is very supportive and encourages her to go to the counseling center. There a therapist could evaluate Maria for mental health problems and recommend treatment. The therapist could also provide Maria with a letter explaining how mental health issues affected her school work and how she will address these issues with treatment. With this letter, Maria will likely be able to keep her scholarship.

When Maria meets with the therapist, the therapist agrees to provide the letter because Maria shows signs of depression that include a sad mood, fatigue, poor concentration, and difficulty sleeping. Maria is grateful, but then says, "Maybe I don't deserve the letter. Maybe I don't even deserve to be in college. I've made too many mistakes as it is." The therapist counsels Maria to be less hard on herself and to practice self-compassion. "We all make mistakes, Maria. But I think your depression is causing you to be extra critical of yourself. It's also made it hard for you to do school work this semester. Let's meet to work on coping strategies for the stress you are experiencing. I also want you to meet with a psychiatrist to see if you would benefit from medication for your depression."

When Maria enters my office, I notice she looks tired, thin, and pale. I see dark circles under her eyes and wonder if she is anemic. I ask her if she's been eating enough. "I haven't had enough money for food, so I've been eating only one meal a day. I've lost about ten pounds since school started." When I ask about sleep, she says she is sleeping six hours a night, more than the four hours a night she slept in the fall semester, but still not enough. Sometimes she is up late at her waitressing job, but at other times it can take her two hours to fall asleep. "I just keep thinking about my scholarship being at risk, the money I still owe on my credit card, and how I let my father down. I feel really depressed. Maybe I should take medication."

I tell Maria that she does have symptoms consistent with depression, and certainly the financial and academic stress she is experiencing could trigger depression. But the lifestyle she is leading—not sleeping enough, not eating enough, and losing weight—could also be fueling her depression. I wondered if she might feel better after making lifestyle changes that involve regular sleep, a healthful diet, and therapy to talk about her feelings. She might not even need medication.

"That sounds like a good idea. I'm going to quit my job so I can get enough sleep, and work full time this summer to pay off my credit card." I tell her how to access food through our campus food bank.

I then recommend Maria meet with a student health care center primary care doctor to do a medical workup. "He can do some lab work and test for any vitamin deficiencies." Maria sees the doctor the next day, and it turns out she is deficient in Vitamin D, most likely due to her poor diet and lack of exposure to sunlight. She also has iron deficiency anemia as she has extremely heavy periods and is not eating enough foods that contain iron. The primary care doctor prescribes a birth control pill that will make her periods lighter and recommends iron and vitamin D supplements. Maria is borderline underweight, and the primary care doctor encourages her to gain weight.

I meet with Maria a week later and she is already feeling more optimistic. She is eating better, taking her supplements, and sleeping regularly. She feels she can get Bs on her finals. If she continues to improve her GPA in the coming school year, she can keep her scholarship. She is looking forward to a fresh start in the fall. But she does have one concern. "I know it's important for me to see a therapist over the summer, but I don't know if I can afford it. My insurance plan has a high deductible." I arrange for Maria to meet with a case manager in our counseling center to help her locate a therapist in her area who bills on a sliding scale.

Maria's depression may have a variety of causes: psychological factors like financial and academic stress and biological factors like nutritional deficiencies and poor sleep. Low iron can contribute to fatigue and low vitamin D levels are linked to depression. I recommend she treat her depression with therapy, regular sleep, and reversing her nutritional deficiencies. I could offer her an antidepressant, but I believe she will recover without medication.

Maria e-mails me midway through the summer. "I wanted to let you know I'm feeling much better and am no longer depressed. I've been talking with a therapist and I've learned that it's okay to ask for help from my father and people on campus when I'm facing a problem. I don't have to handle everything on my own."

Maria comes back to school with restored confidence and motivation. She mentors other students in her scholarship program and tries to give them financial advice so they will not make the same mistakes she did. In the meantime, she and her father check in every few weeks about finances and he helps her set up a monthly budget.

FINANCIAL WELLNESS INTERTWINES
WITH MENTAL WELLNESS

Maria has all the best intentions when she starts college, but her financial choices send her down a rabbit hole of financial failure and depression. Maria's story touches on the theme that financial wellness directly impacts mental wellness. Maria is already facing financial stress, knowing she can lose her scholarship and loans with a few bad grades. Maria's decisions increase this stress: She spends too much money, gets into credit card debt, and works to pay it off, leaving her little time to do school work or sleep adequately. She also does not have enough money to obtain sufficient nutrition. Her financial troubles contribute to her depression, and the depression makes it harder for her to concentrate in school, putting her scholarship at risk.

The end of this story illustrates another point: financial wellness affects access to mental health care. Maria is concerned about paying for her care during the summer, and a counseling center case manager links her to affordable resources. Later in this chapter, I will discuss how you can help your child cope with rising health care costs.

One recent study of college students looked at how financial strain affected psychological health.[5] Financial strain was rated based on whether students had enough money to live on each month, how their financial situation compared with other people their own age, and whether they had sufficient spending money. Having financial strain alone did not lead to a significantly higher number of psychological symptoms like depression and anxiety. But when students under financial strain also viewed their lives as stressful and had difficulty coping with stress, their psychological symptoms increased. They also had increased academic and social difficulties. This study recommended that low-income students received not only help in financial management, but also meditation and stress management classes to ensure their psychological, academic, and social health.

The economy has a major impact on a community's mental health. Several studies have shown suicide rates correlate with poverty and high unemployment.[6] More recently, counties in the Midwest with high rates of poverty and unemployment have seen an increase in depression, suicides, and deaths related to narcotic overdoses.[7] The Great

Recession of 2008 has been linked to an increase in suicides in several countries.[8] The effect of the economy on mental health is profound.

You have a critical role in starting out your child on a financially healthy path, but what can you do, when legally your child is an adult responsible for tuition and other bills? There are a series of steps you can take to promote your child's economic well-being. New technologies are your friend in preventing and detecting financial problems.

USE TECHNOLOGY TO TRACK YOUR CHILD'S FINANCES

In November, you get a call from your son. "I can't pay this month's rent because I had unexpected expenses. Could you send me money?"

Before college started, you and your son agreed that you would deposit a certain amount of money in the bank each month, and he would be responsible for paying his bills. You trusted him because he never overspent in the past. You told him you wanted access to his online accounts to help him track his expenses, but he said he could handle it. Now you must decide if you should come to your son's financial rescue.

Before you do anything, ask your son questions about his unexpected expenses. Is he going out to eat too often? Buying new clothes? Giving money to friends? There can be more troubling reasons for increased spending, like excessive drug and alcohol use. Sometimes people spend more when they feel depressed, seeking short-term pleasure that could be followed by long-term financial pain. People with bipolar disorder may also spend excessively in a manic state. In other words, excessive spending could result from poor judgment, but could also reflect deeper mental health issues. Don't be afraid to ask questions. And don't be afraid to set limits on spending, while encouraging your child to obtain the mental health treatment he needs.

To avoid problems, get involved with your child's finances starting freshman year to encourage sensible spending habits. As time goes on and you see your child behaving responsibly, you will be able to take a less hands-on approach to your child's finances. Current technologies can now assist you in monitoring your child's financial health. Here are some suggestions for fostering your child's financial wellness.

1. Create a dialogue with your college student about finances. Explain to your child, "I know you'll be under a lot of pressure at school, and being responsible for keeping track of all your bills may be a lot to ask when you are a freshman. I want to be involved with your finances until you feel sure you can handle things on your own. Let's create a budget so you know how much I'm going to pay for your expenses and how much scholarship and financial aid you'll need."

If you are going to help pay for college, be consistent with how much money you give. Be open if something changes—if you lose your job, your child might need to take out more loans. Things might also change if you are going through a divorce. Sometimes students feel caught in the middle, and it might be unclear who will pay for college costs. Make it a priority to map out for your child who will pay for each expense.

Discuss what you are willing to pay for, and help your child prioritize what is important to him or her. I am willing to pay for items that promote my children's health. I will support my children buying organic food or taking yoga classes at an off-campus studio. I will assist with health care expenses not covered by insurance. But if I find out money I am giving my children is being used for drugs, my children know there will be serious repercussions that will include a cessation of financial help. I have seen too many instances of parents giving their children money, unaware that it is going toward the purchase of drugs. You don't want any money you give your children to be used in any way that is harmful to them, so it's important to express your values regarding how that money should be spent even before your child sets foot on campus.

Be clear what you won't pay for. I gave drugs as one example of something that I would not support. You should also reconsider paying for school if your child has a consistently poor academic performance. Freshmen will struggle; there may be a failing grade or poor grades at the beginning of school. But students regularly getting Cs or worse and showing no signs of improvement, despite taking the steps outlined in chapter 4, should make you reevaluate your financial support of your child's college career. Working for a few years may give your child the motivation to better meet the demands of school in the future.

2. Obtain online access to college financial statements and bills. Each college has a different way parents can get involved in billing. I encouraged both my children to sign forms at their respective schools so I could call the college billing office and see financial statements. You or your child could be the one to pay the bills. You could say, "Let's talk about how you want to do payments for tuition. I could put money in your account so you can pay. Or you can sign a form through the university so I can be added as a payer. But let's decide what makes sense so there are no surprises."

It's important for you to see the bills and statements whether you are paying tuition or not. You might catch errors that a college student could miss. One time my daughter was billed for university health insurance, even though she already had health insurance through our family plan. I thought I had filled out the required waiver of insurance, but it turns out there was another form to complete. After I made a few phone calls and completed the form, the situation was straightened out and the bill was removed. I kept my daughter fully apprised of the situation. She appreciated my help at a busy time in the semester.

3. *Monitor your college student's bank accounts and credit cards.* Again, this is something your child will need to agree to because he or she is an adult. But it can be helpful to see what your child is doing with money when he or she is on his or her own for the first time. Even if your child is on full scholarship or other financial aid, it's important you help him or her set a budget, as Maria's father learned. If you are providing money for college, your child should allow you to review bank and credit card statements. You need to reinforce the boundaries you've set regarding what he or she can and cannot buy. One time my son made a relatively inexpensive video game component purchase with a joint credit card, but I had him return the item because I had told him the card was for the purchase of food and essential clothing. Having your child on a joint credit card with a spending limit is the best way to go. Opening a joint bank account where you can monitor spending is also a good idea.

4. *Don't be too hard on yourself if you make mistakes. Learn from these mistakes and change your behavior accordingly.* My friend once said, "The bigger your children, the bigger your worries." That statement especially applies to financial worries. One big potential area for error is apartment rentals. Some colleges have four-year housing, but many do not. If your college student is renting an apartment, many complexes require that parents co-sign leases, and often these leases are not breakable for a year, making you liable for payments if your child moves out for any reason.

Beware of co-signing a lease that requires your child to find roommates. I know of instances in which parents co-signed a lease for an apartment or house with the idea that their child would find roommates to divide the rent. But other roommates did not materialize, and the parents ended up paying the full rent. One time I co-signed for a four-bedroom apartment with my daughter for the following academic year. She found three great roommates, but not right away. The last roommate signed the contract a few weeks before moving in. Until that last signature, I feared that I would be responsible for the additional rent. Although the risk we took paid off, I would not take that risk again. In the future, I would want all roommates to sign at the same time, guaranteeing a full house of compatible people.

5. *Help your college student create a long-term financial plan.* Encourage your child to visit the career resource center on campus, where he or she can assess his or her strengths and explore career paths. The campus resource center can help with resumes, interviewing techniques, and alumni connections. One study looked at a group of college graduates and found that a positive experience at the career resource center correlated with a good job after college, whereas a bad experience or no experience generally had a worse outcome.[9]

WHEN THERE ARE TOO MANY STRINGS ATTACHED

"I want to change my major from biology to sociology. I've decided I want to be a sociology professor instead of a doctor. My parents think that's a crazy idea and are considering not paying for school."

"I was going to stay with my friend for part of spring break, but my father says if I don't come home for the whole vacation, he's going to stop paying my tuition."

Do you use finances to control what your college student does? To some extent, we all do. I've already recommended parents not pay for college when there is ongoing drug use or poor academic performance. I would not help my children pay for college if they behaved in dangerous or destructive ways. However, we must be careful about how much control we exert. While we want to reinforce positive behaviors, we don't want to control every aspect of behavior. We want to foster independence, even while our children may rely on us financially during the college years.

For example, if your child chooses a major or a career you don't approve of, resulting in an urge to stop paying tuition, I would ask you to reconsider. A college degree, regardless of major, generally leads to a higher salary and better job advancement than having only a high school degree. Furthermore, your child will do better and be happier in a career of his or her choosing.

Avoid using money to keep your child close all the time. If your child wants to spend some or all of spring break away visiting friends, be glad he or she has friends he or she feels connected to. We want our children to visit us of their own free will, not because they fear they will not get financial help.

Offer as much financial help as possible, while letting your child become the person he or she is meant to be. You can foster financial independence as time goes on. Encourage your child to apply for a job or internship during the summer to help with expenses. A job is likely to make your child appreciate the value of money. Unfortunately, we live in an era of unpaid internships, so your college student may not always have a paying job.

Allow your children to increasingly make their own decisions and face consequences if they make mistakes. They might have to work extra hours or cut back on expenses if they buy an item they truly cannot afford.

Two areas you should stay involved with are health insurance and health care access. Health care costs and complexities continue to mount, and most college students are not ready to face the challenges endemic to our country's health care system. In fact, I've seen many fellow health care professionals—people in the know—struggle to access care for themselves. As our health care system continues to go through upheavals, you need to be a guiding force in dealing with the costs of care.

BATTLING THE HEALTH INSURANCE BLUES

You might wonder why your children would be dealing with health insurance. Doesn't the student health fee that is part of tuition cover their physical and mental health care needs? The answer varies widely from university to university. In some schools, the fee will cover the basic costs of primary care, counseling, and psychiatry, but there can be limits to the number of visits or the kinds of problems college personnel will treat. Students may be referred to health care providers off campus, especially if their problems are more complex and/or require longer-term follow up. Insurance becomes a necessity for off-campus visits. Even if your child gets all of his or her care on campus, insurance may be billed by the campus student health care center. For medications and laboratories, insurance is generally a necessity. It is very likely your child will be using insurance for his or her health care at some point during the college years.

From my perspective as a doctor, dealing with insurance can be a complex and difficult task. As one of my friends said to me, "Doctors and health insurance companies are not getting along." She made this observation after facing a medical crisis exacerbated by the insurance company's initial refusal to pay for life-saving treatment recommended by her doctor.

Since our college psychiatry services started billing insurance companies a few years ago, my practice has drastically changed. I spend much more time completing my notes to meet insurance requirements. I consider some of the information extraneous. What frustrates me the most is that the increased documentation requirements have reduced the number of patients I can see in a day, a less than ideal situation when the demand for psychiatry services has risen. Insurance companies are also increasingly requiring health care providers to complete prior authorization forms in order for the insurance companies to pay for medications. These forms have to be filled out yearly, even if nothing in the patient's status has changed. Many physicians find that these prior authorization forms are a time-consuming burden, interfering with rather than promoting patient care.[10]

Sometimes insurance companies will pay for medications and later decide they will no longer cover the cost of the medication. The medications without insurance may cost hundreds of dollars per month; the costs have risen in inexplicable ways. If a patient is doing well on his or her medication, it is extremely difficult to change him or her to something else. I have seen patients change medication because of insurance company decisions, and the new medication does not work for them.

These medications are not interchangeable; they have unique effects based on a person's symptoms and genetics.

Psychotherapy is another treatment that may not be fully covered by insurance. As I stated earlier, many counseling centers have limits on the number of sessions offered or the kinds of problems they treat. Eating disorders, obsessive compulsive disorder, and substance abuse can require specialized care. Even if your child does not have a complex problem, some counseling centers might see your child one semester and refer him or her to a community therapist. If your child is advised to get therapy off campus, his or her insurance may cover part of the treatment, but there may be co-pays or high deductibles. Your child may not even tell you he or she wants to see a therapist because he or she does not want you to have to pay.

In situations in which students cannot afford their medications or therapy, I will routinely urge them to talk with you, their parents, to provide financial assistance. Early and comprehensive treatment of most mental health problems will lead to recovery, but the longer problems are left to linger, the larger they can grow.

The bottom line: Do your best to help pay for medications and psychotherapy that insurance does not fully cover.

Even though insurance companies can pose challenges to the delivery of care, it is better for your child to have insurance than not have it. I continue to see students without insurance, despite the passage of the Affordable Care Act in 2010: their parents might lose the family's insurance when they are laid off; the students might sign up for the Affordable Care Act but miss monthly payments; they might try to sign up for the Affordable Care Act but feel overwhelmed by the process. If I have students without insurance, I have them meet with a social worker to help them find an insurance plan that works for them.

What are the consequences of not having insurance? Many students delay getting the medical or mental health care they desperately need. I recently worked with a patient who had a serious medical problem that she delayed treating because she had no insurance. When I met with her for the first time, we did not even discuss her depression. I sent the patient straight to the ER, and she underwent surgery for her life-threatening medical problem. Most of the depressive symptoms she was experiencing were in fact a result of her untreated medical condition.

Other patients who don't have insurance might have trouble affording medication, like costly ADD medications, antipsychotics, and mood stabilizers. Sometimes there are coupons and patient assistance programs for people who need medication and don't have insurance. Your child's psychiatrist may be able to direct you to the appropriate program.

The bottom line: Do all that you can to make sure your child has insurance. Help pay for it even if it is expensive. The cost of emergency care will far exceed what you pay in health insurance.

Your child might have more urgent issues that require inpatient care. Eating disorders, psychosis, and suicidal thoughts or behaviors can sometimes lead to a psychiatric hospitalization. What if insurance companies recommend discharge from the hospital before the inpatient psychiatrist feels the patient is ready to leave? If your child is in a psychiatric hospital and you feel he or she is being discharged too soon, you can advocate for a longer stay.

Insurance companies might not want to pay for the hospitalizations at all, even when students are at high risk of harm. I worked briefly with a young woman with bulimia that caused life-threatening medical problems. Psychiatric hospitalization was recommended to treat her bulimia, but the insurance company would not agree to pay for hospitalization. Her father, primary care doctor, and I had to go through two rounds of verbal and written appeals until the insurance company agreed to pay for treatment. I admired this father's advocacy for his daughter to receive life-saving treatment. I advise you to appeal and advocate if you feel your child needs to be admitted to a psychiatric hospital but the insurance company refuses care.

Insurance companies generally provide limited coverage for more severe mental illness, such as chronic psychotic disorders or chronic suicidal behaviors. People with these problems may benefit from intensive outpatient treatment or longer-term residential treatment. I encourage you to do whatever you can to help your child obtain this intensive level of care. I have seen parents take out second mortgages or loans to pay for their children's care. Occasionally, these treatment programs will provide funding for people who are in need.

Several advocacy organizations help parents connect with resources for more challenging problems. If your child has more chronic problems, organizations like the National Alliance on Mental Illness (http://

www.nami.org) and the Depression and Bipolar Support Alliance (http://www.dbsalliance.org) offer wonderful free resources including support groups to parents and their children. The National Institute of Mental Health (https://www.nimh.nih.gov/index.shtml) also describes treatments and has links to resources in the community where your child resides.

The bottom line: Collaborate with your child, the psychiatrist, and a campus case manager to help your child find the care he or she needs for more serious mental health problems.

As a frontline practitioner, I have seen parents deal with a national health care system that sometimes seems to be in disarray. You can be the guiding light in this hodgepodge of health care. You have to be an advocate and a fighter. I have advocated for patients, and I also have had the experience of standing up for both my children and parents. When a hospital wants to discharge a family member too soon or an insurance company wants to deny payment for a procedure they said they would cover, I immediately take action for my loved ones, going from supervisor to supervisor until an appropriate outcome is achieved. I want to give you the fighting spirit to ensure your child gets the care that he or she needs.

Your child might be bearing many financial burdens. Health care costs are becoming increasingly challenging. Students may be facing day-to-day challenges in meeting expenses for food and rent. They may be worried about paying off loans in the future. They may be concerned about creating a stable and successful career. Here are some final tips to relieve financial pressures.

TIPS FOR FINANCIAL FIRST AID

1. *Discuss a budget before your child sets foot on campus.* Look at income and expenditures. Be clear how much you are going to spend.
2. *Encourage your child to plan for his or her financial future by visiting the campus career resource center.*
3. *Get online access to your student's college bills, banking accounts, and credit cards.* Monitor spending, at least at the beginning of

college. Decide who will pay which bills, and with time give your child more responsibility for payments and budgeting.

4. *Set limits with the money you give, to a point.* Do not give money if you feel it is used for self-destructive purposes like excessive drinking or drug use. But don't use money to control all behavior, such as what your child is majoring in or what career he or she is pursuing.

5. *Make sure your child has ongoing health insurance.* An unexpected and uncovered medical expense can lead to life-long debt. A lack of insurance will delay your child from seeking care.

6. *Help your child pay for health care expenses not covered by insurance.*

When your child is in college, you and your child are beginning a new financial journey. Whatever your contribution is to his or her finances, you are an important guide as he or she encounters detours and roadblocks along the way. Encourage sound spending habits now to ensure a brighter, happier, and healthier future.

Part III

Crises

9

SUICIDAL BEHAVIORS

A Parent's Worst Fear

"I want to go home. I don't fit in at school and my friends are never there for me when I need them. Sometimes I feel so bad I want to kill myself."

You get a call from your son, Dev, on a Sunday night in December, the day before his first final exam of sophomore year. He is in his dorm room. You tell him he will be home in a week for winter break and he'll be fine. You've heard these statements before and he's never carried through with them. But you feel uneasy. Should you get in the car and drive two hundred miles to check on him? Should you call the resident advisor?

What would you do?

This chapter may be the most important chapter you read. With suicides now the second leading cause of death in adults aged fifteen to thirty-four, every parent needs to be informed about actions they would take if their children had suicidal thoughts, threatened suicide, or attempted suicide.[1] Just as a new parent might learn infant CPR, you need to have a set of responses to this all too common psychiatric crisis.

Many parents cannot imagine the child they have loved and nurtured could feel suicidal. But suicidal behaviors and thoughts are much more common in the college population than you might think. One of ten college students seriously considered suicide in the past year and 1.5 percent attempted suicide.[2] Sadly, the suicide rate among adults aged fifteen to twenty-four has steadily risen in the past fifteen years and is now at 13/100,000 per year, according to a report by the Centers for Disease Control and Prevention.[3]

Disturbing gender trends can be found in these statistics. While women in the fifteen to twenty-four age group attempted suicide more often than men, men died by suicide at four times the rate of women. But women's suicide rates are increasing at a faster pace than men's. For women ages fifteen to twenty-four, suicides increased by 53 percent in the past fifteen years versus 8 percent for men. The rate of suicide for women ages ten to fourteen has increased even more dramatically, tripling in the past fifteen years. Whether we have sons or daughters, we have cause for concern.

It has been reported that college students end their own lives at a lower rate than similarly aged adults in the general population, at 8/100,000 students per year.[4] However, this statistic may underrepresent the true number of college-related suicides because some students may harm themselves while on leave from college. In addition, certain highly competitive colleges have seen higher suicide rates. The *Boston Globe* reported data showing annual suicide rates for MIT undergraduates of 12.6/100,000 and Harvard undergraduates of 11.8/100,000.[5]

Suicidal thoughts and behaviors in your college student are distress signals that call for you and your child to take action, including an evaluation by a mental health care professional. Suicidal thoughts and behaviors are often linked to depression and other mental health disorders, and treatment of these disorders can increase your child's safety. Staying in touch with your child and the treatment team to help with safety planning and treatment decisions is essential, especially when the best course of action is not clear, as we learn in the following vignette.

DEV'S DILEMMA

Dev's mom Anju does not want to overreact to Dev's suicidal thoughts. She asks him more questions, and he says he would not hurt himself right now, but he keeps getting more thoughts about it. Maybe if a car hit him he'd be better off. Dev has been on an antidepressant for a few years now, prescribed by his pediatrician for the treatment of depression. Anju thinks it's time to make a change in medication. She urges

Dev to meet with a campus psychiatrist tomorrow and have the psychiatrist call her during the appointment.

When Dev meets with me the next day, the first thing he does is pose the question, "Should I stay or should I go?" I'm not sure what he means by this statement: Stay alive or die? Stay in school or go home? He affirms that he is referring to school, not death, but he is also thinking more about death lately and that it would be easier not to be alive.

These thoughts are more likely to come when he is alone in his dorm room late at night. During his darkest moods, he sometimes superficially cuts his wrist with a plastic knife. He does not want to kill himself in that moment, but cutting can make him feel calmer by distracting him from his emotional pain.

When I ask him to tell me what is distressing him, he responds, "I loved school when I first got here. I made friends and was doing well in my classes. But then things started to upset me. My roommates would make plans and not tell me. A professor gave me a C on a paper that I thought deserved an A on. Everything that I thought was great was now terrible. People have told me I see everything as black or white, all good or all bad. I can be feeling good until one small thing makes me angry or sad. Then I'll totally isolate myself from my friends and stop doing the things I enjoy. I felt this way my senior year of high school, and after starting an antidepressant I felt better. I thought I would enjoy college, but instead I just keep feeling worse the longer I stay here."

I ask Dev what he believes would help him feel better. Dev tells me he wants to move back home and commute to a university nearby. He thinks that living with his family will give him a greater sense of security; he does not feel ready to be on his own. "But my mother wants me to stay in school. She says it will build up my self-esteem if I can overcome my problems. She will pay for me to see an off-campus therapist every week and wants me to try a different medication." Dev requests I call Anju so the three of us can discuss what is best for Dev. He signs a release of information form that allows me to have ongoing discussions with his mother. I call Anju and put her on speaker phone.

Anju tells me, "I have two older children, and it took them a few years to adjust to school. I think Dev will be fine if he gets treatment. I'll also speak with him every day by phone and I'll visit him once every few weeks to support him."

Should I disagree with his mother? Maybe he should give treatment time to work. She knows her son better than I do. And Dev is doing well academically. But Dev's chronic suicidal thoughts and superficial cutting concern me. If Dev believed that school was the best place for him to be right now, I would support his staying in school. However, Dev is giving the message that home is where he wants to be.

I tell Anju, "I'll work with Dev if he decides to stay in school. But I'm not sure that will be enough to address all the issues he's struggling with. He seems overwhelmed. Staying home next semester and taking classes locally might be a good way to decide whether he should return here or transfer to a school closer to home."

Anju says, "Dev, it's your decision." Dev takes a deep breath. "I want to give school another chance next semester. I think I can make it work this time." I prescribe Dev a new antidepressant to treat his depression and ask him to make an appointment with his pediatrician over winter break to check his response to the medication. As I wrote in chapter 2, antidepressants can at times increase suicidal thinking, especially at the beginning of treatment, so close monitoring is important.

When I meet with Dev at the start of the spring semester, he is feeling markedly better. However, his mood sinks after a student he dated a few times decides not to continue seeing him. He texts her that he feels suicidal. The student notifies campus administrators, and Dev is asked to see me. Dev tells me that he had no intention of hurting himself that night, but considers suicide as an escape from pain in the future. He's working with a therapist to develop coping strategies to deal with disappointments, but he's starting to worry it will not be enough to keep him safe. He wants to go home. I support his going home as well to obtain more intensive therapy and receive family support. I am also starting to think that he has an additional diagnosis of borderline personality disorder, given his ongoing mood instability, reactivity, relationship instability, and chronic suicidal thoughts. I'll write more about this disorder later in the chapter.

I call Anju and put her on speaker phone; I tell her that I recommend Dev go home for treatment and support. Anju says, "I'll come and visit you this weekend, Dev, and we can decide what the best answer is. If you're not feeling better by the end of the weekend, I'll bring you home." Anju's visit is enough to lift Dev's mood, at least for a time. However, soon Dev is again struggling with relationship problems and reactive moods. His stress escalates as he approaches spring semester final exams. During reading week, I receive a call from a campus administrator that Dev was brought to the hospital the night before after his roommate walked in on Dev in the bathroom using a razor to make multiple cuts on his thighs. Dev told his roommate that cutting relieved his stress. He did not intend to die, but if he did, it would not matter. Dev was first brought to the emergency room, where his cuts were cleaned but did not require stitches. He was then transferred to the psychiatric hospital. I called the psychiatrist who was working with Dev at the hospital and told him about Dev's struggles. We both recommend Dev return home to receive intensive outpatient dialectical behavior treatment, a therapy especially helpful for people with chronic suicidal behaviors and borderline personality disorder. Group therapy, individual therapy, and other activities would teach Dev to find coping skills for stress so he does not turn to self-destructive behaviors and suicidal thoughts.

I call Anju, who is already on her way to the hospital to meet with Dev and the treatment team. She wants Dev to come home as soon as he is discharged from the hospital and is grateful to find out from the dean of students office that Dev can take his final exams online from home. Anju expresses regret for not bringing Dev home sooner, but I tell her that it is difficult to know the best course of action when a college student struggles emotionally, especially if he has suicidal thoughts. Is he safer in school or at home? Dev has been ambivalent as well, telling me he wants to go home while telling his mother that he wants to stay in school. Encouraging independence while providing emotional support for mental health problems can be a tough balancing act for a parent. Anju is acting with love through each step of the process, which bodes well for Dev's recovery. I am certain she will ensure Dev gets the care he needs.

If your child has suicidal thoughts or makes a suicide attempt, you'll want to consider where he or she can flourish, be safe, and get the most effective treatment. The best way you and your child can make that decision is through careful and thoughtful collaboration with his or her treatment team.

HOW PARENT COLLABORATION CAN HELP IN THE CARE OF SUICIDAL STUDENTS

When I have worked with students like Dev who frequently struggle with suicidal thoughts, they generally want parents to be involved in treatment. Sometimes parents will ask to come to the first appointment. One time, I met with a daughter and her father for the first time. The daughter did not want to come in for treatment for depression and some mild suicidal thoughts. She said she had no intention of hurting herself. But the father had lost his mother to suicide and wanted to ensure his daughter got help. With her father's encouragement, the student decided to take medication and saw a dramatic improvement in her sense of well-being.

Your collaboration can encompass a wide range of behaviors, and it will depend on the seriousness and frequency of your child's suicidal thoughts. It could be checking in with your student in ways he or she finds supportive. Your student may not want you to call multiple times a day, but a once a day check in through text or phone is probably a good idea. If your student feels like he or she cannot be safe on his or her own, stay with him or her for a few days until treatment has begun or has been intensified. Otherwise, you will want to encourage him or her to enter the hospital until he or she feels safe.

Here are some ways your collaboration can be extremely beneficial to your child's treatment for suicidal thoughts and behaviors.

1. *Social support.* Your involvement strengthens your child's social safety net. Social support is a critical factor in reducing suicide risk. One study of college freshmen showed that parent support reduced suicidal thinking in college students.[6]
2. *Developmental, psychiatric, and family history.* When you provide information, the mental health provider can make a more informed diagnosis and treatment plan. You can give insight into current problems your child is experiencing and significant events in your child's development, like bullying or the loss of a loved one. If your child has previously taken psychiatric medication, you can provide information about diagnoses and medication. It is also helpful for the mental health provider to know

about any family history of suicide, depression, bipolar disorder, psychosis, and substance abuse.

3. *Education.* The mental health provider can educate you about the mental health problem your child is experiencing and ways to be supportive. He or she will talk with you about how to distinguish between normal adolescent angst and dangerous ways of thinking. He or she will recommend an action plan if your child becomes more suicidal. Increased contact with you may be part of the plan, and admission to the hospital can be a final step if social support is not enough to keep your child safe.

4. *Decision making.* When is it too unsafe for your child to remain on campus? This can be an extremely tough decision to make, as Dev's mother discovers. After a hospitalization for a suicide threat or attempt, I may recommend a student go home to a more supportive environment, but the student may believe school is the most supportive place to be. Talking with your child and his or her mental health provider will help you decide what path to take. Your input is extremely important.

I've reviewed your critical role in treatment if your college student has suicidal thoughts. Unfortunately, there are several barriers that may keep you from getting involved.

BARRIERS TO PARENT INVOLVEMENT

"I just found out from my daughter's roommate that my daughter was involuntarily placed in a psychiatric hospital yesterday after expressing suicidal thoughts. Why didn't anyone tell me? Was anyone from the university or the hospital going to let me know?"

Parents are getting mixed messages regarding parent involvement in their children's mental health, especially when it comes to suicidal thoughts and behaviors. On the one hand, organizations like the Jed Foundation and the National Alliance of Mental Illness promote parent involvement in the care of the suicidal college student.[7] The American Psychiatric Association has guidelines that promote family involvement and support for a patient who is suicidal.[8]

At the same time, there are laws that place barriers to family involvement. The Family Educational Rights and Privacy Act (FERPA) allows university administrators to contact family in the case of a health or safety emergency, but it does not require notification. Let's say the student in the example above was taken from campus to the emergency room by campus police due to suicidal thoughts. Each university has different guidelines related to FERPA. Some universities will immediately notify parents, and others will never tell them. Parents may find out about hospitalizations from roommates or friends. In giving talks at various national meetings, I've seen a wide range of practices in involving families in these emergencies.

HIPAA, the federal health care privacy law, is even stricter when it comes to a mental health or medical professional notifying you if your child is suicidal. Your child would need to provide consent for you to be notified. If your child does not consent, you can only be notified if your child is at imminent risk of suicide and your involvement will benefit your child. You would think that if your child is involuntarily hospitalized, these criteria for notification would be met. But your child might be judged to be safe in the hospital if he or she says he or she is no longer suicidal. Or your child might express that involving you would not be beneficial. In fact, a small minority of students come from homes where parents are abusive and parental notification would be detrimental to a student's well-being.

To make matters even more challenging, mental health providers have a wide range of behaviors when it comes to involving parents in the treatment of suicidal college students. In general, we may not involve parents if we judge a student to be at low risk of suicide. For example, if the student seeks treatment for depression and has occasional fleeting thoughts of suicide but continues to engage in school and have supportive friends, we may not ask the student to involve parents. But if we judge a student to be at a higher risk of suicide—for example, he or she is socially isolated, is abusing alcohol, and has a history of a suicide attempt—we are more likely to involve parents. In my own practice, I lean toward involving parents, but there are other mental health providers who lean the other way. There is no "line in the sand" telling practitioners when they should notify parents, but it may be worthwhile for college psychiatrists as a group to develop clearer guidelines.

In rare instances, I will go against a student's wish and notify parents of an emergency when I believe this will benefit the student. I've done this a few times when I've involuntarily hospitalized someone for an imminent threat of suicide and I am concerned the person will be discharged too quickly from the hospital at a continued risk of suicide. In these cases, I will let the parent and the hospital physicians know that I recommend the student receive longer-term care and explain why, like a specific well-thought-out plan for suicide or multiple previous suicide attempts. When I did inform a father about his son's hospitalization, he arranged for the son to transfer to a psychiatric hospital closer to home for a few more weeks. Both the son and father were grateful I involved the father, even though the son originally opposed the idea. Before going against a patient's wishes, I will consult with a colleague and possibly a lawyer to ensure I am within bounds of the law and sound clinical practice. Whether or not to notify parents against a student's wishes can be a very challenging clinical decision.

Ideally, your student will want to involve you in treatment if he or she is in distress. There have been tragic news reports of parents not being fully informed of a young adult's mental health problems, with parents later being devastated when the young adult dies by suicide.[9] Sadly, these parents did not have the chance to help their child at a time of most critical need. With suicide rates on the rise, we as parents need to do all we can to recognize the risks and signs of suicidal behaviors and take action to get our children help.

PREVENTION OF SUICIDE

If your child is having suicidal thoughts, encourage him or her to get mental health treatment. Suicidal thoughts increase the risk of suicide attempts; suicide attempts in turn increase the risk of death by suicide.[10] Unfortunately, a study of college-aged adults with suicidal ideation showed only one of three was getting mental health treatment.[11] The top reasons these eighteen to twenty-five year olds did not receive treatment were unaffordability, desire to handle issues on their own, not knowing where to get treatment, and fear of being committed, in other words, involuntarily admitted to the hospital. The fear of involuntary commitment is a legitimate one: different mental health providers have different thresholds for forcing someone into a hospital. Ideally, the provider will explore multiple ways of increasing support and safety before hospitalization becomes necessary. Most providers I know use commitment as a last resort and will try to provide treatment to people with suicidal thoughts in an outpatient setting.

Another fear college students express about getting treatment for suicidal thoughts is that they will get asked to leave school. This concern was highlighted by a 2016 *Today Show* report featuring students who say they were forced to leave school due to mental health issues. In response to this report, the *Psychiatric Times* published an article noting that most students who are treated for suicidal thoughts will be able to stay in school, although there have been students who were forced to leave and then successfully sued their universities for violating their civil rights.[12] The Americans with Disabilities Act confers rights on students with mental health issues to be able to remain in school even if they are experiencing suicidality. Each university handles these situations differently. If someone takes a medical leave of absence for mental health reasons, some universities might want them to undergo a mental health evaluation and submit a report before returning to school. The university where I work does not require such an evaluation. As a psychiatrist, I will work with suicidal college students and encourage them to stay in school if I think that is the safest environment to be in; I will encourage them to leave school and return home if I believe that is a safer and more healing environment. However, I have no administrative authority to decide whether they remain in school or leave. Wherever they go, I will encourage them to get treatment for their problems.

Getting comprehensive treatment for mental health disorders can be life saving for college students. Of people who die by suicide, 90 percent have a mental illness, often untreated or inadequately treated. Mood disorders like depression and bipolar disorder are involved in 50 percent of suicides, substance abuse in 25 percent of suicides, anxiety disorders and PTSD in 15 to 20 percent of suicides, psychosis in 10 percent of suicides, and personality disorders in 5 to 10 percent of suicides.[13] Other risk factors for suicide include a history of suicide attempts, a family history of suicide, and a medical illness.

Are there unique dynamics that put college students at risk for suicide? In previous chapters, I've discussed how loneliness, perfectionism, and financial problems—common challenges in the college years—can increase the risk of suicide. A study that looked at risk factors for suicidal thoughts in college freshmen showed several factors were associated with suicidal thoughts: depressive symptoms, low social support from parents, low social support at school, mood problems, and alcohol abuse.[14] Another study of university students with suicidal ideation found 42.8 percent had major depression and 24.1 percent had other kinds of depression.[15] Depression is the most prominent mental health disorder associated with suicidal behaviors in college students.

There is another unique and concerning phenomenon about college student suicide: the cluster or contagion effect that has been seen on some campuses.[16] Suicide clusters mean one suicide leads to more suicides in an academic year at an alarmingly high rate. Due to the close-knit nature of campus life, college students have a particular vulnerability to identifying with the person who died by suicide. As a result, colleges have developed strategies to decrease the risk of suicide following a campus death. I see firsthand how my campus handles these deaths, both as a psychiatrist and a parent, because my daughter is a student on the campus where I work. Students are notified of the death by e-mail and given information about campus resources where they can access help if they are in distress; parents are sent similar information. When I have received one of these notifications, I will usually check in with my daughter to see if she knew the student who died and to understand how this death impacts her. Every parent should check in with a child after a campus suicide.

On many campuses, mental health professionals or administrators might reach out to students most impacted by the death of a student by suicide. Media outlets are discouraged from sensationalizing or romanticizing the death by making it a prominent feature and are encouraged to be sensitive to the family's feelings and wishes.

What if your child does not bring up feelings of suicidality, but he or she is more distressed than you have ever seen him or her? He or she was rejected by a sorority or fraternity his or her heart was set on, he or she just failed a class, he or she just broke up with a boyfriend or girlfriend. Tell him or her you are concerned at how overwhelmed he or she seems and ask if it ever gets so bad he or she doesn't want to live. Does he or she ever think of ending his or her life? If the answer is yes, listen with love and empathy. Talk about a plan for getting help. Be supportive and caring, but don't show extreme distress yourself. Some of my patients who have suicidal thoughts do not want to tell their parents because they are afraid their parents will be overwhelmed or will overreact. Let your child know you can handle it.

TREATMENT FOR SELF-DESTRUCTIVE OR SUICIDAL BEHAVIOR

I've talked about the necessity of treating the underlying mental health disorder that is causing the suicidal thoughts and behaviors. There are even more specific treatments for people who experience these symptoms chronically.

When Students Are Chronically Suicidal: Borderline Personality Disorder

If your college student has ongoing self-destructive or suicidal behaviors, he or she should be evaluated for borderline personality disorder. If you remember, Dev is diagnosed with this disorder. People with borderline personality disorder have ongoing instability in interpersonal relationships, identity, and mood. More specifically, they make efforts to avoid abandonment, idealize or devalue relationships, have an unstable self-image, may be impulsive, and, of most concern, make repeated suicidal threats or act in self-destructive ways.[17]

The prevalence of borderline personality disorder in adults ranges from 1.6 to 5.9 percent, but it's unclear what the rate is in college students.[18] It can also be a tough diagnosis to make in college students because their personalities are still evolving. Some college students have some symptoms without the full disorder. People with borderline personality disorder may have higher rates of depression, bipolar disorder, eating disorders, PTSD, and substance use disorders. While they have an increased risk of suicide in the young adult years, this risk decreases with age. Engaging in effective therapy can reduce suicidal behaviors.

Dialectical behavior therapy (DBT) and psychodynamic therapy are the two most effective treatments in reducing suicidal thoughts and behaviors in people with borderline personality disorder.[19] Many campuses, including my own, offer groups in dialectical behavior therapy. DBT teaches students a variety of skills to manage suicidal thoughts and behaviors that include mindfulness, emotional regulation, distress tolerance, and interpersonal effectiveness.[20] For example, if someone is prone to cutting as a way to distract him- or herself from distressing feelings, he or she will work on developing a new list of coping strategies for distress that could include calling a friend, going for a run, or writing in a journal. Both dialectical behavior therapy and psychodynamic therapy help patients understand what internal states put them at risk for suicide and ways to alter these states to decrease risk.

Do medications reduce suicidality in people with borderline personality disorder? While there are no FDA-approved medications for the treatment of borderline personality disorder, a review of studies showed mild benefits to the use of mood stabilizers and second-generation antipsychotics (more about these in chapter 12) and more minor benefits to antidepressants.[21] In my work with people with borderline personality disorder, I have focused on treating their underlying mood disorder, while simultaneously strongly recommending psychotherapy.

Hospitalization and Beyond

Psychiatric hospitalizations of college students have increased dramatically, tripling in the past twenty years.[22] This is yet another indication of the extreme stress and increased rates of mental health problems that college students are experiencing.

If your child is hospitalized for a suicidal threat or attempt, it is essential that you get to the hospital as soon as possible. This may seem like an obvious statement, but in my experience parents sometimes do not fully understand the seriousness of a suicide threat or attempt. Offer your child love and support and also meet with your child, the psychiatrist, and the social worker. Hospital stays may be as short as a few days; it is essential that you be part of the discharge planning. Whether your child stays in school or goes home, you should ensure comprehensive treatment and support are in place for your child.

Be aware that the days and months post–psychiatric hospitalization may be an extremely vulnerable time. In fact, suicide risk is elevated up to ninety days after discharge from a psychiatric hospital, especially for depression, but also for bipolar disorder and schizophrenia.[23] Some hospital programs are instituting calls or letters to ensure patients are following up with outpatient treatment.

Responding in a Crisis

If your child makes a suicide threat and you feel he or she is in imminent danger, you should call the police immediately. This could be the campus police if your student is currently on campus or lives on campus or the local police if he or she lives off campus. Our dean of students office has an emergency number that anyone can call if they are concerned about a particular student. The dean of students office has access to your student's schedule and might be able to locate him or her if it is a day he or she is in class. Campus police have special training to talk with students who are in distress. Campuses may also have response teams made up of therapists and police to assist a student who is expressing strong suicidal thoughts. I hope you are never in a situation of imminent concern, but if it does happen, reach out to campus administrators or police for help.

THE MYSTERY OF COLLEGE STUDENT SUICIDE

It is incomprehensible that a young, healthy person with friends and in college would die by suicide, but it happens all too often. What seems like a minor event in perspective—a breakup, a bad grade—can take on huge proportions in the adolescent mind. Part of this is biological. Suicidal thoughts may be especially dangerous in your child's still developing adolescent brain. While the prefrontal cortex or executive functioning part of the brain has not completed development, the limbic system or impulsive part of the brain is going at full force. The adolescent brain sometimes functions like a car with a gas pedal that lacks working brakes. If your child is distressed, he or she could try to hurt him- or herself, not pausing to think that he or she might feel better in the future.

Biology in general has been shown to play a large role in suicide. People who have died by suicide have been found to have low levels of a serotonin metabolite, thus indicating low levels of serotonin in their brain.[24] Serotonin is a brain chemical that I talked about in chapter 2;

dysregulation in the serotonin system is associated with depression. Most antidepressants work by raising serotonin levels in the brain. There may be a strong genetic component to suicide that tends to run in families.[25] Relatives of people who have ended their own lives are at much higher risk of suicide and should take extra care of their own mental health.

Suicide is a catastrophic confluence of biological, psychological, and social factors. Parents can be the most loving and caring parents in the world, mental health providers can be highly empathic and employ safety planning, and suicide still happens. I write this with the understanding that we can all do our best to prevent suicide, but it can still happen. If you know anyone who has lost a family member or friend to suicide, they need love, support, and the reassurance that it is not their fault.

As a psychiatrist, it is my goal to prevent suicide in any way I can. One of the reasons I have written this book is so that parents can help college students prevent common mental health problems and pressures from snowballing into crises and emergencies. While there is a temptation to not talk about painful subjects like suicide, I think there is a need to increase awareness and prevention. In the next section, I will offer some final tips to help you be aware of how to help your child with these issues.

FINAL TIPS FOR SUICIDE PREVENTION AND TREATMENT

1. *Reassure your child that he or she can come to you with any problem.* Many students will not tell parents that they are feeling suicidal because they do not want to upset their parents. If your child admits to suicidal thoughts, respond with a calm voice, even if you're not sure what to do. Together, you and your child can consult the counseling center or another campus crisis line to choose the next course of action. There may be times when you want to directly ask your child if he or she has thoughts of self-harm. If you are aware of a campus suicide or the suicide of a friend from home, ask your child how this impacts him or her. If your child was close to the victim, encourage him or her to speak with a counselor. You might also ask your child about suicidal

thoughts if he or she seems very depressed or lonely. If your child is experiencing suicidal thoughts or behaviors, the next steps are especially important.

2. *Encourage your child to take action by seeing a therapist and/or psychiatrist.* Suicidal thoughts or behaviors are signals of emotional distress that indicate the need for assessment and treatment by a mental health professional. Depression, unstable moods, anxiety, and loneliness are all risk factors for suicidal thinking in college students. Counseling centers offer individual and group therapy to address these issues. Some provide psychiatric care, while others refer students off campus for medication treatment.

3. *Request that your child sign a release of information form.* If I believe a student is at risk for self-harm, I'll request he or she sign a release of information form so I can talk openly with parents and coordinate treatment. You as a parent can also encourage your children to sign this form. After this form is signed, I can have parents join their child for an office visit or call in by speaker phone to discuss treatment options. You can share any concerns that I may not be aware of. I would be able to let parents know if I think they should increase social support by a visit or phone call. It's important for you to partner with your child and your child's psychiatrist during times of crisis.

4. *Pursue a more intensive level of care if your child's suicidal thinking escalates .* If you believe your child cannot maintain his or her safety, you should contact the local police, who will do a wellness check. Your child may benefit from a short-term hospitalization in which he or she can receive immediate treatment. Alternatively, it may be enough for your child to take a break from school and come home, where he or she can pursue mental health treatment in a supportive environment. For people with chronic suicidal thinking, programs that offer DBT have been helpful in reducing self-destructive behavior.

When we bring our children to college, we expect they will have the time of their lives, but are surprised to find they may also have times of darkness and despair. If your child is experiencing suicidal thoughts, encourage him or her to seek mental health treatment. Let him or her know that there is hope beyond the pain.

If you or someone you love is suicidal, call the National Suicide Prevention Hotline at 1-800-273-8255. The Jed Foundation (jed foundation.org) provides valuable information for parents about the prevention of suicide in college students.

10

SEXUAL ASSAULT AND INTIMATE PARTNER VIOLENCE

Being There in Their Darkest Hour

One time I was telling someone I was writing a book about college mental health and I would be describing how parents should talk about sex and relationships with their children before and during college. His response was, "Once they turn sixteen they have made up their mind how they are going to act. Nothing I say after that point will make a difference."

To me, that sounds like a fatalistic way to parent. Children, especially college students, are taking in what you say all the time and are having strong responses. I hear it every day in my office. You are their educator in chief when it comes to sex and relationships. You are their protector when it comes to sexual assault and intimate partner violence.

I'll admit that talking about these topics with your children can be uncomfortable for you and especially uncomfortable for them. I had only mild discomfort bringing up these topics with my children because I am discussing these topics with students frequently. My children, on the other hand, were mortified. But I believe my talks with them influenced them to make healthier choices.

Students don't always have the knowledge or experience to understand when physical intimacy crosses the line into forced sex, or when normal ups and downs of relationships evolve into abuse. You will have opportunities to discuss these topics when your children bring up something they see on television, read online, or hear from their friends. Unfortunately, they themselves may experience these difficult events. Sexual assault and intimate partner abuse occur all too often on college campuses.

If your child is a victim of sexual assault or intimate partner violence, he or she may suffer in silence, blaming him- or herself for events that are beyond his or her control. If your daughter has been assaulted, you might not find out until she starts to show signs of PTSD or depression. If your son has been physically or emotionally abused, he might be too embarrassed to tell you.

This chapter will offer you ways to talk with your children about healthy relationships and healthy sex in an effort to prevent problems. If the worst occurs and your child is abused or assaulted, you can take steps to help your child start his or her journey toward healing.

HEALTHY RELATIONSHIPS AND HEALTHY SEX: NO SHADES OF GREY

I never read the book *Fifty Shades of Grey* or saw the movie. Given my line of work, the last thing I wanted to see was a movie about a college student in a physically abusive and sexually violent relationship with an older man. After the movie came out, I saw a strange phenomenon. A few students—both male and female—described allowing themselves to be choked or hit during sex. But they had not learned about these behaviors from the movie. They had seen them on Internet porn. I counseled these students on the physical dangers of these behaviors and the potential harm to their sense of self-worth. These students grew to dislike these experiences and stopped. But hearing their stories made me realize how impressionable young adults are from media and Internet images.

With our children bombarded by disturbing media images, we as parents need to educate our children about healthy relationships and healthy sex long before they set foot on campus. You can brainstorm with your child what makes a healthy relationship and what will make him or her happiest. Here are a few principles that you can share with your children.

1. *Kindness. Sharing. Laughter. Love. These joyful elements are the glue that holds the relationship together.*
2. *Trust is the foundation, the cornerstone, the basis of all relationships.* If your child catches his or her partner lying more than a few times, it is time to question the strength of the relationship.
3. *Respect is another building block of a relationship.* If your child's partner is reading your child's texts or hacking into his or her computer to see what he or she is doing, your child's privacy is being disrespected.
4. *There should never be ongoing verbal abuse in a relationship.* Name calling, cursing, and constant criticizing have no place in a healthy relationship.
5. *There should never be any kind of hitting at any time in any relationship.*
6. *Sex should be an enjoyable, pain-free experience.*
7. *Sex is even better when it occurs between two people who care about each other.*
8. *Sex must be consensual, with both parties agreeing.*[1] Laws differ from state to state about the need for an explicit verbal agreement. But it is advisable that consent to sexual activity be stated by both parties. Individuals cannot provide consent if they are under the influence of drugs or alcohol. Sober sex is best.
9. *If someone wants to stop having sex, stop.*
10. *If your children are freshmen, inform them that freshman year is the highest-risk time for sexual assault.* They should always go to a party with a friend so they can look out for each other.
11. *Binge drinking puts college students at an increased risk of being sexually assaulted.* Drinks can also be tampered with. Encourage your child not to leave any drinks unattended or accept a drink that he or she has not seen poured.
12. *Taking a self-defense course before or during freshman year can be an empowering step toward safety.*
13. *Mistrust and caution can be protective when your children are meeting or dating people for the first time.* Encourage your children to get to know someone well before they are alone with them. Sadly, seven of ten sexual assault survivors have had some previous contact with the perpetrator.[2]

SEXUAL ASSAULT

Your daughter, Lisa, comes home from school one weekend unexpect-edly. She does not seem like herself and is listless and unhappy. You hear her in her room at night pacing, and then she sleeps the whole next day. You ask her if anything is wrong. Her eyes well up with tears and she says she drank too much last weekend. She needed to get away from all the partying that was going on in the dorm. What is she not telling you? You ask, "Did something upsetting happen last weekend?" She starts to cry and says she passed out after drinking too much. When she woke up, she was being sexually assaulted.

What would you say?

If your daughter has been sexually assaulted, she may not tell you right away. She might blame herself if she was drinking or want to forget the whole thing. She may be afraid that you'll be upset or insist she prosecute the perpetrator. If you sense she has been assaulted or if she tells you, responding in a calm and supportive way will make a big difference in her recovery process.

Every parent, especially parents of daughters, needs to be prepared in case their child is a victim of sexual assault. The numbers of college students who are sexually assaulted may shock you, but they do not surprise me after years of working with college students. I hear too many stories of unwanted sexual encounters, from fondling of breasts and genitals to forced penetration, to be surprised by the latest sexual assault statistics. In fact, nearly one of four female college students reported that at some point while in college they experienced sexual assault or sexual misconduct that could range from forced touching to penetration.[3] One of ten women experienced forced penetration. While women make up the majority of sexual assault victims, one of twenty men reported being victims of sexual misconduct or sexual assault. One of four transgender, gender queer, and nonconforming students were victims of sexual assault or misconduct.

I usually see a sexual assault survivor three to six months to a year after the event. She may be experiencing symptoms of depression, anx-iety, or posttraumatic stress disorder, and her grades may have de-clined. She thought she could handle the event by not talking about it and forgetting about it. I'm going to use the feminine pronoun to talk about survivors of sexual assault because they make up the majority, but a person of any gender can be assaulted.

You as a parent may be the first person she reveals this trauma to. You have an important role in helping her through the journey of recovery. Here is how I would advise you to advocate for your daughter.

How You Can Be Your Child's Advocate

You should help your daughter focus on safety, physical health, and emotional health. Here are steps you can take.

1. *Tell your daughter you love her and the assault was not her fault.* Your main concern is her safety and well-being.
2. *Ask your daughter if she is in any danger from the perpetrator of the assault.* Does he live in the dorm? Is he a student? She should immediately contact her school, campus police, or community police about any safety concerns.
3. *Let her decide if she wants to report the assault to the university administration (if he is a student) and/or to the police.* Understand that even in the case of more serious assaults involving penetration, under one-third of students will report this to any agency.[4] There are victim advocates she can consult with on campus to make this decision. You may naturally want to send anyone who would hurt your daughter to jail. But conviction rates are very low, and your daughter may not want to go through the process of filing charges.
4. *If the assault was recent, talk with your daughter about the possibility of doing a rape kit at the nearest facility that has trained personnel to do this.* This kit does not have to be used in an immediate prosecution, but can be used later if she decides to prosecute.
5. *Make sure your daughter has been tested for pregnancy and sexually transmitted diseases through her student health care center or local women's clinic if the assault involved penetration.*
6. *Urge your daughter to speak with a therapist and/or join a sexual assault survivor group for support.*
7. *Encourage your daughter to see a psychiatrist if she is overwhelmed by symptoms of depression, anxiety, or PTSD.*

8. *Promote self-care through physical exercise, healthful eating, and avoidance of drugs and alcohol.*
9. *Let her know that she will feel better with time. Assure her that you will be there every step of the way.*

Posttraumatic Stress Disorder and Sexual Assault

"I haven't been able to focus on school since I was raped. I'm having trouble falling asleep, and I keep having nightmares about it. When I am walking on campus I am scared I'll run into the student who did this to me; sometimes I'll get scared thinking it's him but it's someone else. When I'm not scared, I feel numb inside. I'm really worried about how much my grades have dropped this semester."

I see many women who have been sexually assaulted a few to several months after the act. Like Lisa, they are traumatized, and often they want to forget the event, but their stress response goes into overdrive. They are in a hyperalert and hypervigilant state, trying to avoid further danger. Any level of sexual assault increases the risk of PTSD. One-third to one-half of people who have been raped (sexual assault with penetration) have posttraumatic stress disorder.[5]

Most people who experience a trauma will have a stress response, but with PTSD symptoms last longer than a month and interfere with a person's ability to function. PTSD involves a range of symptoms, including difficulty falling asleep, nightmares, trouble concentrating, difficulty enjoying any activities, feelings of shame and numbness, and being on edge or fearful. They may feel detached from others or even detached from their own bodies. These symptoms are so strong that a student may have trouble concentrating in school and completing assignments. Often students with PTSD also have diagnoses of depression and anxiety.

If your child does not seem like herself and is suddenly experiencing a range of unusual symptoms, you can ask, like Lisa's father does, if any stressful event happened recently. She herself might not fully connect her symptoms with the event. Encourage her to speak with a campus counselor about what happened. Several studies show cognitive behavioral therapy is highly beneficial to people with PTSD.[6] CBT can help your child process and cope better with the memories of these painful events.

Many students will respond to psychotherapy for PTSD, but sometimes symptoms are so severe, particularly sleep disturbances or difficulty concentrating, that they will want to take medication as well. They may also want to take medication if they are experiencing strong depressive or anxiety symptoms. The SSRIs sertraline and paroxetine are FDA approved for the treatment of PTSD. Fluoxetine and the NSRI venlafaxine have also been shown to be helpful. Mirtazapine, an antidepressant that affects the serotonergic and noradrenergic system, is also beneficial. If insomnia or nightmares are a particular problem, prazosin improves sleep by impacting the adrenergic system.[7]

Rapid treatment for PTSD is essential because sleep and concentration problems will especially impact academics. If your child is having strong symptoms of PTSD, she may want to reduce her courseload to give herself the time needed to recover.

Sexual assault is one kind of violence on campus that can lead to PTSD and other mental health issues. But another all too common kind of violence—intimate partner violence—can lead to emotional and physical harm.

INTIMATE PARTNER VIOLENCE

Your son, Tony, calls you. He sounds like he has been crying. He needs you to send rent money. Last night his girlfriend moved out of the apartment and took $500 out of his checking account. He had given her an extra debit card in case she had any emergency bills, and now the money is gone. Earlier in the evening, she was angry at him for spending time with another female student on a project. She has always been a jealous person, but this is the worst he has ever seen her. She made an ultimatum that he stop working with the female student. When he refused, she started punching and scratching him. He locked himself in the bathroom until she left. He did not want to fight back out of fear that she would accuse him of domestic violence.

What would you tell your son?

Intimate partner violence occurs on college campuses with surprising frequency. It is something I hear about in my office on a regular basis. In fact, one of five college students reports having experienced domestic violence with a current partner.[8] Intimate partner violence consists of both physical and emotional abuse.[9] It can include hitting, punching, and shoving as well as threats of violence, stalking, financial abuse, and degrading language. Surprisingly, men and women commit interpersonal violence at about equal rates. But women are much more likely than men to die due to interpersonal violence. No amount of interpersonal violence should be tolerated in any relationship.

How would you know if your child was in an abusive relationship? Sometimes there are overt signs of physical abuse. Ask about any unexplained marks or bruises. If a student comes into my office scratched or bruised, I will always ask what happened. He or she might have been playing intramural soccer, fallen off a scooter, or stumbled after drinking on a Saturday night. But sometimes he or she will describe getting into a fight with his or her partner. The student might have come to see me to talk about medication for depression, but I will switch gears and talk about the relationship problems. Interpersonal violence can lead to depression, anxiety, and PTSD. No amount of medication will help if they are in a dangerous situation.

Other signs of abuse can be more subtle. A partner can be controlling and want to know where your child is at all times. He or she may not want your child to spend time with you. He or she may be jealous of your child's other friendships and worry your child will become intimate with someone else. The partner may say he or she will kill him- or herself if your child ever leaves. Your child will take the blame if his or her partner is upset. Your child will always feel like he or she is walking on eggshells in the relationship. When your child does not fulfill all the demands of the partner, he or she may curse at your child and eventually hit him or her.

If you see any early red flags of controlling or abusive verbal behavior, say something. Tell your child he or she does not deserve to be treated this way. When a student describes abusive behavior, I will pull up a domestic violence website like the one provided by the Center of Relationship Abuse and Awareness (http://stoprelationshipabuse.org/educated/warning-signs-of-abuse/) and review common signs of abuse. After even a single episode of violence, I always recommend the partners separate. There is a caveat in this bit of advice: physical danger increases when someone breaks up with an abuser. The separation must happen in a safe way. Your child, if he or she feels in danger, can work with a victim advocate or a domestic violence organization to find the best way to end the relationship. You or your child can call the campus counseling center, campus police, or dean of students office for a referral to the person or agency who can provide your child this support.

Some students will have trouble leaving a verbally or physically abusive relationship, fearing they will be alone or unable to cope. Keep promoting your child's strengths and let him or her know he or she doesn't need a partner to be whole. Encourage your child to meet with a therapist at the campus counseling center to talk about the relationship and treat any underlying anxiety or depression. Your child might try to work out his or her problems with the partner in couple's therapy. There are some studies that show that the risk of violence can be lowered through couple's therapy and individually treating the perpetrator's underlying mental health or substance abuse problems.[10] But if it were my child, I would tell him or her to leave immediately once any kind of violence takes place. Our college students have their whole lives ahead of them and many chances to find a safe and healthy relationship.

Let's say you are Tony's father. You can be glad that at least part of Tony's problem is solved because his abusive girlfriend has moved out and Tony never wants to see her again. Fortunately, she is not a student on campus. But Tony still has some work to do. He needs to immediately call the bank to protect the remaining money in his bank account. He needs to call the landlord to get his locks changed. You should also encourage Tony to talk to a victim advocate to see if it makes sense to file charges or take other action to keep him safe. Tony should consider blocking his ex-girlfriend's phone number and access to any of his social media sites.

If you could visit Tony for moral support, that would be great. As abusive as the relationship may have been, Tony might feel lonely. He may need some additional support and phone calls until he connects with other friends.

Technology: Sexual Cyberbullying and Stalking

What role does technology have in sexual violence and relationship abuse?

Technology has provided new ways for abusers to stalk and sexually harass their victims. For several years now, I have heard more and more from students about cyberstalking and sexual harassment. In fact, one of four women aged eighteen to twenty-four experienced online stalking and one of four experienced online sexual harassment.[11]

I've seen many students whose ex-partners stalk them through social media sites using fake identities or by looking on a friend's page. This kind of contact can be upsetting and disruptive to a student's work, especially if the ex-partner was abusive. Students might need to limit their contacts on social media. Students have been stalked when someone uses phone technology to monitor their location. Another form of abuse is someone sending a nude picture around of an ex-partner to humiliate him or her. We can't emphasize enough to our children the importance of not having any nude pictures out there. Our children can be overly trusting of people who can later turn on them.

If your child is being cyberstalked or sexually harassed online, he or she should consult with a victim advocate or campus police to see what his or her rights are. If another student is abusing him or her, your child should contact university administration for protective action on your child's behalf.

FINAL WORDS

We should do our best to promote healthy relationships and healthy sex in our children. But we should also know that despite ours and our children's best efforts, sexual assault and intimate partner violence occur all too often on college campuses. Share your concerns if you think your child has been assaulted or abused. Let him or her know you don't judge him or her and that it is not his or her fault. Focus on physical safety and emotional wellness. Link your child to campus resources like the counseling center and the victim advocate office. Text him or her numbers for the Domestic Violence Hotline (1-800-799-7233) or the National Sexual Assault Hotline (1-800-656-4673) if he or she needs advice. Your love and guidance will lift up your child in his or her darkest hour.

11

EATING DISORDERS

Drunkorexia and Other Dangerous Trends

You are at work and the phone rings. Emma, your daughter, is calling, which worries you because she never calls you this early in the day. You answer the phone and Emma says, "Mom, I'm in the psychiatrist's office. This morning I went to the campus health care center because I had a cold, and the doctor who evaluated me had me meet with a psychiatrist. Both doctors are concerned about my weight, and the psychiatrist wants to talk to you." The psychiatrist tells you that Emma weighs 100 pounds at 5'5", making her BMI 16.6, which is underweight. You tell the psychiatrist Emma has always been thin, as is everyone in your family.

The psychiatrist says being thin is only part of the problem. Emma has been vomiting most of her meals to lose weight. The doctor at the campus health care center ran some labs. Emma's potassium is lower than normal, which can happen when someone vomits frequently. If the potassium level gets too low, Emma could have a heart rhythm problem. To make matters worse, Emma sometimes drinks alcohol after she has vomited to get drunk more quickly. Emma is upset with herself, feeling like she cannot control her purging or drinking. She has been feeling down over the past few weeks and sometimes wishes she were dead. Emma would be best admitting herself to an eating disorders residential program for treatment of anorexia with purging features and depression.

You are shocked to hear all of this. Emma was home for December vacation and seemed to be in a good mood. She ate well, although she did look thinner than usual. You also did not see her drink any alcohol. You wonder if the psychiatrist is exaggerating the seriousness of the problem.

What would you do?

EATING DISORDERS ARE TRENDING ON CAMPUS

When I started working with college students two decades ago, I predicted that the high rate of eating disorders that I was seeing among college women would decrease over time. Women would come to accept who they are and embrace their body type. The media would stop promulgating unattainable images of female beauty. My feminist dream did not pan out, and even worse, both men and women are now showing higher rates of eating disorders than they did in the past. One survey of college students showed eating disordered behaviors consistent with diagnosable eating disorders increased from 7.9 percent to 25 percent for males and 23 percent to 32 percent for females over a thirteen-year period.[1] While many of these students may not have full-blown anorexia or bulimia, they are experiencing increasing rates of subclinical forms of these disorders or binge eating disorder. The college years, in fact, are the peak time for eating disorders to begin.

If your child has an eating disorder, getting early and effective treatment is critical because all eating disorders—anorexia, bulimia, binge eating disorder—are associated with elevated mortality rates. Medical problems, suicide, and substance abuse are the main causes of death in people with eating disorders. People with bulimia may suffer cardiovascular complications related to electrolyte abnormalities, and people with anorexia can have permanent heart damage.[2] People with anorexia have a death rate twelve times that of others aged fifteen to twenty-four.[3]

One campus trend may further increase the risk of physical harm to people with eating disordered behaviors. It goes by the name of "drunkorexia," a term that describes eating disordered behaviors used in combination with binge drinking for the purpose of getting intoxicated more quickly. In one study, eight of ten college students starved themselves, made themselves vomit, or used laxatives before drinking to allow themselves to get drunk more quickly.[4] Lately, I have asked more of my patients about these behaviors, allowing me to educate them about the high risks of drinking on an empty stomach, including blackouts and alcohol poisoning.

As alarming as some of these statistics are, I want to give you a message of hope as someone who has worked with many people with eating disorders over the years. In addition, I used to coordinate our university eating disorder treatment program that consisted of a multidisciplinary team of psychiatric providers, primary care providers, therapists, and nutritionists. I can tell you that I've seen many people make remarkable recoveries from eating disorders. You are an essential part of the team in encouraging treatment and helping your child when he or she faces barriers to treatment, as you'll learn in this story.

EMMA SEEMS FINE

When I call Emma's mother Claire to tell her about Emma's eating disorder and recommend inpatient treatment, Claire sounds like she is in shock. Emma was home only a month ago, and Claire did not notice any unusual behaviors.

"How long has this been going on?" Claire asks.

Emma explains, "Mom, I've been feeling stressed out since the summer, when I realized how much work I still had to do to get my physical therapy school applications in. Everything felt out of control. I thought I'd feel better about myself if I lost some weight, and I started dieting. One time I overate, and I made myself throw up. Before I knew it, I was vomiting after every meal. Throwing up calmed me down; I felt I could focus better afterward and I thought I could lose weight more quickly. But I was still so stressed out that I started drinking on the weekends, and I've blacked out a few times already. Now I'm just feeling really depressed, and I know I need help, but I'm not sure I want to go into the hospital."

Claire agrees. "The hospital does seem like a big step. Is there an alternative?"

I tell Claire and Emma that there is an eating disorders program affiliated with our local hospital, and Emma can be evaluated there.

They have an intensive outpatient program that also might work for Emma, where she can go for three hours a day for individual and group therapy, psychiatric treatment, medical monitoring, and nutritional counseling. Emma likes this plan, and I schedule an appointment for her that week to meet with an intake nurse. I am relieved when the nurse calls me to say Emma has been accepted into the program.

My relief turns to frustration when Claire calls me the next day to tell me the insurance company would not authorize payment for the treatment program. With calm determination, she says, "The insurance company wants Emma to try standard outpatient treatment first. Will you write a letter of appeal? She and I are appealing as well. I'm not going to stop until she gets the treatment she needs."

I am glad that Claire is advocating for her daughter. I write my letter of appeal, citing Emma's frequent purging, suicidal thoughts, alcohol abuse, and my concern that once a week therapy or psychiatry appointments will not be enough to change these life-threatening behaviors. I cite American Psychiatric Association eating disorders treatment guidelines that show intensive outpatient or even inpatient treatment is indicated for Emma's symptoms. While waiting to hear from the insurance company, I prescribe fluoxetine for Emma's depression, and she starts therapy with a counseling center therapist. The primary care doctor will monitor her potassium levels.

A week later, Claire calls me. Over the weekend, Emma's roommate brought her to the emergency room; Emma almost passed out after binge drinking without eating all day, and her blood alcohol level was very high. Emma is feeling better now, but Claire and I know it is only a matter of time before something worse happens. Both Claire and I agree to call the insurance company to expedite the appeal. When I call, I insist on speaking to a physician representative. I describe the emergency room visit as additional evidence that Emma needs intensive outpatient treatment. When the doctor says he still wants to give standard outpatient treatment a chance to work, I want to yell expletives at him. Instead I mention the mortality rate for anorexia and cite the particular risks Emma faces due to her alcohol abuse, purging, and depression. I state that if the insurance company continues to deny treatment, it will be their responsibility if something happens to Emma. Suddenly, the physician says the insurance company will authorize treatment. Guilt, or maybe the fear of a lawsuit, is a powerful force.

Three months later, Emma comes back to my office at a healthy weight. She says the intensive outpatient program was extremely helpful, and now she is ready to come back for treatment at the counseling center. She has completely stopped purging, and her potassium is back to normal. She has also stopped drinking alcohol. She is continuing to take fluoxetine, which helps with her depression. She has followed her therapist's advice to do Tai Chi, which makes her feel much more balanced and centered. She has also decided to defer going to graduate school for a year. She wants to feel less rushed before she starts graduate school and will live and work at home. I am thrilled to see Emma doing so well, and I'm glad to know she has a strong advocate in her mother if she ever encounters a problem again.

Emma's story illustrates something I have seen with every parent of a student with an eating disorder that I've worked with: they might not realize their child has an eating disorder, but when they are informed, they will go to the ends of the earth to get them the treatment they need.

BARRIERS TO THE TREATMENT OF EATING DISORDERS

Emma's story could also be called "A Tale of Two Denials." The story highlights two barriers to timely treatment for eating disorders. One is psychological denial—your child's belief that he or she does not have a significant problem. Emma has symptoms for months before she seeks treatment at the urging of a primary care doctor. Students with eating disorders hide symptoms from their parents or deny having problems when their parents ask. Parents might believe these denials, not wanting to suggest their children are not being truthful. Claire and Emma both come to realize the seriousness of Emma's problem and her need for treatment.

The second denial comes from the insurance companies. I find that my patients who have eating disorders are more likely to get denied coverage for inpatient or outpatient treatment than people with other disorders, and I am not alone in this experience. The problem of insurance company denial is noted on the National Eating Disorders Association website (https://www.nationaleatingdisorders.org/insurance-resources), along with advice on how to battle specific denials by insurance companies.[5]

When an insurance company will not authorize payment for intensive treatment, I and a family member appeal. I will appeal a second time if the first one does not go through, and I have always managed to get authorization. My appeal usually begins like this: this patient is at an increased risk of death without treatment and here are the reasons why. Depending on the patient, I will talk about electrolyte abnormalities, a low heart rate, low weight, rapid weight loss, frequent vomiting, increasing suicidal thoughts, substance abuse, severe depression, and inability to recover on an outpatient basis. I will refer to the American Psychiatric Association practice guidelines, which have established clear criteria for intensive outpatient or inpatient treatment of eating disorders.[6]

I share this information because I want parents to fight for the treatment their children need. Be factual and firm. Work with your child's treatment team. Don't give up if treatment is denied.

WHAT ARE EATING DISORDERS?

When does unhealthy eating cross the line into eating disorder territory?

Unhealthy eating that causes serious distress or dysfunction in one's daily life qualifies as an eating disorder. People with eating disorders generally use food to regulate emotions and have a preoccupation with their body image that goes to unhealthy extremes. While anorexia, bulimia, and binge eating disorder may be the most common eating disorders you hear about, many people have "unspecified eating disorders."[7] They might have some but not all the symptoms of anorexia or bulimia, while still having significant health risks.

People with anorexia live by the motto, "I feel fat." They will look at themselves in the mirror and think they are not thin enough; they incessantly count calories to see how they can lose more weight to the point that they are dangerously underweight. They may have a low heart rate and a low bone mass. If they have the purging type of anorexia, like Emma, they are at higher risk of having electrolyte problems.

I've heard some people with bulimia say, "I can't get started studying until I've binged and purged." For some students, binging and purging is a ritual that helps them manage the stress they are experiencing. They can even feel calmer after purging. People with bulimia will eat large amounts of food when they are distressed or upset and then compensate by inducing vomiting, using laxatives, or even overexercising. These behaviors occur at least once a week. Some students might be at increased risk of binging at night after not eating all day. I am frequently telling my patients with and without eating disorders to eat breakfast to improve their general health. Vomiting, which is the most common way someone will purge, can cause damage to tooth enamel and also cause electrolyte abnormalities, which in turn can cause heart problems. People with bulimia tend to have a normal body weight.

"I feel really out of control when I eat." People with binge eating disorder have a feeling of shame and loss of control when they binge and do not have the purging behaviors seen in bulimia. When they binge, they will eat a large amount of food within a two-hour period to the point of extreme discomfort, and they will usually feel guilty afterward. This behavior occurs at least once a week over a three-month period. People with binge eating disorder tend to be overweight.

People with an "unspecified eating disorder" may not fall neatly into the category of anorexia, bulimia, or binge eating, but they can have serious problems. They might be starving themselves to be thin, but their weight may not yet have fallen below normal range. They might be purging less than once per week, while using dangerous levels of ipecac to induce vomiting when they do. If they are binging less frequently than once a week but doing so in the presence of diabetes, they could also be putting their health at risk.

How would you know if your child has an eating disorder? Extreme weight loss or weight gain, dental problems, fainting, visits to the bathroom after every meal, eating much less or much more than usual are ways to know. People with eating disorders will often not want to admit what is going on out of shame. People with anorexia might fear you are going to intervene and make them gain weight. If you have any concern your child has an eating disorder, the first step you can take is to tell your child about the changes you've noticed and ask that he or she see his or her primary care doctor at home or at school. See if you can find someone who has some expertise in adolescent medicine and eating disorders. Ask your child to sign a release of information form so you can talk to the doctor. The doctor can measure his or her weight and look for common signs and symptoms of eating disorders. You can also go on the counseling center's website and tell your child what services are available for the evaluation and treatment of eating disorders. Later in this chapter, I'll talk about your critical role in the comprehensive treatment of eating disorders.

While eating disorders have been documented in various cultures for thousands of years, they seem to be increasing in our current culture. Media, particularly social media, may be fueling the rise of eating disordered behaviors in college students.

THE COMBUSTIBLE MIX OF TECHNOLOGY, BIOLOGY, AND PERFECTIONISM

A friend recently told me a story about high school women putting pictures of themselves in the bare minimum of clothes on Snapchat. Because pictures "disappear," a parent may not even know that picture was out there. Meanwhile, other students might make vicious or demeaning comments that could be devastating to these young women.

Selfies abound. People of all ages, but especially teenagers, are taking pictures of themselves constantly and posting them on Facebook, Instagram, and Snapchat. They may photoshop these pictures to get the perfect image, usually making themselves looking thinner than they are. They may compete to get high numbers of views to affirm their self-worth. This preoccupation with appearance may be contributing to the increase in eating disorders we are seeing in both men and women on college campuses. Some studies, in fact, have found a correlation in young adults between disordered eating and the amount of time spent on Facebook.[8] In addition, there are several websites that are "pro-ana"—promoting anorexic behaviors. The National Eating Disorders Association has worked with social media groups to remove websites that promote dangerous eating disordered behaviors.

Media, even before social media, has been pushing both women and men to new levels of unattainable body proportions. The dramatic increase in eating disorders since the 1950s may be fueled by the media's focus on thinness.[9] Actresses on television are impossibly slender, and it seems like full-figured female newscasters have short careers. Men are more muscled; Montgomery Clift was no Mark Wahlberg. Many of my male patients talk about not being muscular enough and are thinking about ways they can lose weight while building up muscle. It's worth asking your children if social media or any media makes them feel like they don't look good enough. Taking a break from social media might help improve their body image.

Given the social pressure to be thin, you would expect everyone to have an eating disorder, but this is not the case. Biology, of course, always plays a role. Having a relative with an eating disorder increases your risk of having one. Psychology plays a major role, as people who are perfectionists are more likely to have an eating disorder. I wrote more about the increasing problem of perfectionism in college students in chapter 6.

With such a cultural push to be thin, is there any way you can push back as a parent? How you talk about food and weight may have a big influence on your child's eating habits and body image.

TALKING WITH OUR CHILDREN ABOUT WEIGHTY MATTERS

"You look like you've gained weight."

"You need to go on a diet."

These are words college students do not want to hear from their parents when they come home from school for vacation. But college students hear it all the time. You may be trying to help your child be healthy, which is laudable, but your child may feel like you are overemphasizing the importance of looks and weight. In fact, several studies looked at the outcomes of parents telling teens they need to lose weight, even if their weight was in normal range. These teens later experienced higher rates of being overweight or of having highly critical thoughts about their weights.[10] Some of my patients with eating disorders note that a critical comment by a family member, friend, or coach triggered the start of their unhealthful eating behaviors.

Years ago, when I read the book *Battle Hymn of the Tiger Mother*, I cringed at the statement, "Chinese mothers can say to their daughters, 'Hey fatty, lose some weight,'" implying people should be brutally blunt with their children.[11] Was the author, Amy Chua, saying it is alright to call your child fat? In her book's afterword, she talked about the book being a satirical memoir, a self-parody. I will admit, it was a very funny book, as long as you consider it more fiction than fact. Unfortunately, I think some people took the book at face value. I'm sure the author would agree that it is unwise to tell any child he or she is fat. Parents should avoid being harshly critical of their child's weight and eating habits. But what else can you do to positively promote wellness in your child?

Start with how you talk about your food and weight. How many of us have said, "I'd love to lose five pounds"? Or have discussed our gluten-free, bread-free, or sugar-free diets? If you find yourself talking about food and weight all the time, stop yourself and try to enjoy the experience of having a nice meal with your child. Enjoy the moment. Practice mindful eating.

A growing number of books and articles have described the benefits of mindful eating, also known as intuitive eating. Mindful eating has been associated with healthier weights and lower rates of eating disorders.[12] Mindful eating involves choosing to eat by responding to your hunger signals rather than emotional cravings. It involves savoring and enjoying your food while eating in an unrushed manner. Some proponents of mindful eating talk about eating silently to fully enjoy the dining experience. Silent eating may run counter to what I promoted in chapter 5—more social interactions by eating meals with other students. Your child should eat in whatever way promotes a positive and relaxing dining experience.

Making exercise a part of your family's life can also promote wellness for everyone. When my children are visiting, we will sometimes take a walk after dinner, a great way to talk and reconnect. Sometimes my husband and I will work out with our children at the gym, or my husband and daughter will go cycling. You can also encourage your child to participate in fun activities like Zumba or intramural sports at his or her school. If your child is struggling with being overweight, some universities, my own included, offer structured wellness programs that include collaboration with a personal trainer, a nutritionist, and a primary care doctor.

However, discourage your child from taking exercise to an extreme. If your child overexercises to the point of losing too much weight, encourage moderation. Give your child the message that eating and exercise should be about wellness, not about being thin or sculpted.

EATING DISORDERS TREATMENT: WHEN TEAMWORK SAVES LIVES

Teamwork. Communication. Parent involvement. These are essential components to eating disorders treatment. You might be able to obtain treatment through your child's university, which may already have a team consisting of a primary care doctor, nutritionist, therapist, and psychiatrist. Or your child may need to obtain part or all of these services off campus, as many counseling centers provide short-term treatment. If your child has a more severe eating disorder, he or she might need to attend an intensive outpatient or residential treatment program. What is most important is that you assemble a team of people who have expertise in eating disorders. Ask your child to sign a release of information form with each of these providers so you can stay in touch with them.

These providers should be communicating with each other and with you on a regular basis. If the primary care doctor finds your child with anorexia has lost weight, he or she should inform you and the rest of the treatment team. You will all want to agree on how much weight your child should gain for you to support remaining in school. Not gaining weight or dropping below a certain weight may cause you and the team to encourage your child to leave school for more intensive help. Generally, treatment providers have no administrative authority to force your child to leave school. You have the most leverage in encouraging your child to get the help he or she needs.

Each provider has a unique role in your child's recovery from an eating disorder.

1. *The primary care doctor: keeping your child safe.* This doctor will weigh your child on a regular basis, particularly if your child has anorexia, and will notify you and the rest of the treatment team regarding weight changes. The primary care doctor will also monitor for electrolyte and other lab abnormalities, arrhythmias, bone loss, tooth damage, and amenorrhea in women. The primary care

doctor is on the front lines of your child's recovery and will notify you of improvements or the need for additional treatment.

2. *The psychiatrist: covering all the bases.* The psychiatrist will evaluate for and treat other diagnoses common in people with eating disorders like depression, bipolar disorder, anxiety, obsessive compulsive disorder, and substance use disorder. The psychiatrist will evaluate your child's safety and assess for suicidal thoughts and behaviors. They can also treat bulimia with certain antidepressants, like fluoxetine or sertraline. There are no FDA-approved medications for the treatment of anorexia.[13]

3. *The psychologist: teaching your child healthy coping skills.* Some people view eating disorder behaviors as a maladaptive way of coping with stress, so teaching alternative ways to cope can help people recover from eating disorders. Many eating disorder programs incorporate yoga and art therapy as part of the treatment to help your child expand his or her range of coping skills. Cognitive behavioral therapy is a mainstay of treatment for all eating disorders. Interpersonal therapy is also shown to be beneficial for eating disorders, and psychodynamic therapy has some benefits for people with anorexia.[14] Family-based therapy, when parents are more involved in encouraging a child to gain weight, has been shown to be helpful in adolescents with anorexia. I have seen some students go home to receive this kind of therapy with positive results.

4. *The nutritionist: changing your child's relationship with food.* The nutritionist can help your child establish a healthy weight range and a food schedule that will help him or her gain weight if he or she has anorexia or avoid binging if he or she has bulimia or binge eating disorder. The nutritionist will work on helping your child eat mindfully, recognizing the difference between true physiologic and emotional hunger.

There is great hope for women and men with eating disorders. The earlier they get treatment, the more likely they are to make a full recovery. For example, if bulimia is treated within five years of onset, there is an 80 percent chance of recovery.[15] If you believe your child has an eating disorder, you can find treatment resources by calling the campus counseling center or the National Eating Disorders Helpline at 1-800-

931-2237 (nationaleatingdisorders.org). With prevention and early treatment, let's lower the prevalence of these all too common and potentially deadly disorders.

FINAL TIPS: DOS AND DON'TS FOR A POSITIVE BODY IMAGE

Here is some advice you can give to your child to encourage a healthy relationship with food and his or her body.

1. *Don't let your moods depend on a number on a scale or what you have eaten that day.*
2. *Do eat to nourish yourself.* Eat your meals slowly and mindfully, savoring the taste of the food. Try to eat most of your meals with others rather than alone.
3. *Do accept your body.* Focus less on weight and more on health. Join a gym and work on your strength and fitness.
4. *Don't try to follow the impossible standards of actors and actresses who might exercise multiple hours a day.*
5. *Do set realistic goals if you need to lose weight for health reasons.* Lose weight slowly; don't crash diet because that will lead to a binge.

Eating disorders continue to be a major problem on college campuses, but I am still hopeful that as people develop greater body acceptance and a better relationship with food, eating disorders can become a thing of the past. As parents, you can give your message about healthy eating and exercise and explain that our self-worth is not based on a number a on a scale. If your child experiences an eating disorder, your advocacy is essential in ensuring he or she gets the comprehensive care he or she needs.

12

PSYCHOSIS

Heartbreak and Hope

You notice your son, Noah, seems quieter lately when you call him at school. You decide to visit Noah at his apartment and notice he hasn't cleaned it in weeks. You ask him how school is going, and he says fine, but he seems to nap a lot during your weekend visit. He goes into the bathroom sometimes and you think he is talking to someone; maybe he is calling someone on the phone and doesn't want to tell you. Something isn't right, but you can't place it. You wonder if he is going through a "sophomore slump" because it is the spring semester of his sophomore year and he is questioning whether he wants to continue majoring in psychology or become a psychologist in the future.

A few weeks after your visit, you get a call from a social worker at the local hospital. "Your son has been hospitalized for a psychotic episode." You ask the social worker what that means, and she says, "He's been hearing voices telling him the NSA is following him. Sometimes the voices tell him he is worthless and should die. He's been afraid to leave his apartment, and won't eat or sleep. His roommate brought him to the ER."

You visit Noah at the hospital and together meet with the social worker and psychiatrist. Your son is already feeling better after starting an antipsychotic medication and an antidepressant, but he admits he is having trouble focusing. He wants to return to school, but you want him to come home.

What would you do?

Psychotic experiences happen in college more often than you might think. About three in one thousand college students report being diagnosed with or treated for schizophrenia, a chronic psychotic disorder, annually.[1] But people can have psychotic experiences unrelated to schizophrenia. They might have bipolar disorder, psychotic depression, a drug-induced psychotic episode, or a stress- or trauma-induced episode. In fact, one in eight hundred adults aged fifteen to twenty-nine will have a first-time psychotic episode in a year's time.[2] Three of one hundred people will have a psychotic episode in their lifetime.[3]

You can't predict whether or not your child will have a psychotic episode, although if schizophrenia or bipolar disorder occurs in your family, he or she might be at increased risk. *Knowing about psychosis is critical for all parents because if psychosis strikes, early comprehensive treatment is essential to your child's recovery.* I have seen many students who have had psychotic episodes go on to complete college. However, untreated psychosis could lead to dropout and an increased risk of self-harm. The stigma of having psychosis as well as difficulties in functioning in school or work can contribute to suicidal thoughts. One of fifty people with a first episode of psychosis die by suicide within two years of the diagnosis.[4] Your involvement is essential to getting your child effective treatment. Your support and a sense of hope can be lifesaving.

PSYCHOSIS: DIFFERENT EXPERIENCES FOR DIFFERENT PEOPLE

Have you ever heard voices as you were falling asleep or waking up? These are called hypnogogic and hypnopompic hallucinations. They are normal experiences. Even hearing voices when you are fully awake occurs in about 2.5 percent of the population at some point in their lives. These voices are not necessarily part of a psychotic disorder and don't always have associated symptoms like paranoia or depression.[5]

But imagine if you heard voices all the time. They might be the voices of people you know or people you don't know. They could be saying you are bad and worthless or they could be commenting on your every action. They could even be telling you to do something you do not want to do, like harm yourself. Psychotic experiences can be very frightening, especially if they are occurring for the first time. If the voice is negative, distressing, interfering with school work, or accompanied by other symptoms like paranoid thoughts and depression, your child should be evaluated by a professional.

Psychosis can appear to strike suddenly, but more likely a person has some depressive symptoms or school problems before a full-blown psychotic episode occurs. A person's twenties is the prime time for psychosis to appear, and college mental health personnel regularly work with people with psychosis. The psychosis I see in students differs widely from individual to individual. Some students may have a few mild symptoms, like hearing voices that berate them and make them feel fearful, that respond to outpatient treatment. Others have several severe, life-threatening symptoms, like Noah, that require hospitalization. How would you recognize if your child is experiencing psychosis?

Psychosis, according to the *Diagnostic and Statistical Manual of Mental Disorders* (DSM-5), is defined by abnormalities in thinking and perception.[6] Psychosis includes the presence of one or more of the following: hallucinations, delusions, disorganized speech, disorganized behavior, or negative symptoms. I've already talked about auditory hallucinations, which are the most frequent kind of hallucination. People can have visual hallucinations as well, like seeing a friend or relative who is not present. Delusions are false beliefs. An example of a paranoid delusion is the belief that school officials have bugged your room. A grandiose delusion is the belief that you are going to make billions of dollars on a recent invention. Hallucinations and delusions are the most common psychotic symptoms I see in my office.

Disorganized speech is less frequent, but does occur. A student might jump from subject to subject, with only a slight thread holding the topics together. He or she might invent words or use grammar that doesn't make sense. Disorganized behavior can happen when a student gets agitated and paces or sits without moving, frozen like a statue.

Negative symptoms can be of great concern for college students and in the long term can cause the most impairment in day-to-day functioning. Lack of motivation is a very distressing negative symptom, as a previously highly motivated student may no longer be studying or going to class. The most painful negative symptom a person may suffer from is anhedonia, an inability to enjoy what he or she previously liked to do, whether it is doing intramural sports or hanging out with friends. Other negative symptoms include socializing less, talking less, and having a reduction in facial expression.

What causes these psychotic experiences? Diagnosing the cause of psychosis is not always easy, as you'll learn in the following story.

NOAH'S REALITY

When Jack meets with his son Noah and the hospital social worker, Jack is still in a state of shock. How did Noah become psychotic? Would he recover completely? Jack's fear turns into relief when Noah says he is feeling much better after sleeping the previous two nights and eating regularly. Noah is taking a low dose of an antipsychotic and an antidepressant. Noah reveals that he was feeling depressed for months before he became psychotic. He is diagnosed as having psychotic depression. When Jack asks Noah if he wants to go home or stay in school, he replies, "I want to stay. I know I can get through this."

Noah and Jack meet with me at the college counseling center the day after he is discharged from the hospital. Noah wants to review his options and to connect with campus services. I look at Noah, who is very thin after eating poorly for at least a month. He seems distracted when I talk, and I ask if he is hearing voices inside his head that are making it hard to focus. "Yes," he says. "But they are not nearly as loud or frightening as before."

Jack sighs, his eyes filled with anxiety and sadness. "Noah, I think you should come home for the semester. You've been through a lot. You can return in the fall when you're feeling 100 percent."

Noah looks at his father with frustration. "I can't leave now. I have a leadership position in the psychology club. I don't want to let my friends down." Noah looks at me intently, as if he is wondering what I will recommend about school.

"Noah, when someone has a psychotic episode like you had where it is hard for you to take care of yourself, I think going home to a safe and supportive environment is the best thing. But I will also tell you that many students want to recover at school near their friends. The deciding factor might be whether you can handle your course work. Do you feel you can concentrate in school right now?"

"My thinking can feel slowed down at times, but I want to finish the semester. I hate to lose all the work I've put in so far. I'm already feeling better."

I recommend Noah and Jack meet with a case manager in the dean of students office to review his schedule. "Noah, I think it's best if you drop a class or two to ease your way back into course work."

Noah, Jack, and I create a circle of support. I will meet with Noah every week and will call Jack every few weeks as we keep each other in the loop. Jack and Noah will speak by phone every day. Noah will meet with a therapist to talk about how to cope with the voices and how to relieve stress when it builds up. I tell Noah and Jack that the combination of medication and therapy is the best way to recover from psychosis.

After Noah and Jack leave, I take a deep breath. I worry about Noah having a relapse. Will he take his medication? Will the stress of school overwhelm him?

I see Noah over the next month, and he gradually looks more relaxed. He smiles more often and says he is doing well in the two classes he is now taking. But then he becomes more depressed and the hallucinations return on a daily basis. He is having trouble sleeping. We increase the dosages of his medications, but he finally says to me, "I think I need to go home. I'm just feeling down and I can't concentrate. I need to recover without the stress of school." I put Jack on speaker phone and Noah states his plan. I applaud Noah for making his health and well-being a priority, and I ask Jack to make an appointment for Noah with a local therapist and psychiatrist.

Noah takes the rest of the semester off and returns home. He uses the time to consider his future career choice. He decides psychology may not be the right major for him. In a way, it made him feel more depressed to study some of the problems he had been experiencing. Over the summer he does an internship working with a forest ranger and decides to pursue a forestry major when he returns in the fall. He wants to work in conservation. He realizes he likes working outdoors and finds friends in a hiking club.

Noah also sees a psychiatrist who changes his antidepressant and antipsychotic medications. After a few months, Noah feels he can think as clearly as he did before his psychotic episode. His mood is good and the voices have stopped.

When Noah returns to school, I continue to prescribe his antidepressant and the antipsychotic medications. After about six months of Noah being free of psychotic symptoms, I start to taper the antipsychotic. We lower the dose, but when he stops the antipsychotic completely, he hears a muffled voice telling him he is an awful person. It becomes hard for him to concentrate in school. We agree he will remain on a low dose of antipsychotic medication for now. We try to stop the medication six months later, with similar results. Noah stays on the medication, but will explore getting off the medication in the future.

Noah and I meet every month until his graduation. His father Jack comes to the last visit. It's been two years since I saw him, and he looks much more relaxed. He presents me with a beautiful purple orchid, thanking me for supporting his son through his college journey. Whenever I look at that orchid, I think about Noah's resilience and his father's love.

WHAT CAUSES PSYCHOSIS? DIAGNOSES AND CONTROVERSIES

What is Noah's diagnosis? At the beginning of this story, I described a scenario that sounded like psychotic depression, when depression becomes so severe that psychotic symptoms develop. What makes Noah's story different is that usually people with psychotic depression are eventually able to stop taking antipsychotic medication.[7] With Noah, depressive and psychotic symptoms return when I try to stop his antipsychotic. Does he have schizophrenia?

For college students who experience psychosis, I generally do not diagnose schizophrenia. Schizophrenia is a chronic psychotic disorder including in its criteria that people will not return to the functioning they had before the onset of schizophrenia or will not achieve their expected level of educational or social functioning.[8] A diagnosis of schizophrenia means a person meets at least two out of five of the criteria for psychosis (hallucinations, delusions, disorganized speech, disorganized behavior, or negative symptoms) for a month and an at least six-month period of milder forms of these symptoms. Schizophrenia is a hard diagnosis to make in a college student. With the first-episode psychosis we see in the college years, we don't know what the outcome will be, and studies are showing that outcomes are heavily influenced by the kind of mental health treatment the patient receives early on (see "The Comprehensive Evaluation and Treatment of Psychosis").

In Noah's case, he seems to be reaching his potential. He does not have a downward course, although he could without medication or therapy. Noah does not neatly fit into a specific diagnosis in the DSM-5. I diagnose him with "Unspecified schizophrenia spectrum and other psychotic disorder." This is a term for diagnoses that may not fall into a specific category.

In the future, I would like to see the term "schizophrenia" be replaced with a term that carries fewer stigmas. People with chronic psychosis have a wide range of outcomes. The term "schizophrenia" has many negative connotations, and for someone receiving the diagnosis, the implied downward course could be a self-fulfilling prophecy. In fact, some countries like Japan have replaced the term for schizophrenia with a less stigmatizing term, making it easier for people with psychotic symptoms to seek help and feel more optimistic about their futures.[9]

Other countries have a more hopeful approach when treating people with first-episode psychosis, not assuming the patients will have a chronic course. In Finland, there is a program called Open Dialogue that involves family in the care of the young adult with a psychotic episode. Treatment may be done in the hospital or at home, where the treatment team will visit. Family therapy is employed, and family members learn how to understand the psychotic experience and support their loved one. Low dose antipsychotics are used, and patients generally have higher recovery rates than they do in the United States.[10]

Our country needs to improve in the treatment of first-episode psychosis. Unfortunately, public mental health funding has continued to decline, especially since the Great Recession of 2008.[11] People with psychosis might have access to medication, but not to the support they need through intensive individual and family therapy. Our prisons and streets are filled with people who likely did not receive the comprehensive care they needed. There are more and more programs providing comprehensive care for first-episode psychosis, but in my own state of Florida there are only two programs that use the gold standard treatment of coordinated specialty care (CSC). The RAISE study (Recovery

After an Initial Schizophrenia Episode) demonstrated that coordinated specialty care for first-episode psychosis that includes antipsychotic medication, family therapy, individual therapy, and vocational/educational counseling improved long-term functioning. I'll talk more later about getting effective treatment for your child even if you do not have a CSC program in your area.

One thing I have learned as a college mental health psychiatrist is that psychosis comes in many forms. Treatment needs to be tailored to the underlying causes of the psychosis.

Lainey has felt down for about a year and starts exercising more to see if she can improve her mood. She wants to avoid medication because her friend had a bad experience on an antidepressant. She finds her mood getting darker every day, and as she walks on campus, she wonders if she is being stalked and someone is planning to kill her.

Diagnosis: psychotic depression.

About 5 to 19 percent of people with depression have psychotic symptoms.[12] Lainey recovers from her symptoms after treatment with an antidepressant and an antipsychotic. She successfully tapers off her antipsychotic after six months and remains on her antidepressant.

Anna, an engineering student, has been acting irritable, worrying her roommates. What worries them more is when she starts staying up every night cleaning the apartment, getting very little sleep and keeping her roommates awake. At the end of the week she tells them she is leaving school to drive to New York City to become an actress on Broadway. She says the voice of God told her acting was in her future.

Diagnosis: bipolar I disorder, manic episode, with psychotic features.

Anna is treated with a combination of a mood stabilizer and an antipsychotic. She stops her medications after a few months and has a recurrence of symptoms, so she decides to stay on medication while in college but hopes to lower the dose of her medication eventually.

Dixon is at a campus party where cocaine is being passed around. At first, he says no when his friend offers it to him, but decides to try some as a reward for doing well on exams that week. He immediately feels elated, but then becomes paranoid and starts running through campus in the middle of the night, shouting that his friends are imposters and trying to kill him. He is brought to the ER by campus police.

Diagnosis: substance-induced psychotic disorder.

Dixon recovers from his brief psychotic episode after an overnight stay in the emergency room. He is not prescribed an antipsychotic, but he could be at risk for another psychotic episode if he uses drugs again.

DRUGS AND PSYCHOSIS: A DANGEROUS COMBINATION

If your child has a psychotic disorder, using drugs or alcohol can exacerbate his or her psychotic symptoms. For some people, even one episode of drug use can act like a fuse that will set off an eruption of psychotic symptoms, potentially landing them in the emergency room or jail. Unfortunately, as many as 37 to 70 percent of people with first-episode psychosis are misusing substances.[13]

Some people who are prone to psychotic disorders might use drugs or alcohol to self-medicate when they feel uncomfortable. One thing is certain: continued substance use and abuse will send them on a downhill course.

The worst situations of chronic psychosis I see are in people who regularly use alcohol and multiple drugs like marijuana, cocaine, and LSD. The end result can be devastating. They tend to have repeated psychotic episodes related to these substances. The few times I have had patients who were arrested or hospitalized for violence involved a psychotic episode associated with drug use.

How do drugs cause psychosis? Dysfunction in dopamine and serotonin are implicated in psychosis. Some drugs, like LSD and mushrooms (psilocybin), cause psychosis by raising serotonin levels. Other drugs like cocaine raise dopamine levels, causing delusions and hallucinations. I have had patients become psychotic after taking excessive quantities of amphetamine/dextroamphetamine, an ADD medication that raises dopamine levels.

You might wonder how marijuana sets off psychosis in some people because most people view marijuana as a "mellowing" drug. For people who are genetically predisposed to psychosis, marijuana has the opposite effect, making them paranoid. It is not completely understood how marijuana causes paranoia, but it is thought that the THC in marijuana impacts dopamine. Adolescent use of marijuana has been implicated in an earlier onset of psychotic disorders like schizophrenia.[14]

If your child has psychosis and addiction, it is critical he or she get into a rehabilitation program to address his or her psychotic symptoms and substance abuse problems. Drugs complicate everything.

BIPOLAR DISORDER AND PSYCHOSIS: WHEN DISORDERS OVERLAP

Bipolar disorder, which was mentioned in chapter 2, affects 1.7 percent of college students annually.[15] Psychosis is a common occurrence in people with bipolar I disorder, affecting 50 to 60 percent of people.[16] Bipolar I disorder means someone has episodes of depression and episodes of mania at different times. A manic episode means that for at least a week a person experiences an energetic or irritable mood along with at least three other symptoms that could include a decreased need for sleep, increased self-esteem, pressured speech, racing thoughts, increase in activity, and impulsive behaviors. Someone who is manic could spend excessive amounts of money, engage in random sexual encounters, or drive recklessly. People with bipolar I disorder may have some of the same genetic characteristics as people with schizophrenia, and sometimes symptoms can be overlapping.

Individuals with bipolar I disorder, like people with psychosis, face an increased risk of suicide, accounting for one-quarter of completed suicides.[17] Those with bipolar disorder are most at risk for suicide the more time they spend in a depressed state. Ongoing work with a therapist and psychiatrist is critical to recovery.

Bipolar II disorder is a milder form of bipolar I disorder. People will have depressive episodes and hypomanic rather than manic episodes. Hypomania means a person can have symptoms of mania, but those symptoms cause less dysfunction in daily life. People with bipolar II disorder are at increased risk for attempting suicide, but their attempts are less likely to be lethal compared with people with bipolar I disorder.[18]

TRAUMA AND PSYCHOSIS: THE INTERTWINING OF BIOLOGY AND PSYCHOLOGY

The link between childhood trauma and psychosis is stunning. I see this every day in my office.

A young man who was frequently hit by his father growing up will hear his father's voice telling him he is worthless. Often he thinks the voice is real and will have a panic attack when he hears it. The voice makes it almost impossible to concentrate in school.

A young woman was beaten up many times in middle school by other classmates. When she is depressed, she imagines she can see in the distance a woman from high school preparing to assault her. She does not want to leave her room.

Bullying, sexual abuse, and physical abuse have strong associations with later episodes of psychosis. In fact, people with schizophrenia and bipolar disorder also have high rates of posttraumatic stress disorder.[19] Women who have been sexually assaulted or people who have been in combat in general have increased rates of psychosis.

There are biological reasons trauma can lead to psychosis. Cortisol levels can be dysregulated if trauma occurs during childhood, increasing the risk of psychosis. People with a certain mutation of a gene that impacts brain connectivity are at increased risk of psychosis when exposed to traumatic events.[20]

If your child has experienced trauma growing up or even more recently, the therapist working with your child will need to assess how and when to address that issue in the healing process. The therapist will help your child develop coping skills for daily stress as well as events that trigger symptoms.

THE COMPREHENSIVE EVALUATION AND TREATMENT OF PSYCHOSIS

Psychosis, like the eating disorders reviewed in the previous chapter, requires a team approach. The primary care doctor, psychiatrist, therapist, disability resource center, case manager, and you are all important parts of that team.

When the Medical Evaluation Counts Most

Years ago, when I was on call for my clinic, the campus police wanted me to evaluate a young woman who had been wandering on campus in a confused state. She had recently started medication for bipolar disorder. When I saw her, I noted that she had trouble answering my questions and her thinking was slowed. Was she having a thought disorder related to a psychotic episode? Then I noticed her sclera, the whites of her eyes, were light yellow, a sign of liver problems. I asked the police to bring her to the emergency room for a medical evaluation. It turns out she had hepatitis, liver inflammation, from the medication she was taking. She had psychotic symptoms, but they were caused by a medical condition.

If your child has a first episode of psychosis, chances are it is related to a psychiatric condition. But medical conditions must always be evaluated for because they can mimic psychosis and might be reversible. Untreated, they can sometimes evolve into life-threatening conditions. Sometimes psychotic symptoms will appear when people have conditions like epilepsy, lupus, and thyroid problems; take commonly prescribed medications like steroids; or have deficiencies in vitamins B12 and folate.

If your child is psychotic, the medical provider will take a history that includes a family history of medical and psychiatric issues. A physical exam will help the provider decide what labs to order. Suggested labs are a complete blood cell count, a comprehensive metabolic panel that includes liver function tests, a thyroid test, a B12 level, a folate level, and a vitamin D level. If indicated, tests for syphilis and HIV could be done. Tests for autoimmune diseases like lupus could be considered. A CT or MRI scan could be considered, and further neurological testing could be done based on the symptoms your child is having. A urine drug screen should be done as well.

The Psychiatrist's Role: It's Complicated

Let's say your child is having a psychotic episode. The primary care doctor gives him or her a clean bill of health. Now your child's psychiatrist will begin his or her detective work, gathering clues about the cause of your child's psychotic episode. Has anyone in the family had a similar episode? When did your child's episode start and was there a stressful event that led up to it? Did your child take drugs? How often? Did the psychosis come out of the blue or did it start with depression? Sometimes the diagnosis will not be clear, so your child might be diagnosed with an "unspecified psychotic disorder."

Close follow up is the key to treating someone with a psychotic disorder. If someone has a new episode, I will see him or her once or twice a week until he or she has some relief from the symptoms. I will generally prescribe a low dose of an antipsychotic to someone with a first-episode psychosis. If he or she is in the hospital with more severe symptoms, he or she might be placed on a higher dose of antipsychotic medication. In addition to taking an antipsychotic, someone with psychotic depression might be on an antidepressant and someone with bipolar disorder might be on a mood stabilizer like lamotrigine or lithium. Someone with a drug-induced psychotic episode might not need an antipsychotic or may take it for a short period.

What is an antipsychotic? The latest generation of these medications help regulate serotonin and dopamine, which as I mentioned before tend to be dysregulated in psychosis. Commonly used antipsychotics are risperidone, quetiapine, aripiprazole, and lurasidone. If your child is taking one of these medications and is not psychotic, don't be alarmed. Antipsychotics can be used to increase the effectiveness of antidepressants in treating depression. Antipsychotics have mood-stabilizing properties and can be used for bipolar disorders alone or in addition to a more traditional mood stabilizer.

If your child is on an antipsychotic, his or her weight, fasting blood sugar, and other labs should be monitored. Many of these medications are associated with weight gain and can increase the risk of type II diabetes. These medications are an improvement from older antipsychotics, which can cause serious muscle problems and dangerous elevations in body temperature. But I would love to see an even newer generation of antipsychotics that has fewer side effects.

How long should your child stay on antipsychotics? After reading my list of side effects, you may think as short a time as possible. After a first episode of psychosis, many psychiatrists will recommend your child be free of psychotic symptoms for six months before considering a medication taper. In fact, a study out of The Netherlands showed that tapering after six months resulted in better outcomes in functioning seven years later than in staying on medication long term after a first episode of psychosis.[21] It's important to note that in this study, some patients used antipsychotics intermittently when symptoms recurred. If your child wants to stop taking antipsychotic medication, discourage him or her from stopping suddenly. Tapering medication while working with a psychiatrist is important in preventing a relapse.

If your child has repeated psychotic episodes, such as those that occur in schizophrenia or bipolar disorder, most psychiatrists would recommend long-term maintenance medication. But some studies and some patient advocacy groups are challenging this long-held practice.[22] Each situation is unique. Schizophrenia and bipolar disorder are not single disorders but heterogeneous groups of disorders with a wide range of outcomes. An approach needs to be personalized to your child. Your child should work closely with his or her psychiatrist to decide what will promote his or her having the highest level of functioning in school with as few symptoms as possible. But if his or her psychotic symptoms are associated with extreme difficulty functioning or behaviors that are dangerous to him- or herself or other people, long-term maintenance medication should be considered.

Whether your child remains on medication or not, he or she can benefit from therapy to learn to cope with delusions, hallucinations, and other distressing thought patterns.

Therapy: We Need More of It

A patient of mine called me six months after she graduated. I had treated her for bipolar disorder with psychotic features and she came to see me every month for therapy and medication management. She thanked me for my help and told me she was frustrated with the care she was receiving at a community mental health center. She told me she was seen for fifteen minutes every three months; the psychiatrist barely spoke to her.

Medication is not enough to help someone with a psychotic disorder. Even with medication, many people have recurrences of symptoms. Therapy is a great way to receive support and also learn to manage psychotic symptoms, with cognitive behavioral therapy being a very effective treatment.[23] For the patient I just mentioned, she and I worked together to identify triggers for her feeling like she was being watched. It was usually caused by an increase in her workload or not getting enough sleep. She stayed on a low dose of an antipsychotic, and we did behavioral interventions that involved adjusting her schedule to manage her time better and get enough sleep. Her distressing psychotic symptoms lessened with these steps.

The stigma of having psychotic symptoms should be addressed in therapy. Your child is going to feel scared, especially if he or she cannot think as clearly or get his or her work done as quickly. Therapy that educates your child about the process of psychosis and the importance of self-care to promote recovery can go a long way to reducing his or her sense of frustration.

Family therapy can also be beneficial to you and your child. You can learn to understand your child's experience and respond in ways that will reduce distress. Parent education is an important part of the therapy. Parents often feel guilty, thinking they somehow brought on the child's psychosis. Education can reassure parents that the onset of psychosis for many people is in their twenties, and we still do not fully understand why some people develop psychosis and others don't. But genetics, biological events, and social stressors can all play a role. While their past parenting style likely did not trigger psychosis, their current approach to parenting can promote recovery.

There is a unique program of treatment that has been shown to be beneficial to people with psychiatric issues, including those with persistent psychotic illness. With its focus on wellness, lifestyle, and empowerment, it gives your child tools to maintain wellness and intervene when things are not going well. It is called the Wellness Recovery Action Plan (WRAP).[24] Weekly WRAP group treatment can help people learn coping skills from others who might have similar experiences. People identify triggers for their symptoms and develop tools to respond in a healthful way, like calling a friend, exercising, or asking to meet more frequently with their therapist. Having gone to an all-day training in this technique, I can say I think this program is beneficial to everyone because I learned new ways of dealing with my own stress. If your child can find a WRAP group on campus, or other groups like Active Minds, he or she can learn everyday coping skills and get support from his or her peers.

Case Management and the Disability Resource Center

Regular and sufficient sleep is essential to preventing psychosis, but this can be a challenge to many students. It is essential that your child sit with someone who can review his or her classes and assess what kind of schedule will allow for regular sleep. Sometimes taking a reduced course load is the best thing for your child. Usually a case manager from the dean of students office or a counselor from the disability resource center can help your child make these adjustments so your child can get the sleep he or she needs to recover.

Your Role: Working Time and a Half

If your child has a psychotic disorder, you might not be working just full time; you might be working time and a half to help him or her assemble the team that can lead to recovery. There is wonderful support out there for you through groups like National Alliance on Mental Illness (nami.org). Attending a NAMI meeting can give you practical tips on how to help your child and provide a community of support. The National Institute of Mental Health (nimh.nih.gov) has information about treatment and programs in your area.

If your child is being treated for a first-episode psychosis, request that he or she sign a release of information form so his or her psychiatrist can speak with you. As I've said before, the course of first-episode psychosis can be unpredictable, and your awareness of what to expect from treatment can allow you to intervene if things aren't going well. You can also offer support along the way as he or she goes through the recovery process. When I am treating patients for psychosis, I will routinely ask that they sign a release of information form allowing me to speak to parents so I can expand my patients' safety net.

What can you do if you suspect your child is experiencing a psychotic disorder but he or she says he or she is fine? Your child may be hoping the psychotic symptoms go away on their own or believe that the hallucinations are real. You have a few options. You can call the campus counseling center and ask to speak to the counselor on call to get advice. You might want to know if your child is being seen at the counseling center, but it is unlikely you will be informed if he or she has not signed a release of information form. Nonetheless, the counselor will listen to your information and inform any counselor who is currently working with your child. If you have any immediate safety concerns, you can call the counseling center or dean of students office and ask that someone check on your child. Each campus has its own way of conducting these checks. If you don't have immediate safety concerns but you feel something isn't right, you can ask your student's room-mates or friends if they've noticed anything different. You can also visit your child and strongly encourage an evaluation at the counseling center.

HOPE

There is hope for children who experience psychotic disorders. I believe there will be safer and more effective medication treatments for schizophrenia and other psychotic disorders as soon as we better understand the causes and progression of these disorders. Studies have shown markers of increased inflammation and immune dysregulation in schizophrenia, and perhaps future medications that address these processes will improve symptoms.[25] Some people theorize that glutamate and cholinergic dysregulation contribute to psychosis. Memantine, a dementia drug that affects glutamate, was shown in a study to improve the negative symptoms and cognitive problems associated with schizophrenia.[26] Another study showed that a dementia drug that affects the cholinergic system, rivastigmine, improved cognitive function in people with schizophrenia.[27] New studies will shed light on medications that—combined with the therapies and support that we know work—stand to improve the lives of college students who have psychotic disorders.

FINAL TIPS

1. *Remember that young adults are highly resilient.* Stay hopeful if your child has a first episode of psychosis, but also be realistic. Your child may benefit from taking a semester off while developing coping strategies for his or her symptoms.
2. *Help your child get as much comprehensive care as early as possible*, including a medical evaluation, psychiatric treatment, ther-

apy, individual therapy, and educational counseling through the disability resource center.

3. *Get support for yourself* through organizations likes the National Alliance on Mental Illness and the Depression and Bipolar Support Alliance. Attend a family support group.

4. *Don't blame yourself for your child's psychosis.* I talk with many parents who feel sad or guilty. This is not your fault. But if you show too much sadness to your child, he or she will be afraid to open up to you.

5. *Stay in touch with the treatment team until your child's care is solidly established.*

6. *Take good care of yourself.* The course of a psychotic illness can be unpredictable. The uncertainty and fear about the future can take its toll. Maintain your wellness so you can provide the strong support your child might need.

Even as a seasoned psychiatrist, I can get discouraged when I see someone struggling with psychosis. But then I remember some of my patients who struggled most and found hope just around the corner.

EPILOGUE

Every day when I go to work as a psychiatrist at a campus counseling center, I feel fortunate to work with college students who are bright, inquisitive, and kind. Even though these students are experiencing more mental health problems and pressures, they can also experience recovery with early and comprehensive interventions. As parents, you have an important role to play in your child's mental health and wellness, acting as an advocate, cheerleader, teacher, catalyst, and consultant. You can:

- Offer social support, a critical component of treatment for most psychiatric problems.
- Encourage your child to address problems and pressures by using campus resources, like the tutoring center, advising office, counseling center, dean of students office, office of student success, and disability resource center.
- Read up on the problem your child is experiencing so you can offer help.
- Inform the psychiatrist of a family history of mental health problems and the medications that worked for family members.
- Act as an early detection system for new or returning symptoms.
- Fight treatment roadblocks: help your child obtain the mental health care he or she needs and the medications that help him or her.
- Help your child decide whether he or she should continue in school or take a leave of absence.

When more serious problems arise, you should collaborate with university administrators or mental health care providers in your child's care. Consider collaboration when your child is at risk of self-harm, is in great distress, or is not functioning in school. High-risk situations include:

- Increasing suicidal thoughts or behaviors
- A recent psychiatric hospitalization
- Psychosis
- Eating disorders
- Severe depression, anxiety, or substance abuse

Ideally, a mental health care provider will encourage a student struggling with serious mental health issues to sign a release of information so the provider, student, and parent can collaborate in care. On some campuses, college administrators rather than counselors inform parents of serious problems. Under FERPA, administrators have the option but not the requirement to notify parents if their child is having a serious mental health crisis or emergency. There is variability from school to school as to when parents will be notified, so you can't count on this. Tell your child you want to know if he or she is having a problem so you can help.

Anyone who knows me realizes how passionately I feel about parent support and collaboration when a child faces a major problem or pressure. Sometimes I have seen students who are completely on their own due to a lack of a parental figure in their lives; they can survive and thrive, but it is a tough road. Your guidance is essential. I hope the studies and stories I have offered will convince you of the important role you have to play in your child's college journey. If you know of someone who doesn't have a parent figure in his or her life, you can provide these young adults support as well.

Parents, you are not the only audience to whom I am delivering this message of collaboration. I have also encouraged college personnel to think more about reaching out to parents. This year I gave a talk at a conference for Student Affairs Professionals in Higher Education titled "College Student Depression: The Importance of Collaboration with Psychiatrists and Parents." I also co-presented a talk at the American College Counseling Association annual meeting called "Emerging Adults in the Odyssey Years: Should Parents Be a Greater Part of the

Journey?" I chaired a workshop at the American Psychiatric Association annual meeting called "Is It Helicopter Parenting? Collaborating with Parents in College Mental Health according to the Law, Best Practices, and a Personal Story." I see more and more counselors and psychiatrists receptive to the idea of collaborating. I hope by sharing studies and stories of collaboration that college students, their parents, and university personnel will be convinced of the benefits of teamwork.

Here are some wishes for the future. I want this book to serve as a catalyst for discussions among parents of college students about their children's mental health, thereby decreasing stigma and increasing support for these parents, who often feel alone. I also want this book to empower parents to get more involved in their child's mental health, while opening up a dialogue between parents and mental health professionals about how much involvement is enough. With psychiatric hospitalizations of college students tripling in the last few decades, there need to be better guidelines for how parents and mental health professionals work together. I hope this book is a start.

As a parent of a college student, you will have many bright days and a few dark ones. Even though your child might fumble and fall sometimes, always be mindful of his or her strengths, resilience, and capacity for change. Remember that college campuses are filled with people who have dedicated decades of their lives to launching competent, creative, and caring young adults into the world. Many innovative programs are looking at ways to reduce substance abuse and sexual assault on campus. Students are being offered classes for credit on coping strategies and mindfulness techniques. Every year when I see data showing high levels of mental health problems in college students, I know it doesn't have to be this way. I am optimistic that this trend of increasing mental health problems will reverse itself and that we can turn campuses into the centers of wellness and growth they are meant to be. Your support, love, and collaboration are a major part of the campus cure.

NOTES

INTRODUCTION

1. Alex Williams, "Move Over Millennials, Here Comes Generation Z," *New York Times*, September 18, 2015, accessed December 27, 2016, http://www.nytimes.com/2015/09/20/fashion/move-over-millennials-here-comes-generation-z.html?_r=0.

2. American College Health Association National College Health Assessment II: Spring 2016 Executive Group Reference Summary, accessed December 29, 2016, http://www.acha-ncha.org/docs/NCHA-II%20SPRING%20 2016%20US%20REFERENCE%20GROUP%20EXECUTIVE%20SUMMA RY.pdf.

3. Mallika Marshall, "New Concerns Arise About Mental Health of College Students," August 25, 2016, accessed January 2, 2016, http://boston. cbslocal.com/2016/08/25/new-concerns-mental-health-college-students-suicide/.

4. American College Health Association National College Health Assessment II.

5. Ibid.

6. Barbara Hollingsworth, "Less than 40 Percent of H.S. Seniors Academically Prepared for College," *CNS News*, May 14, 2014, accessed May 21, 2016, http://cnsnews.com/news/article/barbara-hollingsworth/less-40-hs-seniors-academically-prepared-college.

7. "Fast Facts," National Center for Education and Statistics, accessed May 21, 2016. https://nces.ed.gov/fastfacts/display.asp?id=40.

8. Josh Mitchell, "Student Debt Is About to Set Another Record, But the Picture Isn't All Bad," *Wall Street Journal*, May 2, 2016, accessed December 9,

2016, http://blogs.wsj.com/economics/2016/05/02/student-debt-is-about-to-set-another-record-but-the-picture-isnt-all-bad/.

9. "Increase in Suicide Rates in the United States, 1999–2014," Centers for Disease Control and Prevention, April 2016, accessed May 21, 2016, http://www.cdc.gov/nchs/products/databriefs/db241.htm.

10. 2015 Campus Climate Survey on Sexual Assault and Sexual Misconduct conducted by the American Association of Universities, accessed May 19, 2016, https://www.aau.edu/uploadedFiles/AAU_Publications/AAU_Reports/Sexual_Assault_Campus_Survey/AAU_Campus_Climate_Survey_12_14_15.pdf.

11. Center for Collegiate Mental Health 2015 Annual Report, accessed May 21, 2016, http://ccmh.psu.edu/wp-content/uploads/sites/3058/2016/01/2015_CCMH_Report_1-18-2015.pdf.

12. "College Students: Coping with Stress and Anxiety on Campus," American Psychiatric Association, August 27, 2015, accessed December 30, 2016, https://psychiatry.org/news-room/apa-blogs/apa-blog/2015/08/college-students-coping-with-stress-and-anxiety-on-campus.

13. American College Health Association National College Health Assessment II.

14. Ibid.

15. Aude Henin and Noah Berman, "The Promise and Peril of Emerging Adulthood," *Cognitive and Behavioral Practice* 23, no. 3 (2016): 263–69, accessed June 16, 2016, http://dx.doi.org/10.1016/j.cbpra.2016.05.005.

16. Allie Grasgreen, "Parents: Help or Hindrance?" *Inside Higher Ed*, March 28, 2012, accessed May 18, 2016, https://www.insidehighered.com/news/2012/03/28/naspa-survey-finds-parental-involvement-isnt-always-bad-thing#.Vz3wGUKZbhs.mailto.

17. "Mental Health Facts: Children and Teens," National Alliance on Mental Illness, accessed December 31, 2016, https://www.nami.org/getattachment/Learn-More/Mental-Health-by-the-Numbers/childrenmhfacts.pdf.

I. ANXIETY

1. American College Health Association National College Health Assessment II: Spring 2016 Executive Group Reference Summary, accessed December 29, 2016, http://www.acha-ncha.org/docs/NCHA-II%20SPRING%202016%20US%20REFERENCE%20GROUP%20EXECUTIVE%20SUMMARY.pdf.

2. Center for Collegiate Mental Health 2015 Annual Report, accessed July 18, 2016, http://ccmh.psu.edu/wp-content/uploads/sites/3058/2016/01/2015_CCMH_Report_1-18-2015.pdf.

3. American College Health Association National College Health Assessment II.

4. Facts and Statistics, Anxiety and Depression Association of America, accessed January 13, 2017, https://www.adaa.org/about-adaa/press-room/facts-statistics.

5. Ibid.

6. Josh Nepon et al., "The Relationship Between Anxiety Disorders and Suicide Attempts: Findings from the National Epidemiologic Survey on Alcohol and Related Conditions," *Depression and Anxiety* 27, no. 9 (2010): 79, accessed January 13, 2010, http://doi.org/10.1002/da.20674 https://www.ncbi.nlm.nih.gov/pmc/articles/PMC2940247/.

7. Murray B. Stein et al., "Panic Disorder," in *Gabbard's Treatments of Psychiatric Disorders, Fifth Edition*, ed. Glen O. Gabbard (Arlington, VA: American Psychiatric Association, 2014), 343–56, iPad edition.

8. Ibid.

2. DEPRESSION

1. American Psychiatric Association, *Diagnostic and Statistical Manual of Mental Disorders*, fifth edition (Washington, DC: American Psychiatric Association, 2013), 157.

2. American College Health Association National College Health Assessment II: Spring 2016 Executive Group Reference Summary, accessed December 29, 2016, http://www.acha-ncha.org/docs/NCHA-II%20SPRING%202016%20US%20REFERENCE%20GROUP%20EXECUTIVE%20SUMMARY.pdf.

3. Center for Collegiate Mental Health 2015 Annual Report, accessed July 18, 2016, http://ccmh.psu.edu/wp-content/uploads/sites/3058/2016/01/2015_CCMH_Report_1-18-2015.pdf.

4. Increase in Suicide Rates in the United States, 1999–2014, Centers for Disease Control and Prevention, April 2016, accessed May 21, 2016, http://www.cdc.gov/nchs/products/databriefs/db241.htm.

5. Peter Gray, "The Decline of Play and Rise in Children's Mental Disorders," *Psychology Today*, January 26, 2010, accessed January 14, 2017, https://www.psychologytoday.com/blog/freedom-learn/201001/the-decline-play-and-rise-in-childrens-mental-disorders.

6. Brian Primack, "Social Media and Depression," *Psychiatric Times*, May 25, 2016, accessed June 5, 2016, http://www.psychiatrictimes.com/depression/social-media-and-depression.

7. Boadie W. Dunlop, "Evidence-Based Applications of Combination Psychotherapy and Pharmacotherapy for Depression," *Focus* 14, no. 2 (2016): 156–74.

8. National Institute of Mental Health, "Antidepressant Medications for Children and Adolescents: Information for Parents and Caregivers," accessed September 24, 2016, National Institute of Mental Health, "Antidepressant Medications for Children and Adolescents: Information for Parents and Caregivers," accessed September 24, 2016, http://www.nimh.nih.gov/health/topics/child-and-adolescent-mental-health/antidepressant-medications-for-children-and-adolescents-information-for-parents-and-caregivers.shtml.

9. Robert M. A. Hirschfeld, "The Comorbidity of Major Depression and Anxiety Disorders: Recognition and Management in Primary Care," *Primary Care Companion to The Journal of Clinical Psychiatry* 3, no. 6 (2001): 244–54, accessed October 1, 2016, https://www.ncbi.nlm.nih.gov/pmc/articles/PMC181193/.

10. American College Health Association National College Health Assessment II.

11. Victor Schwartz and Jerald Kay, "The Crisis in College and University Mental Health," *Psychiatric Times*, October 10, 2009, accessed October 1, 2016, https://www.jedfoundation.org/press-room/news-archive/Psychiatric_Times_The_Crisis_in_College_and_University_Mental_Health.

3. SUBSTANCE USE DISORDERS

1. FERPA Frequently Asked Questions, Family Policy Compliance Office, accessed March 6, 2017, http://familypolicy.ed.gov/faq-page#t39n410.

2. HIPAA Privacy Rule and Sharing Information Related to Mental Health, U.S. Department of Health and Human Services, accessed March 6, 2017, https://www.hhs.gov/hipaa/for-professionals/special-topics/mental-health/.

3. American College Health Association National College Health Assessment II: Spring 2016 Executive Group Reference Summary, accessed December 29, 2016, http://www.acha-ncha.org/docs/NCHA-II%20SPRING%202016%20US%20REFERENCE%20GROUP%20EXECUTIVE%20SUMMARY.pdf.

4. College Drinking, National Institute on Alcohol Abuse and Alcoholism, accessed March 4, 2017, https://pubs.niaaa.nih.gov/publications/CollegeFactSheet/CollegeFactSheet.pdf.

5. American College Health Association National College Health Assessment II.

6. Ibid.

7. Ibid.

8. Simon E. Aberg, "Study Drug Abuse by College Students: What You Need to Know," *National Center for Health Research*, 2016, accessed March 2, 2016, http://center4research.org/child-teen-health/hyperactivity-and-adhd/study-drug-abuse-college-students/.

9. Joseph A. Califano Jr., "Wasting the Best and the Brightest: Alcohol and Drug Abuse on College Campuses," May 28, 2007, accessed March 4, 2017, http://www.centeronaddiction.org/newsroom/op-eds/wasting-best-and-brightest-alcohol-and-drug-abuse-college-campuses.

10. "Prescription Drug Misuse Among College Students," Substance Abuse and Mental Health Services Administration, accessed March 10, 2017, http://publichealth.hsc.wvu.edu/media/4239/college_students_no-samhsa-logo.pdf.

11. Injury Prevention and Control: Opioid Overdose, Centers for Disease Control and Prevention, accessed March 4, 2107, https://www.cdc.gov/drugoverdose/.

12. William Brangham, "Is Pot Getting More Potent," *PBS Newshour*, April 2, 2014, accessed March 4, 2017, http://www.pbs.org/newshour/updates/pot-getting-potent/.

13. L. M. Squeglia et al., "The Influence of Substance Use on Adolescent Brain Development," *Clinical EEG and Neuroscience: Official Journal of the EEG and Clinical Neuroscience Society* 40, no. 1 (2009): 31–38, https://www.ncbi.nlm.nih.gov/pmc/articles/PMC2827693/.

14. Ibid.

15. Celia Vimont, "College Marijuana Use Linked with Skipped Classes, Lower Grades, and Late Graduation," Partnership for Drug-Free Kids, January 27, 2016, accessed March 4, 2017, http://www.drugfree.org/news-service/college-marijuana-use-linked-skipped-classes-lower-grades-late-graduation/.

16. Ibid.

17. Lisa Hefernan and Jennifer Breheny Wallace, "For Freshman, Campus Life Poses New Risks," *New York Times*, August 17, 2016, accessed March 4, 2016, https://well.blogs.nytimes.com/2016/08/17/for-freshmen-campus-life-poses-new-risks/?hpw&rref=health&action=click&pgtype=Homepage&module=well-region&region=bottom-well&WT.nav=bottom-well&_r=1.

18. Rob Turrisi and Anne E. Ray, "Sustained Parenting and College Drinking in First-Year Students," *Developmental Psychobiology* 52, no. 3 (2010):

286–94, accessed March 3, 2017, http://www.ncbi.nlm.nih.gov/pmc/articles/PMC3937263/.

19. Lindsey Varvil-Weld et al., "Hurting, Helping, or Neutral? The Effects of Parental Permissiveness toward Adolescent Drinking on College Student Alcohol Use and Problems," *Prevention Science: The Official Journal of the Society for Prevention Research* 15, no. 5 (2014): 716–24, doi:10.1007/s11121-013-0430-6, http://www.ncbi.nlm.nih.gov/pmc/articles/PMC3919881/#!po=7.81250.

20. Fact Sheets—Binge Drinking, Centers for Disease Control and Prevention, accessed March 4, 2017, https://www.cdc.gov/alcohol/fact-sheets/binge-drinking.htm.

21. Alcohol and Public Health, Centers for Disease Control and Prevention, accessed March 5, 2017, https://www.cdc.gov/alcohol/faqs.htm.

22. Maria Paul, "Casual Marijuana Use Linked to Brain Abnormalities," *Northwestern News*, April 16, 2014, accessed March 5, 2014, https://news.northwestern.edu/stories/2014/04/casual-marijuana-use-linked-to-brain-abnormalities-in-students.

23. 8 Ways to Talk with Your Teen about Drugs and Alcohol, Partnership for a Drug-Free Kids, accessed March 4, 2017, http://www.drugfree.org/resources/8-ways-to-talk-with-your-teen-about-drugs-and-alcohol/.

24. Lisa Hefernan and Jennifer Breheny Wallace, "For Freshman, Campus Life Poses New Risks," *New York Times*, August 17, 2016, accessed March 4, 2016, https://well.blogs.nytimes.com/2016/08/17/for-freshmen-campus-life-poses-new-risks/?hpw&rref=health&action=click&pgtype=Homepage&module=well-region&region=bottom-well&WT.nav=bottom-well&_r=1.

25. Student Health, Drugwatch, accessed March 4, 2017, http://www.drugwatch.com/students/.

26. Association of Recovery in Higher Education, accessed March 4, 2017, http://collegiaterecovery.org.

4. ACADEMIC FAILURE TO THRIVE

1. Barbara Hollingsworth, "Less than 40 Percent of H.S. Seniors Academically Prepared for College," *CNS News*, May 14, 2014, accessed May 21, 2016, http://cnsnews.com/news/article/barbara-hollingsworth/less-40-hs-seniors-academically-prepared-college.

2. "Fast Facts," National Center for Education and Statistics, accessed May 21, 2016. https://nces.ed.gov/fastfacts/display.asp?id=40.

3. American College Health Association National College Health Assessment II: Spring 2016 Executive Group Reference Summary, accessed Decem-

ber 29, 2016, http://www.acha-ncha.org/docs/NCHA-II%20SPRING%202016
%20US%20REFERENCE%20GROUP%20EXECUTIVE%20SUMMARY.
pdf.

4. "How to Finish College in 4 Years: What Parents Need to Know,"
Grown and Flown Blog, accessed February 24, 2017, http://grownandflown.
com/how-to-finish-college-in-4-years/.

5. "Parents' Guide to the Family Educational Rights and Privacy Act:
Rights Regarding Children's Education Records," U.S. Department of Education, October 2007, accessed February 24, 2017, https://www2.ed.gov/policy/
gen/guid/fpco/brochures/parents.html.

6. Allie Grasgreen, "Parents: Help or Hindrance?" *Inside Higher Ed*,
March 28, 2012, accessed May 18, 2016, https://www.insidehighered.com/
news/2012/03/28/naspa-survey-finds-parental-involvement-isnt-always-bad-
thing#.Vz3wGUKZbhs.mailto.

7. David Dekok, "Missing Penn State Student Found After Parents at
Graduation Learned He Dropped Out," *Reuters*, May 11, 2015, accessed February 24, 2017, http://www.reuters.com/article/us-usa-pennsylvania-missing-
idUSKBN0NW20G20150511.

8. Barbara K. Hofer, "Student-Parent Communication in the College
Years: Can Students Grow up on an Electronic Tether?" *The Bulletin* 79, no. 2
(2011), accessed June 3, 2015, http://www.acui.org/publications/bulletin/
article.aspx?issue=28134&id=14773.

9. Dominic Barton, "The Most Important Factor in a College Student's
Success," *Wall Street Journal*, September 26, 2016, accessed February 28,
2017, http://blogs.wsj.com/experts/2015/09/16/the-most-important-factor-in-a-
college-students-success/.

10. American College Health Association National College Health Assessment II.

11. Ibid.

12. Simon E. Aberg, "Study Drug Abuse by College Students: What You
Need to Know," *National Center for Health Research*, 2016, accessed March 2,
2016, http://center4research.org/child-teen-health/hyperactivity-and-adhd/
study-drug-abuse-college-students/.

13. American Psychiatric Association, *Diagnostic and Statistical Manual of
Mental Disorders*, fifth edition (Washington, DC: American Psychiatric Association, 2013), 59–65.

14. Edward M. Hallowell, MD, and John J. Ratey, MD, *Delivered from
Distraction* (New York: Ballantine Books, 2005).

15. Cecilia Simon, "Major Decisions," *New York Times*, November 2, 2012,
accessed April 23, 2015, http://www.nytimes.com/2012/11/04/education/edlife/
choosing-one-college-major-out-of-hundreds.html.

16. American College Health Association National College Health Assessment II.

5. LONELINESS

1. American College Health Association National College Health Assessment II: Spring 2016 Executive Group Reference Summary, accessed December 29, 2016, http://www.acha-ncha.org/docs/NCHA-II%20SPRING%202016%20US%20REFERENCE%20GROUP%20EXECUTIVE%20SUMMARY.pdf.

2. Dominic Barton, "The Most Important Factor in a College Student's Success," *Wall Street Journal*, September 16, 2015, accessed December 2, 2016, http://blogs.wsj.com/experts/2015/09/16/the-most-important-factor-in-a-college-students-success/.

3. Louise C. Hawkley and John T. Cacioppo, "Loneliness Matters: A Theoretical and Empirical Review of Consequences and Mechanisms," *Annals of Behavioral Medicine*, 40, no. 2 (2010): 1–14, doi:10.1007/s12160-010-9210-8, accessed May 2, 2015, http://www.ncbi.nlm.nih.gov/pmc/articles/PMC3874845/pdf/nihms538929.pdf.

4. Amelia M. Arria and Kevin E. O'Grady, "Suicide Variation Among College Students: A Multivariate Analysis," *Archives of Suicide Research* 13, no. 3 (2009): 230–46, accessed July 10, 2015, http://www.ncbi.nlm.nih.gov/pmc/articles/PMC2709750/.

5. Hawkley and Cacioppo, "Loneliness Matters," 1–14.

6. Ibid.

7. Julianne Holt-Lunstad, Timothy B. Smith, et al., "Loneliness and Social Isolation as Risk Factors for Mortality: A Meta-Analytic Review," *Perspectives on Psychological Science* 10, no. 2 (2015): 1, http://journals.sagepub.com/doi/full/10.1177/1745691614568352.

8. The American Freshman: National Norms Fall 2014, Cooperative Institutional Research Program at the Higher Education Research Institute at UCLA, accessed July 23, 2015, http://www.heri.ucla.edu/monographs/theamericanfreshman2014.pdf.

9. Ann Almendrala, "More Children with Autism Are Going to College Than Ever Before," *Huffington Post*, March 11, 2014, accessed July 23, 2015, http://www.huffingtonpost.com/2014/03/11/research-autism-spectrum_n_4939200.html.

10. Press Release: Many International Students Have Few Close American Friends, Survey Says, National Communication Association, June 14, 2012, accessed July 23, 2015, http://www.natcom.org/newsroom.aspx?id=2521.

11. Hawkley and Cacioppo, "Loneliness Matters."

12. Martin M. Antony and Richard P. Swinson, *The Shyness and Social Anxiety Workbook* (Oakland, CA: New Harbinger Publications, Inc., 2008).

13. Hawkley and Cacioppo, "Loneliness Matters."

6. PERFECTIONISM

1. Julie Scelfo, "Suicide on Campus and the Pressure of Perfection," *New York Times*, July 27, 2015, accessed March 10, 2017, https://www.nytimes.com/2015/08/02/education/edlife/stress-social-media-and-suicide-on-campus.html?_r=0.

2. Lindsay Mason and Amy Hoch, "Radically Open DBT (RO-DBT): Treating Over-Thinking and the Plight of Perfectionism in College Students" (talk presented at the annual meeting of the American College Counseling Association, Tampa, Florida, February 17, 2017).

3. Melissa Dahl, "The Alarming New Research on Perfectionism," *New York Magazine*, September 30, 2014, accessed March 10, 2017, http://nymag.com/scienceofus/2014/09/alarming-new-research-on-perfectionism.html?mid=emailshare_scienceofus.

4. Etienne Benson, "The Many Faces of Perfectionism," *American Psychological Association Monitor on Psychology*, November 2003, accessed March 10, 2017, http://www.apa.org/monitor/nov03/manyfaces.aspx.

5. Dahl, "The Alarming New Research on Perfectionism."

6. Ibid.

7. American Psychiatric Association, *Diagnostic and Statistical Manual of Mental Disorders*, fifth edition (Washington, DC: American Psychiatric Association, 2013), 237–42.

8. Ibid.

9. American College Health Association National College Health Assessment II: Spring 2016 Executive Group Reference Summary, accessed December 29, 2016, http://www.acha-ncha.org/docs/NCHA-II%20SPRING%202016% 20US%20REFERENCE%20GROUP%20EXECUTIVE%20SUMMARY.pdf.

10. John H. Greist and James W. Jefferson, "Obsessive Compulsive Disorder," in *Gabbard's Treatments of Psychiatric Disorders*, fifth edition, ed. Glen O. Gabbard (Arlington, VA: American Psychiatric Association, 2014), 405–18, iPad edition.

11. Rae Jacobson, "Social Media and Self-Doubt," Child Mind Institute, accessed March 12, 2017, https://childmind.org/article/social-media-and-self-doubt/.

12. Louise Radnofsky and Ben Cohen, "How Simone Biles Achieved Greatness," *Wall Street Journal*, August 12, 2016, D5.

13. Allison J. Lockard et al., "Self-Compassion Among College Counseling Center Clients: An Examination of Clinical Norms and Group Differences," *Journal of College Counseling* 17 (2014): 249–59, DOI: 10.1002/j.2161-1882.2014.00061.x, accessed March 12, 2017, http://self-compassion.org/wp-content/uploads/2015/03/Lockard.Neff_.pdf.

14. Mason and Hoch, "Radically Open DBT (RO-DBT)."

15. Savithiri Ratnapalan and Helen Batty, "To Be Good Enough," *Canadian Family Physician* 55, no. 3 (2009): 239–40, accessed March 12, 2017, https://www.ncbi.nlm.nih.gov/pmc/articles/PMC2654842/

7. CULTURE, SEXUALITY, AND GENDER CHALLENGES

1. "White Supremacists on Campus: Unprecedented Recruitment Efforts Underway," Anti-Defamation League, March 6, 2017, accessed March 24, 2017, https://www.adl.org/blog/white-supremacists-on-campus-unprecedented-recruitment-efforts-underway.

2. Kimberly F. Balsam et al., "Measuring Multiple Minority Stress: The LGBT People of Color Microaggressions Scale," *Cultural Diversity and Ethnic Minority Psychology* 17, no. 2 (2011): 163–74, accessed March 21, 2017, https:/www.ncbi.nlm.nih.gov/pmc/articles/PMC4059824/.

3. Melissa Scholes Young, "The Cost of Being First," *The Atlantic*, October 16, 2016, accessed March 24, 2017, https://www.theatlantic.com/education/archive/2016/10/the-cost-of-being-first/504155/.

4. Fast Facts: Enrollment, National Center for Education Statistics, accessed March 24, 2017, https://nces.ed.gov/fastfacts/display.asp?id=98.

5. Fast Facts: Race/Ethnicity of College Faculty, National Center for Education Statistics, accessed March 24, 2017, https://nces.ed.gov/fastfacts/display.asp?id=61.

6. Beth Han et al., "Prevalence and Mental Health Treatment of Suicidal Ideation and Behavior Among College Students Aged 18–25 Years and Their Non-College Attending Peers in the United States," *Journal of Clinical Psychiatry* 77, no. 6 (2016): 815–23.

7. Sarah B. Oswalt et al., "Beyond Alphabet Soup: Helping College Health Professionals Understand Sexual Fluidity," *Journal of American College Health* 64, no. 6 (2016): 502–8.

8. American College Health Association National College Health Assessment II: Spring 2016 Executive Group Reference Summary, accessed December 29, 2016, http://www.acha-ncha.org/docs/NCHA-II%20SPRING%202016.

9. Caitlin Ryan et al., "Family Rejection as a Predictor of Negative Health Outcomes in White and Latino Lesbian, Gay, and Bisexual Young Adults," *Pediatrics* 123, no. 1 (2009): 346–52, doi: 10.1542/peds.2007-3524, accessed March 25, 2017, https://www.ncbi.nlm.nih.gov/pubmed/19117902.

10. Emily Kroshus and Ann K. Davoren, "Mental Health and Substance Use of Sexual Minority College Athletes," *Journal of American College Health* 64, no. 5 (2016): 371–79.

11. The American Freshman: National Norms Fall 2015, Cooperative Education Research Program at the Higher Education Research Institute at UCLA, accessed July 3, 2016, http://www.heri.ucla.edu/monographs/The AmericanFreshman2015.pdf.

12. Lisa D. Hawley et al., "Baseline Assessment of Campus-Wide General Health Status and Mental Health: Opportunity for Tailored Suicide Prevention and Mental Health Awareness Programming," *Journal of American College Health* 64, no. 3 (2016): 174–83.

13. Jorge Rivas, "Half of Young People Believe Gender Isn't Limited to Male and Female," *Fusion*, February 3, 2015, accessed March 25, 2017, http://fusion.net/story/42216/half-of-young-people-believe-gender-isnt-limited-to-male-and-female/.

14. American College Health Association National College Health Assessment II.

15. Jan Hoffman, "As Attention Grows, Transgender Numbers Are Elusive," *New York Times*, May 17, 2016, accessed March 25, 2017, https://www.nytimes.com/2016/05/18/science/transgender-children.html?_r=2.

16. GLAAD Media Reference Guide, accessed March 25, 2017, http://www.glaad.org/publications/reference.

17. Lauren Booker, "What It Means to Be Gender Fluid," *CNN*, April 13, 2016, accessed March 25, 2017, http://www.cnn.com/2016/04/13/living/gender-fluid-feat/.

18. Robin Marantz Henig, "How Science Is Helping Us Understand Gender," *National Geographic*, January 2017, accessed March 25, 2017, http://www.nationalgeographic.com/magazine/2017/01/.

19. "The Facts on Transgender Student Mental Health," *Active Minds*, accessed March 25, 2017, http://www.activeminds.org/transgender-college-student-mental-health.

20. Elizabeth W. Diemer et al., "Gender Identity, Sexual Orientation, and Eating-Related Pathology in a National Sample of College Students," *Journal of Adolescent Health* 57, no. 2 (2015): 144–49, DOI: http://dx.doi.org/10.1016/

j.jadohealth.2015.03.003, accessed March 18, 2017, http://www.jahonline.org/article/S1054-139X(15)00087-7/fulltext.

21. Jaclyn M. White and Sari L. Reisner, "A Systematic Review of the Effects of Hormone Therapy on Psychological Functioning and Quality of Life in Transgender Individuals," *Transgender Health* 1, no. 1 (January 2016): 21–31, doi:10.1089/trgh.2015.0008, accessed March 25, 2017, http://online.liebertpub.com/doi/full/10.1089/trgh.2015.0008.

8. FINANCIAL STRESS

1. American College Health Association National College Health Assessment II: Spring 2016 Executive Group Reference Summary, accessed December 29, 2016, http://www.acha-ncha.org/docs/NCHA-II%20SPRING%202016%20US%20REFERENCE%20GROUP%20EXECUTIVE%20SUMMARY.pdf.

2. Bob Davis, "Pay Dream Dims for Young," *Wall Street Journal*, December 9, 2016, accessed December 9, 2016, http://www.wsj.com/articles/the-american-dream-is-fading-and-may-be-very-hard-to-revive-1481218911.

3. Lauren Weber, "The End of Employees," *The Wall Street Journal*, February 3, 2017, A1, 10.

4. Josh Mitchell, "Student Debt Is About to Set Another Record, But the Picture Isn't All Bad," *Wall Street Journal*, May 2, 2016, accessed December 9, 2016, http://blogs.wsj.com/economics/2016/05/02/student-debt-is-about-to-set-another-record-but-the-picture-isnt-all-bad/.

5. Danielle R. Adams, Stephen A. Meyers, and Rinad S. Beidas, "The Relationship Between Financial Strain, Perceived Stress, Psychological Symptoms, and Academic and Social Integration in Undergraduate Students," *Journal of American College Health* 64, no. 5 (2016): 362–70.

6. David H. Rehkopf and Stephen L. Buka, "The Association Between Suicide and Socioeconomic Characteristics of Geographical Areas: A Systematic Review," *Psychological Medicine* 36, no. 2 (2006): 145–57, accessed December 10, 2016, https://www.ncbi.nlm.nih.gov/pubmed/16420711.

7. Janet Adamy, "Opioid Epidemic Is an Immediate Test for Donald Trump's Administration," *Wall Street Journal*, December 10, 2016, accessed December 10, 2016, http://www.wsj.com/articles/opioid-epidemic-is-an-immediate-test-for-donald-trumps-administration-1481309696.

8. Mary Elizabeth Dallas, "Recession Linked to More than 10,000 Suicides," *Healthday*, June 12, 2014, accessed December 10, 2016, http://www.cbsnews.com/news/recession-linked-to-more-than-10000-suicides-in-north-america-europe/.

9. Douglas Belkin, "College Career Offices Boost Job Prospects, Alumni Gifts," *Wall Street Journal*, December 13, 2016, accessed December 14, 2016, http://www.wsj.com/articles/college-career-offices-boost-job-prospects-alumni-gifts-1481605260.

10. Jeffrey Bendix, "Curing the Prior Authorization Headache," *Medical Economics*, October 10, 2013, accessed February 26, 2017, http://medicaleconomics.modernmedicine.com/medical-economics/content/tags/americas-health-insurance-plans/curing-prior-authorization-headache.

9. SUICIDAL BEHAVIORS

1. Suicide Facts at a Glance 2015, Centers for Disease Control and Prevention, accessed March 8, 2017, https://www.cdc.gov/violenceprevention/pdf/suicide-datasheet-a.pdf.

2. American College Health Association National College Health Assessment II: Spring 2016 Executive Group Reference Summary, accessed December 29, 2016, http://www.acha-ncha.org/docs/NCHA-II%20SPRING%202016%20US%20REFERENCE%20GROUP%20EXECUTIVE%20SUMMARY.pdf.

3. Increase in Suicide Rates in the United States, 1999–2014, Centers for Disease Control and Prevention, April 2016, accessed May 21, 2016, http://www.cdc.gov/nchs/products/databriefs/db241.htm.

4. Suicide Prevention Resource Center, Suicide among College and University Students in the United States, accessed June 23, 2015, http://www.sprc.org/sites/sprc.org/files/library/SuicideAmongCollegeStudentsInUS.pdf.

5. Matt Rocheleau, "Suicide Rate at MIT Higher Than the National Average," *Boston Globe*, March 17, 2014, accessed June 23, 2015, http://www.bostonglobe.com/metro/2015/03/16/suicide-rate-mit-higher-than-national-average/1aGWr7lRjiEyhoD1WIT78I/story.html?s_campaign=8315.

6. Amelia M. Arria and Kevin E. O'Grady, "Suicide Variation Among College Students: A Multivariate Analysis," *Archives of Suicide Research* 13, no. 3 (2009): 230–46, accessed July 10, 2015, http://www.ncbi.nlm.nih.gov/pmc/articles/PMC2709750/.

7. The JED Foundation and the National Alliance on Mental Illness, "Starting the Conversation: College and Your Mental Health." August 2016, accessed March 7, 2017, https://www.jedfoundation.org/wp-content/uploads/2016/09/jed-nami-guide-starting-conversation-college-mental-health.pdf.

8. Assessing and Treating Suicidal Behaviors, American Psychiatric Association Practice Guidelines, accessed June 25, 2015, http://psychiatryonline.org/pb/assets/raw/sitewide/practice_guidelines/guidelines/suicide-guide.pdf.

9. Mark Moran, "Confidentiality: When Does It Give Way to Other Ethical Imperatives?" *Psychiatric News*, August 29, 2016, accessed March 8, 2017, http://psychnews.psychiatryonline.org/doi/full/10.1176/appi.pn.2016.9a12.

10. Beth Han et al., "Prevalence and Mental Health Treatment of Suicidal Ideation and Behavior Among College Students Aged 18–25 Years and Their Non-College Attending Peers in the United States," *Journal of Clinical Psychiatry* 77, no. 6 (2016): 815–23.

11. Ibid.

12. Victor Schwartz, "Mandatory Leave of Absence for College Students with Suicidal Behaviors: The Real Story," *Psychiatric Times*, August 26, 2016, accessed March 9, 2017, http://www.psychiatrictimes.com/suicide/mandatory-leave-absence-college-students-suicidal-behaviors-real-story.

13. Rebecca W. Brendel et al., "Suicide," in *Massachusetts General Hospital Psychiatry Update and Board Preparation*, ed. Theodore A. Stern et al. (Boston: MGH Psychiatry Academy Publishing, 2012), 427–31.

14. Arria and O'Grady, "Suicide Variation Among College Students," 230–46.

15. Lisa D. Hawley et al., "Baseline Assessment of Campus-Wide General Health Status and Mental Health: Opportunity for Tailored Suicide Prevention and Mental Health Awareness Programming," *Journal of American College Health* 64, no. 3 (2016): 174–83.

16. Victor Schwartz, "Suicide Clusters on College Campuses: Risk, Prevention, Management," *Psychiatric Times*, February 24, 2016, accessed March 9, 2017, http://www.psychiatrictimes.com/suicide/suicide-clusters-college-campuses-risk-prevention-management.

17. American Psychiatric Association, *Diagnostic and Statistical Manual of Mental Disorders*, fifth ed. (Washington, DC: American Psychiatric Association, 2013), 663–66.

18. Ibid.

19. American Psychiatric Association, "Psychotherapies Effective for BPD, But Effects are Small, Study Says," *Psychiatric News Alert*, March 2, 2017, accessed March 9, 2017, http://alert.psychnews.org/2017/03/psychotherapies-effective-for-bpd-but.html.

20. "What Is DBT?" The Linehan Insitute Behavioral Tech, accessed March 8, 2017, http://behavioraltech.org/resources/whatisDBT.cfm.

21. "Drug Treatment for Borderline Personality Disorder," Cochrane Database of Systematic Reviews, January 24, 2010, accessed March 8, 2017, https://www.ncbi.nlm.nih.gov/pubmedhealth/PMH0013611/.

22. Nance Roy and Laura Braider, "College Students and Mental Illness: Strategies for Optimal Results," *Psychiatric Times*, May 30, 2016, accessed July 3, 2016, http://www.psychiatrictimes.com/child-adolescent-psychiatry/college-students-and-mental-illness-strategies-optimal-results.

23. Laura Stiles, "Short-Term Suicide Risk for Discharged Psychiatric Hospital Patients," *Psychiatry Advisor*, December 2, 2016, accessed March 8, 2017, http://www.psychiatryadvisor.com/depressive-disorder/short-term-suicide-risk-in-discharged-psychiatric-patients-with-depression/article/576572/?DCMP=EMC-PA_Depression_Spotlight_RD&cpn=psych_md%2cpsych_all&hmSubId=&NID=1619914256&dl=0&spMailingID=16037641&spUser-ID=MjQzMjY1MTQ5NTAwS0&spJobID=920189089&spRepor-tId=OTIwMTg5MDg5S0.

24. Brendel et al., "Suicide," 427–31.

25. Ibid.

10. SEXUAL ASSAULT AND INTIMATE PARTNER VIOLENCE

1. What Consent Looks Like, Rape, Abuse, and Incest National Network (RAINN), accessed March 23, 2017, https://www.rainn.org/articles/what-is-consent.

2. Key Terms and Phrases, RAINN, accessed March 24, 2017, https://www.rainn.org/articles/key-terms-and-phrases.

3. Association of American Universities Climate Survey on Sexual Assault and Sexual Misconduct, accessed March 23, 2017, https://www.aau.edu/Climate-Survey.aspx?id=16525.

4. Ibid.

5. American Psychiatric Association, *Diagnostic and Statistical Manual of Mental Disorders*, fifth edition (Washington, DC: American Psychiatric Association, 2013), 271–80.

6. Cole G. Youngner et al., "PTSD: Evidence Based Psychotherapy and Emerging Treatment Approaches," *Focus* 11, no. 3 (2013): 307–14.

7. Matthew J. Friedman, "PTSD: Pharmacotherapeutic Approaches," *Focus* 11, no. 3 (2013): 315–20.

8. Jake New, "Deadly Dating Violence," *Inside Higher Education*, December 2, 2014, accessed March 24, 2017, https://www.insidehighered.com/news/2014/12/02/domestic-abuse-prevalent-sexual-assault-college-campuses.

9. Psychiatric Times Editors, "3 Important Facts About Intimate Partner Violence," *Psychiatric Times*, August 17, 2016, accessed March 24, 2017, http://www.psychiatrictimes.com/forensic-psychiatry/3-important-facts-about-

domestic-violence?GUID=1C7ACAB0-88D4-469A-8F24-B709701CA7E6&
rememberme=1&ts=21032017.

10. Christopher I. Eckhardt, Christopher Murphy, and Joel Sprunger, "Interventions for Perpetrators of Intimate Partner Violence," *Psychiatric Times*, August 28, 2014, http://www.psychiatrictimes.com/special-reports/interventions-perpetrators-intimate-partner-violence.

11. Maeve Duggan, "Online Harassment," Pew Research Center, October 22, 2014, accessed March 24, 2017, http://www.pewinternet.org/2014/10/22/online-harassment/.

I I. EATING DISORDERS

1. Eating Disorders on College Campus, National Eating Disorders Association, Collegiate Survey Project, accessed March 19, 2016, https://www.nationaleatingdisorders.org/sites/default/files/CollegeSurvey/CollegiateSurveyProject.pdf.

2. Beatriz Jáuregui-Garrido and Ignacio Jáuregui-Lobera, "Sudden Death in Eating Disorders," *Vascular Health and Risk Management* 8 (2012): 91–98, accessed March 20, 2017, https://www.ncbi.nlm.nih.gov/pmc/articles/PMC3292410/.

3. Marcella Rojas, "Social Media Helps Fuel Some Eating Disorders," *USA Today*, June 1, 2014, accessed March 19, 2017, http://www.usatoday.com/story/news/nation/2014/06/01/social-media-helps-fuel-eating-disorders/9817513/.

4. Jake New, "Drunkorexia," *Inside Higher Ed*, June 30, 2016, accessed March 19, 2017, https://www.insidehighered.com/news/2016/06/30/study-8-10-students-said-they-engaged-behaviors-related-drunkorexia.

5. Insurance Resources, National Eating Disorder Association, accessed March 18, 2017, https://www.nationaleatingdisorders.org/insurance-resources.

6. Practice Guideline for the Treatment of Patients with Eating Disorders, American Psychiatric Association, accessed March 18, 2017, http://psychiatryonline.org/pb/assets/raw/sitewide/practice_guidelines/guidelines/eatingdisorders.pdf.

7. American Psychiatric Association, *Diagnostic and Statistical Manual of Mental Disorders*, fifth edition (Washington, DC: American Psychiatric Association, 2013), 338–54.

8. Rojas, "Social Media Helps Fuel Some Eating Disorders."

9. Wendy Spettigue and Katherine A. Henderson, "Eating Disorders and the Role of the Media," *The Canadian Child and Adolescent Psychiatry Re-*

view 13, no. 1 (2004): 16–19, accessed March 19, 2017, https://www.ncbi.nlm.nih.gov/pmc/articles/PMC2533817/.

10. Roni C. Rabin, "Parents Should Avoid Comments on a Child's Weight," Well Family, *New York Times*, June 16, 2016, accessed March 20, 2017, http://well.blogs.nytimes.com/2016/06/16/parents-should-avoid-comments-on-a-childs-weight/?em_pos=small&emc=edit_ml_20160616&nl=well-family&nl_art=5&nlid=70054023&ref=headline&te=1&_r=0.

11. Amy Chua, *Battle Hymn of the Tiger Mother* (New York: Penguin Books, 2011), iPad edition.

12. Jenni Grover, "Mindful Eating: 5 Easy Tips To Get Started," *The Huffington Post*, November 12, 2013, accessed March 20, 2017, http://www.huffingtonpost.com/2013/11/12/mindful-eating-tips_n_3941528.html.

13. Katherine A. Halmi, "Pharmacotherapy and Physiologic Intervention for Eating Disorders," *Focus* 12, no. 4 (2014): 388–91.

14. Hunna J. Watson and Cynthia Bulik, "Evidence Based Psychotherapy for Eating Disorders, *Focus* 20, no. 4 (2014): 379–84.

15. Securing Eating Disorders Treatment, National Eating Disorders Association, accessed March 20, 2017, https://www.nationaleatingdisorders.org/securing-eating-disorders-treatment.

12. PSYCHOSIS

1. American College Health Association National College Health Assessment II: Spring 2016 Executive Summary, accessed October 29, 2016, http://www.acha-ncha.org/docs/NCHA-II SPRING 2016 US REFERENCE GROUP EXECUTIVE SUMMARY.pdf.

2. Gregory E. Simon et al., "First Presentation with Psychotic Symptoms in a Population Based Setting," *Psychiatric Services*, January 3, 2017, accessed February 21, 2017, http://ps.psychiatryonline.org/doi/abs/10.1176/appi.ps.201600257.

3. Early Psychosis and Psychosis, National Alliance on Mental Illness, accessed October 28, 2016, http://www.nami.org/Learn-More/Mental-Health-Conditions/Early-Psychosis-and-Psychosis.

4. S. Charles Schulz et al., "Early Stage Schizophrenia," in *Gabbard's Treatments of Psychiatric Disorders*, fifth edition, ed. Glen O. Gabbard (Arlington, VA: American Psychiatric Association, 2014), 138–39, iPad edition.

5. Anna M. Miller, "Living With the Voices in Your Head," *U.S. News and World Report*, July 2, 2015, accessed February 21, 2016, http://health.usnews.com/health-news/health-wellness/articles/2015/07/02/hearing-voices-not-always-a-sign-of-mental-illness.

6. American Psychiatric Association, *Diagnostic and Statistical Manual of Mental Disorders*, fifth edition (Washington, DC: American Psychiatric Association, 2013), 87–88.

7. Anthony J. Rothschild and Suzanne E. Duval, "How Long Should Patients With Psychotic Depression Stay on Antipsychotic Medication?" *Journal of Clinical Psychiatry* 64, no. 4 (2003): 390–96, accessed February 22, 2017, https://www.ncbi.nlm.nih.gov/pubmed/12716238.

8. American Psychiatric Association, *Diagnostic and Statistical Manual of Mental Disorders*, fifth edition, 99–100.

9. Norman Sartorius et al., "Name Change for Schizophrenia." *Schizophrenia Bulletin* 40, no. 2 (2014): 255–58, accessed March 17, 2017, https://www.ncbi.nlm.nih.gov/pmc/articles/PMC3932100/.

10. Jaakko Seikkula et al., "Five-Year Experience of First-Episode Nonaffective Psychosis in Open-Dialogue Model," *Psychotherapy Research* 16, no. 2 (2006): 214–28, accessed March 17, 2017, https://www.researchgate.net/publication/252659625_Five-year_experience_of_first-episode_nonaffective_psychosis_in_open-dialogue_approach_Treatment_principles_follow-up_outcomes_and_two_case_studies.

11. Fred Osher, "We Need Better Funding for Mental Health Services," *New York Times*, May 9, 2016, accessed February 22, 2017, http://www.nytimes.com/roomfordebate/2016/05/09/getting-the-mentally-ill-out-of-jail-and-off-the-streets/we-need-better-funding-for-mental-health-services.

12. Brandon Gaudiano et al., "Prevalence and Clinical Characteristics of Psychotic Versus Nonpsychotic Major Depression in a General Psychiatric Outpatient Clinic," *Depression and Anxiety* 26, no. 1 (2009): 54–64, accessed February 20, 2017, https://www.ncbi.nlm.nih.gov/pmc/articles/PMC3111977/.

13. Schulz et al., "Schizophrenia Spectrum and Other Psychotic Disorders," 138.

14. Joseph M. Rey, "Does Marijuana Contribute to Psychotic Illness?" *Current Psychiatry* 6, no. 2 (February 2007): 37–46, accessed November 3, 2016, http://www.mdedge.com/currentpsychiatry/article/62537/does-marijuana-contribute-psychotic-illness.

15. American College Health Association National College Health Assessment II.

16. Carol A. Tamminga and Elena I. Ivleva, "Toward a Dimensional Understanding of Psychosis and Its Treatment," in *Gabbard's Treatments of Psychiatric Disorders*, ed. Glen O. Gabbard (Arlington, VA: American Psychiatric Association), 158–59.

17. American Psychiatric Association, *Diagnostic and Statistical Manual of Mental Disorders*, fifth edition, 131.

18. Ibid., 138.

19. Ingo Schäfer and Helen L. Fisher, "Childhood Trauma and Psychosis— What Is the Evidence?" *Dialogues in Clinical Neuroscience* 13, no. 3 (2011): 360–65, accessed October 29, 2016. https://www.ncbi.nlm.nih.gov/pmc/articles/PMC3182006/.

20. Ibid.

21. Joanna Moncrieff, "Antipsychotic Maintenance Treatment: Time to Rethink?" *PLoS Medicine* 12, no. 8 (2015): e1001861, accessed November 8, 2016, https://www.ncbi.nlm.nih.gov/pmc/articles/PMC4524699/.

22. Ibid.; Robert Insel, "Antipsychotics, Taking the Long View," National Institute of Mental Health, August 28, 2013, accessed February 21, 2017, https://www.nimh.nih.gov/about/directors/thomas-insel/blog/2013/antipsychotics-taking-the-long-view.shtml.

23. Wai Tong Chien et al. "Current Approaches to Treatments for Schizophrenia Spectrum Disorders, Part II: Psychosocial Interventions and Patient-Focused Perspectives in Psychiatric Care," *Neuropsychiatric Disease and Treatment* 9 (2013): 1463–1481, accessed February 22, 2017, https://www.ncbi.nlm.nih.gov/pmc/articles/PMC3792827.

24. Judith A. Cook et al, "Results of a Randomized Controlled Trial of Mental Illness Self-management Using Wellness Recovery Action Planning," *Schizophrenia Bulletin*, 38 (4)(2012): 881–91, accessed February 22, 2017, doi: 10.1093/schbul/sbr012 https://academic.oup.com/schizophreniabulletin/article/38/4/881/1868636/Results-of-a-Randomized-Controlled-Trial-of-Mental#T2

25. Will Boggs, "Chemokine Levels Altered in Schizophrenia," *Psych Congress Network*, October 27, 2016, accessed February 21, 2017, http://www.consultant360.com/story/chemokine-levels-altered-schizophrenia

26. Terry Airov, "Dementia Drug Shown Effective as Adjunctive Treatment in Schizophrenia," *Psych Congress Network*, October 11, 2016, accessed February 21, 2017, http://www.consultant360.com/exclusives/dementia-drug-shown-effective-adjunctive-treatment-schizophrenia.

27. Jolynn Tumolo, "Dementia Drug Shown Effective as Adjunctive Treatment in Schizophrenia," *Psych Congress Network*, October 14, 2016, accessed February 21, 2017, http://www.consultant360.com/exclusives/adjunctive--rivastigmine-improves-cognitive-function-schizophrenia.

BIBLIOGRAPHY

Aberg, Simon E. "Study Drug Abuse by College Students: What You Need to Know." *National Center for Health Research.* 2016. Accessed March 2, 2017. http://center4research.org/child-teen-health/hyperactivity-and-adhd/study-drug-abuse-college-students/.

Active Minds. "The Facts on Transgender Student Mental Health." Accessed March 25, 2017. http://www.activeminds.org/transgender-college-student-mental-health.

Adams, Danielle R., Stephen A. Meyers, and Rinad S. Beidas. "The Relationship Between Financial Strain, Perceived Stress, Psychological Symptoms, and Academic and Social Integration in Undergraduate Students," *Journal of American College Health* 64, no. 5 (2016): 362–70.

Adamy, Janet. "Opioid Epidemic Is an Immediate Test for Donald Trump's Administration," *Wall Street Journal,* December 10, 2016, accessed December 10, 2016, http://www.wsj.com/articles/opioid-epidemic-is-an-immediate-test-for-donald-trumps-administration-1481309696

Airov, Terry. "Dementia Drug Shown Effective as Adjunctive Treatment in Schizophrenia." *Psych Congress Network.* October 11, 2016. Accessed February 21, 2017. http://www.consultant360.com/exclusives/dementia-drug-shown-effective-adjunctive-treatment-schizophrenia.

Almendrala, Ann. "More Children with Autism Are Going to College Than Ever Before." *Huffington Post.* March 11, 2014. Accessed July 23, 2015. http://www.huffingtonpost.com/2014/03/11/research-autism-spectrum_n_4939200.html.

American College Health Association. "National College Health Assessment II: Spring 2016 Executive Group Reference Summary." Accessed December 29, 2016. http://www.acha-ncha.org/docs/NCHAII%20SPRING%202016%20US%20REFERENCE%20GROUP%20EXECUTIVE%20SUMMARY.pdf.

American Psychiatric Association. "Assessing and Treating Suicidal Behaviors." Accessed June 25, 2015. http://psychiatryonline.org/pb/assets/raw/sitewide/practice_guidelines/guidelines/suicide-guide.pdf.

———. "College Students: Coping with Stress and Anxiety on Campus." August 27, 2015. Accessed December 30, 2016. https://psychiatry.org/news-room/apa-blogs/apa-blog/2015/08/college-students-coping-with-stress-and-anxiety-on-campus.

———. *Diagnostic and Statistical Manual of Mental Disorders.* Fifth Edition. Washington, DC: American Psychiatric Association, 2013.

———. "Practice Guideline for the Treatment of Patients with Eating Disorders." Accessed March 18, 2017. http://psychiatryonline.org/pb/assets/raw/sitewide/practice_guidelines/guidelines/eatingdisorders.pdf.

————. "Psychotherapies Effective for BPD, But Effects Are Small, Study Says." *Psychiatric News Alert*. March 2, 2017. Accessed March 9, 2017. http://alert.psychnews.org/2017/03/psychotherapies-effective-for-bpd-but.html.

Anti-Defamation League. "White Supremacists on Campus: Unprecedented Recruitment Efforts Underway." March 6, 2017. Accessed March 24, 2017. https://www.adl.org/blog/white-supremacists-on-campus-unprecedented-recruitment-efforts-underway.

Antony, Martin M., and Richard P. Swinson. *The Shyness and Social Anxiety Workbook*. Oakland, CA: New Harbinger Publications, Inc., 2008.

Anxiety and Depression Association of America. "Facts and Statistics." Accessed January 13, 2017. https://www.adaa.org/about-adaa/press-room/facts-statistics.

Arria, Amelia M., and Kevin E. O'Grady. "Suicide Variation Among College Students: A Multivariate Analysis." *Archives of Suicide Research* 13, no. 3 (2009): 230–46. Accessed July 10, 2015. http://www.ncbi.nlm.nih.gov/pmc/articles/PMC2709750/.

Association of American Universities. "AAU Climate Survey on Sexual Assault and Sexual Misconduct." Accessed March 23, 2017. https://www.aau.edu/Climate-Survey.aspx?id=16525.

Association of Recovery in Higher Education. Accessed March 4, 2017. http://collegiaterecovery.org.

Balsam, Kimberly F., Yamile Molina, Blaire Beadnell, Jane Simoni, and Karina Walter. "Measuring Multiple Minority Stress: The LGBT People of Color Microaggressions Scale." *Cultural Diversity and Ethnic Minority Psychology* 17, no. 2 (2011): 163–74. Accessed March 21, 2017. https://www.ncbi.nlm.nih.gov/pmc/articles/PMC4059824/.

Barton, Dominic. "The Most Important Factor in a College Student's Success." *Wall Street Journal*. September 26, 2016. Accessed February 28, 2017. http://blogs.wsj.com/experts/2015/09/16/the-most-important-factor-in-a-college-students-success/.

Belkin, Douglas. "College Career Offices Boost Job Prospects, Alumni Gifts," *Wall Street Journal*, December 13, 2016, accessed December 14, 2016, http://www.wsj.com/articles/college-career-offices-boost-job-prospects-alumni-gifts-1481605260

Bendix, Jeffrey. "Curing the Prior Authorization Headache." *Medical Economics*. October 10, 2013. Accessed February 26, 2017. http://medicaleconomics.modernmedicine.com/medical-economics/content/tags/americas-health-insurance-plans/curing-prior-authorization-headache.

Benson, Etienne. "The Many Faces of Perfectionism." *American Psychological Association Monitor on Psychology*. November 2003. Accessed March 10, 2017. http://www.apa.org/monitor/nov03/manyfaces.aspx.

Boggs, Will. "Chemokine Levels Altered in Schizophrenia." *Psych Congress Network*. October 27, 2016. Accessed February 21, 2017. http://www.consultant360.com/story/chemokine-levels-altered-schizophrenia.

Booker, Lauren. "What It Means to Be Gender Fluid." *CNN*. April 13, 2016. Accessed March 25, 2017. http://www.cnn.com/2016/04/13/living/gender-fluid-feat/.

Brangham, William. "Is Pot Getting More Potent?" *PBS Newshour*. April 2, 2014. Accessed March 4, 2017. http://www.pbs.org/newshour/updates/pot-getting-potent/.

Brendel, Rebeca W., Amanda S. Green, Roy H. Perlis, and Theodore A. Stern. "Suicide." In *Massachusetts General Hospital Psychiatry Update and Board Preparation*, edited by Theodore A. Stern, John B. Herman, and Tristan Gorrindo, 427–31. Boston: MGH Psychiatry Academy Publishing, 2012.

Califano Jr., Joseph A. "Wasting the Best and the Brightest: Alcohol and Drug Abuse on College Campuses." The National Center on Addiction and Substance Abuse. May 28, 2007. Accessed March 4, 2017. http://www.centeronaddiction.org/newsroom/op-eds/wasting-best-and-brightest-alcohol-and-drug-abuse-college-campuses.

Center for Collegiate Mental Health 2015 Annual Report. Accessed May 21, 2016. http://ccmh.psu.edu/wp-content/uploads/sites/3058/2016/01/2015_CCMH_Report_1-18-2015.pdf.

Centers for Disease Control and Prevention. "Alcohol and Public Health." Accessed March 5, 2017. https://www.cdc.gov/alcohol/faqs.htm.

———. "Fact Sheets—Binge Drinking." Accessed March 4, 2017. https://www.cdc.gov/alcohol/fact-sheets/binge-drinking.htm.

———. "Increase in Suicide Rates in the United States, 1999–2014." April 2016. Accessed May 21, 2016. http://www.cdc.gov/nchs/products/databriefs/db241.htm.

———. "Injury Prevention and Control: Opioid Overdose." Accessed March 4, 2107. https://www.cdc.gov/drugoverdose/.

———. "Suicide Facts at a Glance 2015." Accessed March 8, 2017. https://www.cdc.gov/violenceprevention/pdf/suicide-datasheet-a.pdf.

Chien, Wai Tong, Sau F. Leung, Frederick K. K. Yeung, and Wai K. Wong. "Current Approaches to Treatments for Schizophrenia Spectrum Disorders, Part II: Psychosocial Interventions and Patient-Focused Perspectives in Psychiatric Care." *Neuropsychiatric Disease and Treatment* 9 (2013): 1463–81. Accessed February 21, 2017. https://www.ncbi.nlm.nih.gov/pmc/articles/PMC3792827/ doi:10.2147/NDT.S49263.

Chua, Amy. *Battle Hymn of the Tiger Mother*. New York: Penguin Books, 2011. iPad edition.

Cochrane Database of Systematic Reviews. "Drug Treatment for Borderline Personality Disorder." January 24, 2010. Accessed March 8, 2017. https://www.ncbi.nlm.nih.gov/pubmedhealth/PMH0013611/.

Cook, Judith A., Mary Ellen Copeland, Jessica A. Jonikas, Marie M. Hamilton, Lisa A. Razzano, Dennis D. Grey, Carol B. Floyd, Walter B. Hudson, Rachel T. Macfarlane, Tina M. Carter, and Sherry Boyd. "Results of a Randomized Controlled Trial of Mental Illness Self-Management Using Wellness Recovery Action Planning." *Schizophrenia Bulletin* 38, no. 4 (2012): 881–91. Accessed February 22, 2017. doi: 10.1093/schbul/sbr012. https://academic.oup.com/schizophreniabulletin/article/38/4/881/1868636/Results-of-a-Randomized-Controlled-Trial-of-Mental#T2.

Cooperative Education Research Program at the Higher Education Research Institute at UCLA. "The American Freshman: National Norms Fall 2015." Accessed July 3, 2016. http://www.heri.ucla.edu/monographs/TheAmericanFreshman2015.pdf.

Dahl, Melissa. "The Alarming New Research on Perfectionism." *New York Magazine*, September 30, 2014. Accessed March 10, 2017. http://nymag.com/scienceofus/2014/09/alarming-new-research-on-perfectionism.html?mid=emailshare_scienceofus.

Dallas, Mary Elizabeth. "Recession Linked to More than 10,000 Suicides," *Wall Street Journal*, December 13, 2016, accessed December 10, 2016, http://www.cbsnews.com/news/recession-linked-to-more-than-10000-suicides-in-north-america-europe/.

Davis, Bob. "Pay Dream Dims for Young," *Wall Street Journal*, December 9, 2016, accessed December 9, 2016, http://www.wsj.com/articles/the-american-dream-is-fading-and-may-be-very-hard-to-revive-1481218911.

Dekok, David. "Missing Penn State Student Found After Parents at Graduation Learned He Dropped Out." *Reuters*, May 11, 2015. Accessed February 24, 2017. http://www.reuters.com/article/us-usa-pennsylvania-missing-idUSKBN0NW20G20150511.

Diemer, Elizabeth W., Julia D. Grant, Melissa A. Munn-Chernoff, David A. Patterson, and Alexis E. Duncan. "Gender Identity, Sexual Orientation, and Eating-Related Pathology in a National Sample of College Students." *Journal of Adolescent Health* 57, no. 2 (2015): 144–49. Accessed March 18, 2017. http://www.jahonline.org/article/S1054-139X(15)00087-7/fulltext.

Drugwatch. "Student Health." Accessed March 4, 2017. http://www.drugwatch.com/students/.

Duggan, Maeve. "Online Harassment." Pew Research Center. October 22, 2014. Accessed March 24, 2017. http://www.pewinternet.org/2014/10/22/online-harassment/.

Dunlop, Boadie W. "Evidence-Based Applications of Combination Psychotherapy and Pharmacotherapy for Depression." *Focus* 14, no. 2 (2016): 156–74.

Eckhardt, Christopher I., Christopher Murphy, and Joel Sprunger. "Interventions for Perpetrators of Intimate Partner Violence," *Psychiatric Times*, August 28, 2014, http://www.psychiatrictimes.com/epcial-reports/interventions-perpetrators-intimate-partner-violence.

Family Policy Compliance Office. "FERPA Frequently Asked Questions." Accessed March 6, 2017. http://familypolicy.ed.gov/faq-page#t39n410.

Friedman, Matthew J. "PTSD: Pharmacotherapeutic Approaches." *Focus* 11, no. 3 (2013): 315–20.

Gaudiano, Brandon A., Kristy L. Dalrymple, and Mark Zimmerman. "Prevalence and Clinical Characteristics of Psychotic Versus Nonpsychotic Major Depression in a General Psychiatric Outpatient Clinic." *Depression and Anxiety* 26, no. 1 (2009): 54–64. Accessed February 20, 2017. https://www.ncbi.nlm.nih.gov/pmc/articles/PMC3111977/.

GLAAD Media Reference Guide. Accessed March 25, 2017. http://www.glaad.org/publications/reference.

Grasgreen, Allie. "Parents: Help or Hindrance?" *Inside Higher Ed.* March 28, 2012. Accessed May 18, 2016. https://www.insidehighered.com/news/2012/03/28/naspa-survey-finds-parental-involvement-isnt-always-bad-thing#.Vz3wGUKZbhs.mailto.

Greist, John H., and James W. Jefferson. "Obsessive Compulsive Disorder." In *Gabbard's Treatments of Psychiatric Disorders*, fifth edition, edited by Glen O. Gabbard, 405–18. Arlington, VA: American Psychiatric Association, 2014. iPad edition.

Gray, Peter. "The Decline in Play and Rise in Children's Mental Disorders." *Psychology Today*. January 26, 2010. Accessed January 14, 2017. https://www.psychologytoday.com/blog/freedom-learn/201001/the-decline-play-and-rise-in-childrens-mental-disorders.

Grover, Jenni. "Mindful Eating: 5 Easy Tips to Get Started." *The Huffington Post*. November 12, 2013. Accessed March 20, 2017. http://www.huffingtonpost.com/2013/11/12/mindful-eating-tips_n_3941528.html.

Grown and Flown Blog. "How to Finish College in 4 Years: What Parents Need to Know." Accessed February 24, 2017. http://grownandflown.com/how-to-finish-college-in-4-years/.

Hallowell, Edward M., and John J. Ratey. *Delivered from Distraction*. New York: Ballantine Books, 2005.

Halmi, Katherine A. "Pharmacotherapy and Physiologic Intervention for Eating Disorders." *Focus* 12, no. 4 (2014): 388–91.

Han, Beth, Wilson M. Compton, Daniel Eisenberg, Laura Milazzo-Sayre, Richard McKeon, and Art Hughes. "Prevalence and Mental Health Treatment of Suicidal Ideation and Behavior Among College Students Aged 18–25 Years and Their Non-College Attending Peers in the United States." *Journal of Clinical Psychiatry* 77, no. 6 (2016): 815–23.

Hawkley, Louise C., and John T. Cacioppo. "Loneliness Matters: A Theoretical and Empirical Review of Consequences and Mechanisms." *Annals of Behavioral Medicine* 40, no. 2 (2010): 1–14. Accessed May 2, 2015. doi:10.1007/s12160-010-9210-8. http://www.ncbi.nlm.nih.gov/pmc/articles/PMC3874845/pdf/nihms538929.pdf.

Hawley, Lisa D., Michael G. MacDonald, Erica H. Wallace, Julia Smith, Brian Wummel, and Patricia Wren. "Baseline Assessment of Campus-Wide General Health Status and Mental Health: Opportunity for Tailored Suicide Prevention and Mental Health Awareness Programming." *Journal of American College Health* 64, no. 3 (2016): 174–83.

Hefernan, Lisa, and Jennifer Breheny Wallace. "For Freshman, Campus Life Poses New Risks." *New York Times*, August 17, 2016. Accessed March 4, 2016. https://well.blogs.nytimes.com/2016/08/17/for-freshmen-campus-life-poses-new-risks/?hpw&rref=health&action=click&pgtype=Homepage&module=well-region&region=bottom-well&WT.nav=bottom-well&_r=1.

Henig, Robin Marantz. "How Science Is Helping Us Understand Gender." *National Geographic*. January 2017. Accessed March 25, 2017. http://www.nationalgeographic.com/magazine/2017/01/.

Henin, Aude, and Noah Berman. "The Promise and Peril of Emerging Adulthood." *Cognitive and Behavioral Practice* 23, no. 3 (2016): 263–69. Accessed June 16, 2016. http://dx.doi.org/10.1016/j.cbpra.2016.05.005.

Hirschfeld, Robert M. A. "The Comorbidity of Major Depression and Anxiety Disorders: Recognition and Management in Primary Care." *Primary Care Companion to the Journal of Clinical Psychiatry* 3, no. 6 (2001): 244–54.

Hofer, Barbara K. "Student-Parent Communication in the College Years: Can Students Grow up on an Electronic Tether?" *The Bulletin*. Association of College Unions International 79, no. 2 (2011). Accessed June 3, 2015. http://www.acui.org/publications/bulletin/article.aspx?issue=28134&id=14773.

Hoffman, Jan. "As Attention Grows, Transgender Numbers Are Elusive." *New York Times.* May 17, 2016. Accessed March 25, 2017. https://www.nytimes.com/2016/05/18/science/transgender-children.html?_r=2.

Hollingsworth, Barbara. "Less than 40 percent of H.S. Seniors Academically Prepared for College." *CNS News.* May 14, 2014. Accessed May 21, 2016. http://cnsnews.com/news/article/barbara-hollingsworth/less-40-hs-seniors-academically-prepared-college.

Holt-Lunstad, Julianne, Timothy B. Smith, Mark Baker, Tyler Harris, and David Stephenson. "Loneliness and Social Isolation as Risk Factors for Mortality: A Meta-Analytic Review." *Perspectives on Psychological Science* 10, no. 2 (2015): 1. http://journals.sagepub.com/doi/full/10.1177/1745691614568352.

Insel, Robert. "Antipsychotics, Taking the Long View." National Institute of Mental Health. August 28, 2013. Accessed February 21, 2017. https://www.nimh.nih.gov/about/directors/thomas-insel/blog/2013/antipsychotics-taking-the-long-view.shtml.

Jacobson, Rae. "Social Media and Self-Doubt." Child Mind Institute. Accessed March 12, 2017. https://childmind.org/article/social-media-and-self-doubt/.

Jáuregui-Garrido, Beatriz, and Ignacio Jáuregui-Lobera. "Sudden Death in Eating Disorders." *Vascular Health and Risk Management* 8 (2012): 91–98. Accessed March 20, 2017. https://www.ncbi.nlm.nih.gov/pmc/articles/PMC3292410/.

JED Foundation and the National Alliance on Mental Illness. "Starting the Conversation: College and Your Mental Health." August 2016. Accessed March 7, 2017. https://www.jedfoundation.org/wp-content/uploads/2016/09/jed-nami-guide-starting-conversation-college-mental-health.pdf.

Kroshus, Emily, and Ann K. Davoren. "Mental Health and Substance Use of Sexual Minority College Athletes." *Journal of American College Health* 64, no. 5 (2016): 371–79.

Linehan Institute Behavioral Tech. "What Is DBT?" Accessed March 8, 2017. http://behavioraltech.org/resources/whatisDBT.cfm.

Lockard, Allison J., Jeffrey A. Hayes, Kristin Neff, and Benjamin D. Locke. "Self-Compassion Among College Counseling Center Clients: An Examination of Clinical Norms and Group Differences." *Journal of College Counseling* 17 (2014): 249–59. Accessed March 12, 2017. DOI: 10.1002/j.2161-1882.2014.00061.x. http://self-compassion.org/wp-content/uploads/2015/03/Lockard.Neff_.pdf.

Marshall, Mallika. "New Concerns Arise About Mental Health of College Students." August 25, 2016. Accessed January 2, 2016. http://boston.cbslocal.com/2016/08/25/new-concerns-mental-health-college-students-suicide/.

Mason, Lindsay, and Amy Hoch. "Radically Open DBT (RO-DBT): Treating Over-Thinking and the Plight of Perfectionism in College Students." Talk presented at the annual meeting of the American College Counseling Association, Tampa, Florida, February 17, 2017.

Miller, Anna M. "Living with the Voices in Your Head." *U.S. News and World Report.* July 2, 2015. Accessed February 21, 2016. http://health.usnews.com/health-news/health-wellness/articles/2015/07/02/hearing-voices-not-always-a-sign-of-mental-illness.

Mitchell, Josh. "Student Debt Is About to Set Another Record, But the Picture Isn't All Bad." *Wall Street Journal.* May 2, 2016. Accessed December 9, 2016. http://blogs.wsj.com/economics/2016/05/02/student-debt-is-about-to-set-another-record-but-the-picture-isnt-all-bad/.

Moncrieff, Joanna. "Antipsychotic Maintenance Treatment: Time to Rethink?" *PLoS Medicine* 12, no. 8 (2015): e1001861. Accessed November 8, 2016. https://www.ncbi.nlm.nih.gov/pmc/articles/PMC4524699/.

Moran, Mark. "Confidentiality: When Does It Give Way to Other Ethical Imperatives?" *Psychiatric News.* August 29, 2016. Accessed March 8, 2017. http://psychnews.psychiatryonline.org/doi/full/10.1176/appi.pn.2016.9a12.

National Alliance on Mental Illness. "Early Psychosis and Psychosis." Accessed October 28, 2016. http://www.nami.org/Learn-More/Mental-Health-Conditions/Early-Psychosis-and-Psychosis.

———. "Mental Health Facts: Children and Teens." Accessed December 31, 2016. https://www.nami.org/getattachment/Learn-More/Mental-Health-by-the-Numbers/childrenmhfacts.pdf.

National Center for Education Statistics. "Fast Facts: Enrollment." Accessed March 24, 2017. https://nces.ed.gov/fastfacts/display.asp?id=98.
———. "Fast Facts: Graduation Rates." Accessed May 21, 2016. https://nces.ed.gov/fastfacts/display.asp?id=40.
———. "Fast Facts: Race/Ethnicity of College Faculty." Accessed March 24, 2017. https://nces.ed.gov/fastfacts/display.asp?id=61.
National Communication Association. "Press Release: Many International Students Have Few Close American Friends, Survey Says." June 14, 2012. Accessed July 23, 2015. http://www.natcom.org/newsroom.aspx?id=2521.
National Eating Disorders Association. "Eating Disorders on College Campus." Accessed March 19, 2016. https://www.nationaleatingdisorders.org/sites/default/files/CollegeSurvey/CollegiateSurveyProject.pdf.
———. "Insurance Resources." Accessed March 18, 2017. https://www.nationaleatingidisorders.org/insurance-resources.
———. "Securing Eating Disorders Treatment." Accessed March 20, 2017. https://www.nationaleatingdisorders.org/securing-eating-disorders-treatment.
National Institute on Alcohol Abuse and Alcoholism. "College Drinking." Accessed March 4, 2017. https://pubs.niaaa.nih.gov/publications/CollegeFactSheet/CollegeFactSheet.pdf.
National Institute of Mental Health. "Antidepressant Medications for Children and Adolescents: Information for Parents and Caregivers." Accessed September 24, 2016. http://www.nimh.nih.gov/health/topics/child-and-adolescent-mental-health/antidepressant-medications-for-children-and-adolescents-information-for-parents-and-caregivers.shtml.
Nepon, Josh, Shay Lee-Belik, James Bolton, and Jitender Sareen. "The Relationship Between Anxiety Disorders and Suicide Attempts: Findings from the National Epidemiologic Survey on Alcohol and Related Conditions." Depression and Anxiety 27, no. 9 (2010): 791–98. Accessed January 13, 2017. http://doi.org/10.1002/da.20674. https://www.ncbi.nlm.nih.gov/pmc/articles/PMC2940247/.
New, Jake. "Deadly Dating Violence." Inside Higher Education. December 2, 2014. Accessed March 24, 2017. https://www.insidehighered.com/news/2014/12/02/domestic-abuse-prevalent-sexual-assault-college-campuses.
———. "Drunkorexia." Inside Higher Ed. June 30, 2016. Accessed March 19, 2017. https://www.insidehighered.com/news/2016/06/30/study-8-10-students-said-they-engaged-behaviors-related-drunkorexia.
Osher, Fred. "We Need Better Funding for Mental Health Services." New York Times. May 9, 2016. Accessed February 22, 2017. http://www.nytimes.com/roomfordebate/2016/05/09/getting-the-mentally-ill-out-of-jail-and-off-the-streets/we-need-better-funding-for-mental-health-services.
Oswalt, Sara B., Samantha Evans, and Andrew Drott. "Beyond Alphabet Soup: Helping College Health Professionals Understand Sexual Fluidity." Journal of American College Health 64, no. 6 (2016): 502–8.
Partnership for Drug-Free Kids. "8 Ways to Talk with Your Teen About Drugs and Alcohol." Accessed March 4, 2017. http://www.drugfree.org/resources/8-ways-to-talk-with-your-teen-about-drugs-and-alcohol/.
Paul, Maria. "Casual Marijuana Use Linked to Brain Abnormalities." Northwestern News. April 16, 2014. Accessed March 5, 2014. https://news.northwestern.edu/stories/2014/04/casual-marijuana-use-linked-to-brain-abnormalities-in-students.
Primack, Brian. "Social Media and Depression." Psychiatric Times. May 25, 2016. Accessed June 5, 2016. http://www.psychiatrictimes.com/depression/social-media-and-depression.
Psychiatric Times Editors. "3 Important Facts About Intimate Partner Violence." Psychiatric Times. August 17, 2016. Accessed March 24, 2017. http://www.psychiatrictimes.com/forensic-psychiatry/3-important-facts-about-domestic-violence?GUID=1C7ACAB0-88D4-469A-8F24-B709701CA7E6&rememberme=1&ts=21032017.
Rabin, Roni C. "Parents Should Avoid Comments on a Child's Weight." New York Times. June 16, 2016. Accessed March 20, 2017. http://well.blogs.nytimes.com/2016/06/16/parents-should-avoid-comments-on-a-childs-weight/?em_pos=small&emc=edit_ml_20160616&nl=well-family&nl_art=5&nlid=70054023&ref=headline&te=1&_r=0.

Radnofsky, Louise, and Ben Cohen, "How Simone Biles Achieved Greatness." *Wall Street Journal.* August 12, 2016, D5.

RAINN (Rape, Abuse, and Incest National Network). "Key Terms and Phrases." Accessed March 24, 2017. https://www.rainn.org/articles/key-terms-and-phrases.

———. "What Consent Looks Like." Accessed March 23, 2017. https://www.rainn.org/articles/what-is-consent.

Ratnapalan, Savithiri, and Helen Batty. "To Be Good Enough." *Canadian Family Physician* 55, no. 3 (2009): 239–40. Accessed March 12, 2017. https://www.ncbi.nlm.nih.gov/pmc/articles/PMC2654842/.

Rehkopf, David H. and Stephen L. Buka. "The Association Between Suicide and Socioeconomic Characteristics of Geographical Areas: A Systematic Review," *Psychological Medicine* 36, no. 2 (2006): 145–57, accessed December 10, 2016, https://www.ncbi.nlm.nih.gov/pubmed/16420711

Rey, Joseph M. "Does Marijuana Contribute to Psychotic Illness?" *Current Psychiatry* 6, no. 2 (2007): 37–46. Accessed November 3, 2016. http://www.mdedge.com/currentpsychiatry/article/62537/does-marijuana-contribute-psychotic-illness.

Rimer, Sara. "Today's Lesson for College Students: Lighten Up." *New York Times.* April 6, 2004. Accessed March 11, 2017. http://www.nytimes.com/2004/04/06/us/today-s-lesson-for-college-students-lighten-up.html?_r=0.

Rivas, Jorge. "Half of Young People Believe Gender Isn't Limited to Male and Female." *Fusion.* February 3, 2015. Accessed March 25, 2017. http://fusion.net/story/42216/half-of-young-people-believe-gender-isnt-limited-to-male-and-female/.

Rocheleau, Matt. "Suicide Rate at MIT Higher than the National Average." *Boston Globe.* March 17, 2015. Accessed June 23, 2015. http://www.bostonglobe.com/metro/2015/03/16/suicide-rate-mit-higher-than-national-average/1aGWr7lRjiEyhoD1WIT78I/story.html?s_campaign=8315.

Rojas, Marcella. "Social Media Helps Fuel Some Eating Disorders." *USA Today.* June 1, 2014. Accessed March 19, 2017. http://www.usatoday.com/story/news/nation/2014/06/01/social-media-helps-fuel-eating-disorders/9817513/.

Rothschild, Anthony J., and Suzanne E. Duval. "How Long Should Patients with Psychotic Depression Stay on Antipsychotic Medication?" *Journal of Clinical Psychiatry* 64, no. 4 (2003): 390–96. Accessed February 22, 2017. https://www.ncbi.nlm.nih.gov/pubmed/12716238.

Roy, Nance, and Laura Braider. "College Students and Mental Illness: Strategies for Optimal Results." *Psychiatric Times.* May 30, 2016. Accessed July 3, 2016. http://www.psychiatrictimes.com/child-adolescent-psychiatry/college-students-and-mental-illness-strategies-optimal-results.

Ryan, Caitlin, David Huebner, Rafael M. Diaz, and Jorge Sanchez. "Family Rejection as a Predictor of Negative Health Outcomes in White and Latino Lesbian, Gay, and Bisexual Young Adults." *Pediatrics* 123, no. 1 (2009): 346–52. Accessed March 25, 2017. doi: 10.1542/peds.2007-3524. https://www.ncbi.nlm.nih.gov/pubmed/19117902.

Sartorius, Norman, Helen Chiu, Kua Ee Heok, Min-Soo Lee, Wen-Chen Ouyang, Mitsumoto Sato, Yen Kuang Yang, and Xin Yu. "Name Change for Schizophrenia." *Schizophrenia Bulletin* 40, no. 2 (2014): 255–58. Accessed March 17, 2017. doi: 10.1093/schbul/sbt231. https://www.ncbi.nlm.nih.gov/pmc/articles/PMC3932100/.

Scelfo, Julie. "Suicide on Campus and the Pressure of Perfection." *New York Times.* July 27, 2015. Accessed March 10, 2017. https://www.nytimes.com/2015/08/02/education/edlife/stress-social-media-and-suicide-on-campus.html?_r=0.

Schäfer, Ingo, and Helen L. Fisher. "Childhood Trauma and Psychosis—What Is the Evidence?" *Dialogues in Clinical Neuroscience* 13, no. 3 (2011): 360–65. Accessed February 21, 2017. https://www.ncbi.nlm.nih.gov/pmc/articles/PMC3182006/.

Schulz et al., "Schizophrenia Spectrum and Other Psychotic Disorders," 138.

Schulz, S. Charles, Danielle Goerke, Michael B. O'Sullivan, and Suzanne G. Jasberg. "Early Stage Schizophrenia." In *Gabbard's Treatments of Psychiatric Disorders*, fifth edition, edited by Glen O. Gabbard, 131–56. Arlington, VA: American Psychiatric Association, 2014. iPad edition.

Schwartz, Victor. "Mandatory Leave of Absence for College Students with Suicidal Behaviors: The Real Story." *Psychiatric Times*. August 26, 2016. Accessed March 9, 2017. http://www.psychiatrictimes.com/suicide/mandatory-leave-absence-college-students-suicidalbehaviors-real-story.

———. "Suicide Clusters on College Campuses: Risk, Prevention, Management." *Psychiatric Times*. February 24, 2016. Accessed March 9, 2017. http://www.psychiatrictimes.com/suicide/suicide-clusters-college-campuses-risk-prevention-management.

Schwartz, Victor, and Jerald Kay. "The Crisis in College and University Mental Health." *Psychiatric Times*. October 10, 2009. Accessed October 1, 2016. http://www.psychiatrictimes.com/articles/crisis-college-and-university-mental-health.

Seikkula, Jaakko, Jukka Aaltonen, Birgittu Alakare, and Kauko Haarakangas. "Five-Year Experience of First-Episode Nonaffective Psychosis in Open-Dialogue Model." *Psychotherapy Research* 16, no. 2 (2006): 214–28. https://www.researchgate.net/publication/252659625_Five-year_experience_of_first-episode_nonaffective_psychosis_in_in_open-dialogue_approach_Treatment_principles_follow-up_outcomes_and_two_case_studies.

Simon, Cecila. "Major Decisions." *New York Times*. November 2, 2012. Accessed April 23, 2015. http://www.nytimes.com/2012/11/04/education/edlife/choosing-one-college-major-out-of-hundreds.html.

Simon, Gregory E., Karen J. Coleman, Bobbi Jo H. Yarborough, Belinda Operskalski, Christine Stewart, Enid M. Hunkeler, Frances Lynch, David Carrell, and Arne Beck. "First Presentation with Psychotic Symptoms in a Population Based Setting." *Psychiatric Services*. January 3, 2017. Accessed February 21, 2017. http://ps.psychiatryonline.org/doi/abs/10.1176/appi.ps.201600257.

Spettigue, Wendy, and Katherine A. Henderson. "Eating Disorders and the Role of the Media." *The Canadian Child and Adolescent Psychiatry Review* 13, no. 1 (2004): 16–19. Accessed March 19, 2017. https://www.ncbi.nlm.nih.gov/pmc/articles/PMC2533817/.

Squeglia, L. M., J. Jacobus, and S. F. Tapert. "The Influence of Substance Use on Adolescent Brain Development." *Clinical EEG and Neuroscience: Official Journal of the EEG and Clinical Neuroscience Society (ENCS)* 40, no. 1 (2009): 31–38. https://www.ncbi.nlm.nih.gov/pmc/articles/PMC2827693/.

Stein, Murray B., Calvin T. Yang, and Laura Campbell-Sills. "Panic Disorder." In *Gabbard's Treatments of Psychiatric Disorders*, fifth edition, edited by Glen O. Gabbard, 343–56. Arlington, VA: American Psychiatric Association, 2014. iPad edition.

Stiles, Laura. "Short-Term Suicide Risk for Discharged Psychiatric Hospital Patients." *Psychiatry Advisor*. December 2, 2016. Accessed March 8, 2017. http://www.psychiatryadvisor.com/depressive-disorder/short-term-suicide-risk-in-discharged-psychiatric-patients-with-depression/article/576572/.

Substance Abuse and Mental Health Services Administration. "Prescription Drug Misuse Among College Students." Accessed March 10, 2017. http://publichealth.hsc.wvu.edu/media/4239/college_students_no-samhsa-logo.pdf.

Suicide Prevention Resource Center. "Suicide among College and University Students in the United States." Accessed June 23, 2015. http://www.sprc.org/sites/sprc.org/files/library/SuicideAmongCollegeStudentsInUS.pdf.

Tamminga, Carol A., and Elena I. Ivleva. "Toward a Dimensional Understanding of Psychosis and Its Treatment." In *Gabbard's Treatments of Psychiatric Disorders*, fifth edition, edited by Glen O. Gabbard, 157–68. Arlington, VA: American Psychiatric Association, 2014. iPad edition.

Tumolo, Jolynn. "Dementia Drug Shown Effective as Adjunctive Treatment in Schizophrenia." *Psych Congress Network*. October 14, 2016. Accessed February 21, 2017. http://www.consultant360.com/exclusives/adjunctive-rivastigmine-improves-cognitive-function-schizophrenia.

Turrisi, Rob, and Anne E. Ray. "Sustained Parenting and College Drinking in First-Year Students." *Developmental Psychobiology* 52, no. 3 (2010): 286–94. Accessed March 3, 2017. http://www.ncbi.nlm.nih.gov/pmc/articles/PMC3937263/.

U.S. Department of Education. "Parents' Guide to the Family Educational Rights and Privacy Act: Rights Regarding Children's Education Records." October 2007. Accessed February 24, 2017. https://www2.ed.gov/policy/gen/guid/fpco/brochures/parents.html.

U.S. Department of Health and Human Services. "HIPAA Privacy Rule and Sharing Information Related to Mental Health." Accessed March 6, 2017. https://www.hhs.gov/hipaa/for-professionals/special-topics/mental-health/.

Varvil-Weld, Lindsey, D. Max Crowley, Rob Turrisi, Mark Greenber, and Kimberly Mallett. "Hurting, Helping, or Neutral? The Effects of Parental Permissiveness toward Adolescent Drinking on College Student Alcohol Use and Problems." *Prevention Science: The Official Journal of the Society for Prevention Research* 15, no. 5 (2014): 716–24. http://www.ncbi.nlm.nih.gov/pmc/articles/PMC3919881/#!po=7.81250.

Vimont, Celia. "College Marijuana Use Linked with Skipped Classes, Lower Grades, and Late Graduation." Partnership for Drug-Free Kids. January 27, 2016. Accessed March 4, 2017. http://www.drugfree.org/news-service/college-marijuana-use-linked-skipped-classes-lower-grades-late-graduation/.

Watson, Hunna J., and Cynthia Bulik. "Evidence Based Psychotherapy for Eating Disorders." *Focus* 10, no. 4 (2014): 379–84.

Weber, Lauren. "The End of Employees," *The Wall Street Journal*, February 3, 2017, AI, 10.

White Hughto, Jaclyn M., and Sari L. Reisner. "A Systematic Review of the Effects of Hormone Therapy on Psychological Functioning and Quality of Life in Transgender Individuals." *Transgender Health* 1, no. 1 (2016): 21–31. doi:10.1089/trgh.2015.0008. http://online.liebertpub.com/doi/full/10.1089/trgh.2015.0008.

Williams, Alex. "Move Over Millennials, Here Comes Generation Z." *New York Times.* September 18, 2015. Accessed December 27, 2016. http://www.nytimes.com/2015/09/20/fashion/move-over-millennials-here-comes-generation-z.html?_r=0.

Young, Melissa Scholes. "The Cost of Being First." *The Atlantic.* October 16, 2016. Accessed March 24, 2017. https://www.theatlantic.com/education/archive/2016/10/the-cost-of-being-first/504155/.

Youngner, Cole G., Maryrose Gerardi, and Barbara O. Rothbaum. "PTSD: Evidence-Based Psychotherapy and Emerging Treatment Approaches." *Focus* 11, no. 3 (2013): 307–14.

INDEX

academic failure to thrive, 53–71
acid reflux, anxiety and, 11
addiction, 39–52
adolescent brain, 44–46
advisors, 67–69
Affordable Care Act, 128
alcohol, xi, xii, xiii; depression and, 33;
    social anxiety disorder and, 9, 15
alcohol use disorder, 40–41, 45–46
alprazolam, 41
Americans with Disabilities Act, 144
amphetamine/dextroamphetamine, 41,
    63, 185
amygdala, 9, 47
anhedonia, psychosis, 179
anorexia, 168; transgender individuals,
    111
antidepressant medication: genetic
    testing, 31; power of, 30–31; side
    effects, 30–31; suicidal thoughts, 28;
    use in anxiety, 19; use in depression,
    34–35
antipsychotic medication, 29, 129, 189
anxiety, 3–20; academic struggles, 14–15;
    campus cure, 16–19; definition and
    examples, 8–9; depression with, 19;
    lifestyle changes, 16–17; maladaptive,
    9; medical evaluation, 17; medication
    for, 18–19; new norm on college
    campuses, 4–5; panic attack, 9;
    perfectionism and, 100; physical

symptoms, 11–12; seasons, 12–14;
    social media and, 11; substance abuse
    and, 15; suicidal thinking, 16;
    technology and, 10–12; therapy for,
    17–18; untreated, 14–16
aripiprazole, 189
attention deficit hyperactivity disorder
    (ADHD): academic problems, 63;
    campus controversies and, 63–65;
    evaluation and treatment, 55–57;
    medication for, 17, 41, 129; use of
    campus disability resource center, 62
autism, 85

benzodiazepines, use in anxiety disorders,
    19
binge drinking, 39, 47
binge eating disorder, 169
biology, in suicidal behavior, 148–149
bipolar disorder: psychosis and, 186;
    starting as depression, 32
bipolar I disorder, 184
bipolar II disorder, 186
bisexual, 14, 103, 107
borderline personality disorder, 146–147
brain: biology of, 30; development, xvi; on
    drugs, 44–46; panic attack, 9
brain-derived neurotrophic factor
    (BDNF), 30
breathing techniques, 7
bulimia, 169

bupropion, 30

caffeine, anxiety and, 16
campus counseling center, xii, 5;
    loneliness and social anxiety, 78
campus disability resource center, 35, 62,
    192
childhood trauma, psychosis and, 187
citalopram, 19, 78
clonazepam, use in anxiety disorders, 19
cocaine: depression and, 33; psychosis
    and, 185; substance use disorders, 39,
    46
cognitive behavioral therapy, 6, 29–30; for
    anxiety, 17–18; OCD, 98
coordinated specialty care (CSC), 183
culture, 104–107; mental health
    challenges, 105–106
cyberbullying, 161–162

debt, 115–130
delusions: with depression, 32; psychosis,
    179
depression, 21–37; with anxiety, 19;
    campus disability resource center, 35;
    financial stress and, 115–120; five-
    point plan for, 33–35; hospitalization
    for, 35–36; increasing rates of, 25;
    masking of, 23–24; metaphors for
    description of, 24–25; partners of,
    32–33; power of therapy, 29–30;
    psychotic, 32; sleep disorders, 33;
    social media, 26–27; suicide rates, 22;
    technology and, 26–27; therapy,
    medication, or both, 27–29; therapy
    for, 34; video games and, 26
Depression Bipolar Support Alliance, 194
Diagnostic and Statistical Manual of
    Mental Disorders (DSMV): psychosis,
    179; substance use disorders, 41
dialectical behavior therapy (DBT), for
    suicidal thoughts, 146
disorganized speech, psychosis, 179
dopamine, 32, 33
drug abuse. see substance abuse;
    substance use disorders
drunkorexia, xii, 164
duck syndrome, 93–102

eating disorders, 163–175; barriers to
    treatment, 167–168; perfectionism
    and, 94; substance use and, 47;
    technology, biology, and
    perfectionism, 170–171; transgender
    individuals, 111; treatment, 173–174;
    unhealthy eating, 168; unspecified,
    169
ecstasy, 15
emerging adult, xvi
escitalopram, 19
exercise, treating depression, 33

Family Educational Rights and Privacy
    Act (FERPA), xv, 40, 54, 142
fear of missing out (FOMO), 11
fight or flight reaction, 9
financial pressures, xii, 115–131;
    depression and, 25; too many strings
    attached, 125–126
first-generation college students, 105
fluoxetine, 30

gay, 14, 103, 107
gender, 110–113; fluid, 111; mental
    health challenges, 111–113
generalized anxiety disorder, 10
good enough mother, 102
grades: academic ailments and, 60–62;
    drop in, substance use and, 48; as a
    measure of success, 59; parent
    checking of, 57–58
great recession, 115, 116, 183
grit, 60
group therapy: depression, 30; social
    anxiety, 79–80

hallucinations: auditory, 178–179; with
    depression, 32; hypnogogic and
    hypnopompic, 178; psychosis, 179;
    visual, 179
health insurance, 117, 126–130, 166–167,
    167–168
Health Insurance Portability and
    Accountability Act (HIPAA), 40, 142
healthy relationships, healthy sex and,
    154–155
hearing voices: depression, 32; psychosis,
    178, 179

helicopter parent, xvi, 54, 116
heroin, 42
hospitalization: for depression, 35–36;
    suicidal threat, 147
hydrocodone, 42
hypomania, 186

imposter syndrome, 104–105
international students, 86–87
interpersonal therapy, 29, 174
intimate partner violence, 159–161
irritable bowel syndrome, anxiety and, 11

lamotrigine, 189
legal problems, substance use and, 49
lesbian, 14, 103, 107
LGBTQ (lesbian, gay, bisexual,
    transgender, and queer), 103, 108
lifestyle changes, for anxiety, 16–17
limbic system, xvi, 148
lithium, 189
loneliness, 75–91; autism and, 85; campus
    cure for, 87–88; dangers, 76–77;
    depression and, 25; international
    students, 86–87; social anxiety disorder
    and, 84; stay or go?, 89; triggers for,
    82–83
lorazepam, 6; use in anxiety disorders, 19
lurasidone, 189

major decisions, academics, 65–66
maladaptive anxiety, 9
marijuana, 41, 47; legalization, 47
medical evaluation: for anxiety, 17; for
    depression, 33
medical withdrawal, 36, 63
medication, ix; for anxiety, 18–19; for
    depression, 34–35; with therapy for
    depression, 27–29
meditation, 7
mental health: challenges for minority
    students, 105–106; financial wellness
    and, 121–122; gender and, 111–113;
    sexuality challenges, 108; stigma, 105
mental health issues, academic problems
    and, 62–63
methylphenidate, 41
mindfulness-based cognitive behavioral
    group therapy, 30

minority students, 105
mirtazapine, 159
mood disturbances, substance use and, 49
mood stabilizers, 29, 32, 129, 147, 189
mushrooms, 15, 41, 47, 185

narcolepsy, depression and, 33
Narcotics Anonymous, 51
National Alliance on Mental Illness
    (NAMI), 129, 141, 192
negative symptoms, psychosis, 179
norepinephrine, 32, 33
nucleus accumbens, 47

obsessive compulsive disorder (OCD),
    perfectionism and, 95–98
Open Dialogue, 183
opioids, 42
oxycodone, 42

panic disorder, 5–7, 9
pansexual, 107
paranoid, 42–44
parasympathetic nervous system, in
    anxiety, 9
Parents, Families, and Friends of
    Lesbians and Gays (PFLAG), 109, 113
paroxetine, for PTSD, 159
perfectionism, 93–102; eating disorders
    and, 94, 170–171; fighting one day at a
    time, 99–100; OCD and, 95–98; social
    media role in, 98–99
performance anxiety, 9
positive parenting, 48, 52
posttraumatic stress disorder (PTSD):
    sexual assault and, 158–159; suicide
    and, 144
prazosin, 159
prefrontal cortex, xvi, 45, 148
psilocybin, 185
psychodynamic therapy, 29, 146, 174
psychosis, 177–193; bipolar disorder and,
    186; causes of, 182–185; childhood
    trauma and, 187; comprehensive
    evaluation and treatment, 187–192;
    drugs and, 185–186; hope, 193;
    substance-induced psychotic disorder,
    184
psychotic depression, 32

psychotic symptoms, substance use and,
39

quetiapine, 189

Radically Open Dialectical Behavior
Therapy (RO-DBT), 94, 100
RAISE study (Recovery After an Initial
Schizophrenia Episode), 183
release of information form, xv, 28, 49,
137, 173, 192
risperidone, 189

safe sex, 109
schizophrenia, 182
school discipline problem, substance use
and, 49
sedatives, 41
selective serotonin reuptake inhibitors
(SSRI), 6; OCD symptoms, 98; social
anxiety disorder, 78; use in anxiety
disorders, 19
self-destructive behavior, treatment,
146–148
self-harm, depression, 32, 150, 178
serotonin, 32, 33
sertraline, 6; for PTSD, 159; social anxiety
disorder, 78
sex, healthy relationships, 154–155
sex, safe, 109
sexual assault, xii, 156–159; being your
child's advocate, 157–158; PTSD and,
158–159
sexuality, 107–109; mental health
challenges, 108; spectrum on
campuses, 107
sexually transmitted diseases (STDs), 109
sexual minority, 108
shyness, 9
Shyness and Social Anxiety Workbook, 88
sleep: anxiety and, 10; lifestyle, 16;
substance use disorders and, 48
sleep apnea, depression and, 33
sleep disorders, depression and, 33
social anxiety disorder, 9, 77, 84; alcohol
and, 9
social belonging, 60
social interactions, cure for loneliness, 87
social isolation. see loneliness

social media, 81–82; anxiety and, 11;
depression and, 26–27; perfectionism
and, 98–99
social skills, cure for loneliness, 88
social support (belonging), 76; cure for
loneliness, 88; depression and, 25
spending increase, substance use and, 49
stalking, 161–162
stimulant, 17, 49, 56, 63
substance abuse: anxiety and, 15;
prevention, 46–48
substance-induced psychotic disorder,
184
substance use disorders, 39–52; eating
disorders and, 47; recognition of,
48–50; treatment, family affair, 50–51
suicidal behaviors, xii, 135–151; barriers
to parent involvement, 141–143;
biology in, 148–149; hospitalization,
147; parent collaboration, 140–141;
responding in a crisis, 148; treatment,
146–148; untreated anxiety, 14, 16
suicidal ideation, 105, 143, 145
suicidal thinking: antidepressant
medication, 28; anxiety and, 16;
dialectical behavior therapy, 146
suicide: depression and, 22, 25; loneliness
and, 78, 82
suicide clusters, 145
suicide prevention, 143–145
sympathetic nervous system, in anxiety, 9

technology: as a cause of anxiety, 10–12;
depression and, 26–27; eating
disorders and, 170–171; impact on
academic success, 69–70; sexual
cyberbullying and stalking, 161–162;
tracking finances, 122–125
tetrahydrocannabinol (THC), 44
therapy: for anxiety, 17–18; for
depression, 34; with medication for
depression, 27–29; power of, 29–30;
for psychosis, 190–191
thyroid, anxiety and, 16, 17
transgender, 111; eating disorders and,
111; hormone therapy, 112; transition,
112

venlafaxine, 19, 30, 159

victim advocate, 157, 160, 162
video games, depression and, 26

Winnicott, Donald, 102

ABOUT THE AUTHOR

Marcia Morris, MD, is a psychiatrist at the University of Florida with over 20 years of experience providing care to university students. She is currently an Associate Professor with the College of Medicine Department of Psychiatry and Associate Program Director of Student Health Care Center Psychiatry. Dr. Morris writes a parenting blog for Psychology Today called "College Wellness: Promoting Happiness and Health in the College Years" (https://www.psychologytoday.com/experts/marcia-morris-md). In articles and talks, she promotes preventive care and comprehensive treatment for mental illness in the college years and beyond. Her articles have been published in the *New York Times*, the *Tampa Bay Times, The Conversation, Psychiatric Times*, and *Clinical Psychiatry News*. She has appeared on Huffington Post Live and co-hosted a monthly radio show, Family Matters, on WOCA 96.3 FM/1370 AM in Ocala, Florida. A board-certified psychiatrist and Fellow of the American Psychiatric Association, she has published original research on suicide as well as obsessive compulsive disorder. Dr. Morris has made several presentations on college mental health, eating disorders, anxiety and depression at national professional meetings.